**AMBITIOUS
LIKE A
MOTHER**

ALSO BY LARA BAZELON

Rectify

A Good Mother

AMBITIOUS LIKE A MOTHER

Why Prioritizing Your Career Is **Good** for **Your Kids**

LARA BAZELON

LITTLE,
BROWN
SPARK

New York   Boston   London

Hachette Book Group supports the right to free expression and the value of copyright. The purpose of copyright is to encourage writers and artists to produce the creative works that enrich our culture.

The scanning, uploading, and distribution of this book without permission is a theft of the author's intellectual property. If you would like permission to use material from the book (other than for review purposes), please contact permissions@hbgusa.com. Thank you for your support of the author's rights.

Little, Brown Spark
Hachette Book Group
1290 Avenue of the Americas, New York, NY 10104
littlebrownspark.com

First Edition: April 2022

Little, Brown Spark is an imprint of Little, Brown and Company, a division of Hachette Book Group, Inc. The Little, Brown Spark name and logo are trademarks of Hachette Book Group, Inc.

The publisher is not responsible for websites (or their content) that are not owned by the publisher.

The Hachette Speakers Bureau provides a wide range of authors for speaking events. To find out more, go to hachettespeakersbureau.com or call (866) 376-6591.

Excerpt from "This Week in Fiction: Lauren Groff on the Cult of Motherhood," Cressida Leyshon, The New Yorker, © Condé Nast.

ISBN 9780316429757
LCCN 2021950352

Printing 1, 2022

LSC-C

Printed in the United States of America

This book is for my mother, Eileen Amy Bazelon

Contents

Preface

My mother once told me, "Never be at the financial mercy of anyone else."

More than any other advice she gave me, it stuck.

Throughout her life, my mother worked. She never stopped. Not after having my sister Emily in 1971. Or me in 1974. Not after finishing her medical residency in 1975. Not after having my sister Jill in 1976, and not after having a fourth child, my sister Dana, in 1979.

My mother worked to be independent. She worked so that she would have an identity outside of her marriage and her four children. She worked because it made her happy. She worked to be free from the ever-present stress and misery of the near poverty that defined her childhood. She worked to set an example for her four daughters.

And she did. All four of us went to college and graduate school. We are all mothers who work full-time.

My mother lost her father when she was three. He died of a heart attack early in the morning on February 17, 1948. He was thirty-one. "It was completely shocking," she said, "and devastating." An engineer with the Department of the Navy, he had been the family's sole breadwinner. My mother's mother, Edith, was left alone to raise a toddler. She had no savings, no job, and no money aside from her husband's five-thousand-dollar life insurance policy.

The next two decades of my grandmother's life were marked by her struggling to make ends meet while battling severe anxiety and depression. She could no longer afford the rent for the New Jersey apartment she had shared with her late husband and had no choice but to move with my mother to Baltimore to live with her parents, with whom she had a contentious relationship. Even when my grandmother could finally afford a small garden apartment in a nearby neighborhood, she and my mother shared a bedroom. That remained true until my mother left for college. Edith worried constantly about money, at times relying on her younger sister and brother-in-law for support.

My grandmother had a college degree, but in the late 1940s, the options for women — particularly women with small children — were limited: teacher, nurse, secretary. After substitute teaching for months, she found work as a middle-school English teacher in a Baltimore public school. Her students' previous education had been severely lacking and they struggled with the curriculum. Edith was frustrated by the way that the system had failed them and her; she was grossly underpaid — as most teachers at that time were and continue to be today. From June through September, when school was out, she had no salary at all. Her dream of living a middle-class life with a husband and a houseful of children behind a white picket fence had shattered. She went through bouts of depression and repeatedly threatened suicide. "Not having money drove her crazy," my mother said, "and she could not adjust to her life."

In response, my mother focused on her education. She skipped two grades and got a full scholarship to Bryn Mawr College, a prestigious all-women's school, where she was premed. It was 1961, and she was sixteen years old. A few months later, she met my father — her first and only serious boyfriend. Toward the end of college, she began applying to medical school. Her mother and grandparents advised against it. "They told me I would never get married because no man would want me if I had a career." She ignored them. My father was not put off. Several months into her first year of medical school, he proposed. They were engaged on New Year's Eve 1965 and got married six months later; my mother was twenty-one, my father, twenty-three.

Getting married did nothing to stop my mother's ambition. "We had a saying at Bryn Mawr," she told me: "Only failures *only* get married." From 1966 to 1969, she and my father, a law student at the University of Pennsylvania, lived in a basement apartment next to a country club. My dad was an avid tennis player but he wasn't allowed on the courts; the club barred Jews from admission. But, as my mother pointed out, they couldn't have afforded it anyway. Instead, their lives revolved around school and homework. In 1970, my mother graduated from the Medical College of Pennsylvania. First in her class.

The more I dug into my mother's story — over hours of interviews spanning more than a year — the more it became clear that my father's role, and their relationship, were complicated and complicating factors in her success. On the one hand, my father was supportive of my mother's professional aspirations, which was relatively unusual for their generation. On their first date, at the Bryn Mawr College Inn, my mom, seventeen, told my dad, nineteen, she was going to be a doctor. He said, "I thought it was great. It showed ambition. It showed determination. It showed wanting to do something that was important and useful. It showed independence."

On the other hand, my father made it clear that for the marriage to work, my mother needed to make sure their kids were fed, dressed, and transported to various activities, dinner was on the table on time, and the house was clean. In figuring out that logistical equation, she was mostly on her own. She outsourced the housecleaning and some of the cooking and childcare; we had housekeepers and a babysitter who worked full-time for my family for more than a decade. But my mother also drove the Hebrew school carpool and took us to the pediatrician, the dentist, and — three of us — the orthodontist. She brought cupcakes to school on our birthdays. (Back then, sugary treats in the classroom were still legal.)

Of course, growing up in my parents' house, I was aware of this dynamic. For all of us to thrive, or even function, my mother had to treat the domestic sphere as a second job — and that meant she worked very hard and seemingly nonstop. What I didn't understand until I started writing this book was the sacrifices she made continuously along the way. Some of those sacrifices were professional. Some were personal. My mother spent decades plagued by guilt that she was shortchanging her daughters and her patients. As an ambitious mother, she experienced a peculiar kind of loneliness, part of which stemmed from the decision to keep her angst private for fear of inviting further judgment.

I think of my mother as a pioneer. Still, her story isn't one of linear triumph. She succeeded within the constraints of a marriage that was, at its core, conventional. Her success required yielding: her leisure time, her emotional energy, and some of her aspirations. "I had almost no close friends when you were growing up," she told me. "I never had time, I could never have lunch with anyone, and I felt that Nana [her mother] and Gamma [my dad's mom] disapproved of me. Dad wasn't discouraging as long as it didn't interfere with him." I asked if she resented my dad, who returned late in the evenings from his law firm, regularly worked weekends, and, as far as I could remember, had never cooked a family meal. She said, "Would it have been nice if Dad had been around more? Of course. But that's not Dad. He was never going to be different than who he was."

Although my mother's chosen profession of medicine made her unusual for her time, her story is not unique. Countless working mothers have found joy and fulfillment as well as a vital means of security in their careers. But nearly the same number have felt lonely and suffered quietly from guilt, shame, and the fear that what they wanted for themselves in the workplace was at odds with being a good mother.

It isn't. Professional success is emotionally fulfilling. It is also liberating. It allows us to be role models, to show our children that by pursuing our dreams and ambitions, we are strong, independent, and eminently capable. Think of how much more free and joyful women's lives could be if they accepted this truth: their work benefits themselves *and* their children. But the truth is a hard sell because it runs counter to how we have constructed and enforced gender norms, particularly when it comes to child-rearing. It is vital that we accept — and tell — this truth now.

Millennial and Generation Z women need to hear this message. We know, having lived through the Great Recession of 2008 and now COVID-19, the worst pandemic in a century, that economic circumstances can shift abruptly and for the worse. A partner's once solid job can evaporate. Seemingly perfect marital unions can fall apart. *Opting out* — the much-buzzed-about term to describe wealthy women with elite credentials who chose to leave the workforce to raise children in the early aughts — simply isn't an option for most American women.[1] And that includes some of the women who thought it was.[2] Many of them discovered, years later, that the choice not to work was economically and emotionally unsustainable.

For some of us, work means having the economic freedom to leave unhappy relationships or radically reframe them, to weather divorces, economic downturns, disease, and even widowhood, knowing we can provide for ourselves and our children. That freedom is integral to our ability to be good mothers.

But we don't say so in polite company.

The truth — that striving for success in the workplace has the potential to make women better mothers, not worse ones — remains controversial. It challenges the enduring belief that a "good mother" is a woman who subordinates her own desires to her children's needs. It contradicts stereotypes of what is considered acceptable feminine behavior: being modest, self-effacing, and deferential.

As an ambitious working mother of two young children with multiple professional identities — law professor/litigator/writer — I have found myself judged. Some of that judgment is externally imposed; some of it is self-directed. As a young mother, when I was offered a professional opportunity that separated me from my children — a trip out of state to give an academic presentation, a sought-after writer's residency to finish a book, a legal battle to exonerate a client incarcerated hundreds of miles away — I took it. These opportunities were stepping-stones, yes, but they also fed my brain, which was always hungry for new ideas and professional engagement. They fed my soul — there is nothing as exhilarating and life-affirming as watching the prison gates open and an innocent person walk free, knowing that I played a part in making that happen.

And yet. Because time is finite, the deficits add up on the other side of the ledger. My choices inevitably meant I was less available to my children. One could argue my choices cost me my marriage. What kind of example is that? For more than a decade I struggled with these questions, agonized over them, sought an escape route that would free me from my guilt, shame, and conviction that I was a Bad Mother. For years, I raced like a mouse in a maze in search of the work-life balance finish line that would signal that I had found my way out. I ran and ran, believing that if I rebounded from the dead ends and survived the booby traps, I would arrive in this magical Eden.

But there is no such place. The Work-Life Balance and the Selfless Mother are false gods. I wrote this book in the hope that it will convince you to stop chasing the same mirage and punishing yourselves for failing to attain the impossible. I wrote this book as a resource, a refuge, and a source of reassurance. It isn't selfish to want to feed your brain or your soul. It isn't wrong to think that doing so requires something more than being a mother. It isn't detrimental to focus on the ability to support yourself or your children or to make sacrifices early on for the flexibility that comes with rising higher in your field or having more professional choices.

Quite the opposite. Choosing professional opportunities, prioritizing your career — not all the time, but some of the time — models valuable lessons for your children, including independence, resilience, and the importance of using one's talents and abilities to help other people. Nor need these choices come at the expense of a marriage if a woman chooses her life partner with these truths in mind. There is no glide path to nirvana; there is instead a bumpy road of everyday beauty and mess. Mothers shouldn't go it alone; we should bring our families (in all of their iterations) and our partners (in all of their iterations) as we stride forth, clear and confident about our value and purpose in life.

Recently, a former standout student of mine, newly married, asked me to write her a letter of recommendation for a competitive position. After I sent it off, she wrote to thank me. Referring to a *New York Times* op-ed I had written in 2019 about women and ambition,[3] she said, "Your article . . . was the first time I had ever been told that it was ok to prioritize my work. Hearing that I could be both a (future) mother and a passionate lawyer was so incredibly liberating." She concluded, "Thank you for empowering me and

showing a generation of young women that we don't have to settle."
Reading her note, I blinked back tears. I also thought, *If only someone had said those words to twenty-something-year-old me.*

Now, when American women are both empowered and imper-
iled as never before, it is important to tell this truth. *Ambitious Like
a Mother* delves into the lives of ambitious, economically independent working mothers who are raising happy, healthy kids — my
mother's story, my own, and that of so many others. This book is
a call to tell our stories out loud and with pride. It is a call to put
the antiquated trope that ambitious women are selfish, aggressive
bitches in the junk heap of history where it belongs. And it is a call
to stop trapping professional working mothers in a cycle of shame
and self-recrimination by demanding that they squash their ambition, hide it, or sacrifice it.

We need to change the conversation. Too many women face
the same impediments to success that confronted our mothers and
grandmothers. Entrenched gender bias in the workplace, including
sexual harassment, sexual assault, and the "motherhood penalty,"[4]
presents barriers to advancement. For women of color, these threats
and inequities are compounded by deep-seated racial biases and stereotypes. We live in a political climate where targeted legal assaults
on our reproductive rights are the norm, posing a threat to our
ability to control our bodies. At home, we face additional stresses
and burdens; we're expected to shoulder the lion's share of the labor while being made to feel as if we still aren't doing enough. The
COVID-19 pandemic, which drove women out of the workforce in
record numbers, laid bare the reality that one sidestep in the performance of this high-wire act sends many of us into free fall with no
social safety net to catch us.

Data shows that one-third of households are headed by single
women[5] and that in most two-parent households, both parents must
work to make ends meet.[6] Whether women work by necessity or

out of love of the job or some combination, they are entitled to equal pay and opportunities for advancement. They deserve to live in a world that is responsive to the complexities of their lives as mothers who are also human beings with needs — financial and emotional — that cannot be satisfied solely by mothering.

Of course, there has been progress, most recently with #MeToo, steadily rising numbers of women reaching the apex of their professions, and more parity with male partners in the domestic sphere.[7] But for the most part, society has refused to put working women on an equal footing with working men. And so working women have been stuck. Many professions are still tied to a centuries-old model designed for men with wives at home to take care of the house and the children: early-morning to late-afternoon hours in the workplace with little or no flexibility. In some ways, it has gotten worse; with advances in technology comes the reality that no one is ever more than a text or an e-mail away from work. Before the pandemic, most jobs demanded a strict nine-to-five in person and then more work at home on nights and weekends.[8]

This is not a book that advocates for women to accept these strictures or work themselves to the bone as a prerequisite of being ambitious. It is a book that argues for change from the inside — from inside the home, the workplace, and the institutions that establish hierarchies and norms that set women up to fail. There is strength in numbers when women as a collective push back and say, "No more — we are going to shift the paradigm."

The social and political upheaval of the past five years, culminating in a global pandemic, has made one thing clear: we cannot continue to have the same debates today about work, children, love, and family that we did a generation ago. Working mothers are demanding more support, more flexibility, and more recognition from the government, from partners, and from bosses. But the recent muscular push for gender equality will succeed only if we stop undermining ourselves. We have got to stop buying what social media and other powerful institutions — cultural, political, familial — are selling us: perfectly curated images of svelte, selfless, self-effacing mothers flawlessly executing the work-life balance all on their own.

Let's get real: Achieving the perfect work-life balance isn't any more possible than being the perfectly selfless mother. What we have instead, as one grown son of a full-time working mother put it, is "sliding weights from one end of the scale to the other; family to work, work to family, with rare times in perfect balance." That imbalance is healthy and necessary, and it involves the sharing of sacrifices and burdens that should not be a mother's to bear alone. He went on:

> You can't always give your children your time or full attention (no one can), yet there is little doubt that you always give them your love. While young people can get attached to things and events that society and our culture reinforce as important, nothing is more important than love, safety, and a sense of available support. I like to think of it as the way an AC electrical current is always available and ready, even when something is not plugged in. You yourself, and with the aid of others, ensure this crucial foundation is in place.[9]

What would it take for the electrical-current analogy to take hold in the public imagination so that working women could be supported economically and emotionally by partners, peers, and society? A cultural shift. A legal shift. A reframing that does not pit work and life against each other in a zero-sum game. It is starting to happen. The pandemic is a natural jumping-off point for this high-stakes cross-profession negotiation. It has changed what work looks like for tens of millions of Americans, many of them women. While there is no understating the grossly disproportionate impact and stress the yearlong lockdown inflicted on mothers, who exited the workforce in droves,[10] it also changed the rules about work. There is growing recognition that many aspects of a job that doesn't require face-to-face interaction can be successfully and efficiently performed remotely.

Moving forward, particularly now that a demand for labor has created, at least temporarily, a job seeker's market, women are positioned to bargain for schedules that better accommodate their needs and the needs of their children.[11] These workplace accommodations save time and money by reducing the costs and time-suck of commuting and other expenses associated with a five-day-a-week office schedule. Soft pants mean hard savings in dry-cleaning bills; at-home lunches translate into big savings in meals not eaten out.

The pandemic has also reopened the conversation about expanding the social safety net to provide benefits that would transform the lives of working mothers, such as more robust unemployment insurance, paid family leave, child tax credits, and high-quality, low-cost childcare. The $1.9 trillion American Rescue Plan that President Biden signed into law on March 10, 2021, provided some of those benefits, albeit in temporary form. Even if Congress fails to make these benefits permanent, many states can, and some already have.[12]

But no real change is possible until working mothers let themselves off the hook and stop trying to be all things to all people — perfect at work, perfect as partners, and perfect as mothers, with each role entirely cabined off. Rather than engaging in the futile struggle to always put their children first while treating motherhood as a role that must be kept hermetically sealed from workplace schedules, struggles, triumphs, and woes, women need to embrace the seepage and come to understand that the messiness is a good in and of itself.

I have made that shift in my own life, intentionally choosing to raise children who see why my work is important. That holds true for so many professions — if what you do brings you and other people joy, provides a vital service, puts money in your bank account, or, hopefully, some combination of these things, your children will appreciate that your work makes the world inside and outside of your home a better place. They will understand that they can't — and should not — always come first. At the same time, they will know that their existence inspires and motivates you.

When I was coming up for tenure, a well-meaning colleague advised me never to mention my children or even have their pictures in my office. I was also advised never to say that they were the reason I could not attend a work function or take on an extra assignment. I rejected this advice. I wanted to set a different example for the mothers who would be in my position some day in the future. I wanted to be able to tell those young women, "I was clear and direct about my childcare responsibilities and the limitations they would sometimes impose. I proved through my work ethic and my achievements that being a mother of young children is not incompatible with being an academic worthy of tenure. Yes, at times it was stressful and even scary, but it worked out in the end, and it will for you too."

My mothering isn't perfect. There is no such thing. But it is real and it is good. My children know that my love for my job does not diminish my love for them. They see me pay our bills on time and in full. They see me able to support them and myself through dedication, grit, and hard work that I love. We have had sunny days and darker ones; they have seen me struggle and they have seen me overcome. In the process, they have learned that there is strength to be found in a place of vulnerability. They have learned to be resilient.

I know because they show me. When my daughter was seven, she wrote a poem called "Getting Up." She recited it in front of her entire elementary school at an assembly. It reads:

*If something hard and heavy is weighing you
     down and you fall, get back up.*

*If someone says it is impossible, it makes me
     feel like it is more possible to get back up.*

*If you get back up, don't think I am not
     going to talk to this person ever again.*

*Think I will try again and even if they push
     me again, I will get back up.*

*I don't know if I have learned this the hard
     way or the easy but I have learned, and
     you can learn too.*[13]

This book tells the story of ambitious mothers living in the United States in the twenty-first century who get pushed down and get back up. Diverse across race, age, ethnicity, sexual orientation, class, profession, geography, and country of origin, they are married, single, divorced, and widowed. What they have in common is their fierce love of work, their ability to help support — or, in some cases, solely support — their families, and their belief that striving for professional achievement and economic stability makes them better mothers, not worse ones. They know that a perfect work-life balance is impossible. But rather than apologize for what they can't give their children, they celebrate what they can: a lifelong lesson in independence and self-confidence that will give them the tools to thrive and the courage to chase down their own dreams.

**AMBITIOUS
LIKE A
MOTHER**

CHAPTER ONE

LOVE, MARRIAGE, BABY CARRIAGE

T HE VAST MAJORITY OF ADULT WOMEN IN THE UNITED States become mothers. Eighty-six percent of women between the ages of forty and forty-four have children.[1] When it is a choice, even the culmination of a long-held dream, having a baby should bring unmitigated joy. But for ambitious working women, that joy is often tinged with anxiety. What does becoming a mother mean for women's work lives when time and money become scarcer and priorities shift while work structures remain rigid? For women who want to have biological children, when is the "right" time to have a baby to minimize the impact of these concerns and maximize the chance of getting pregnant and having a healthy child? The anxiety that women experience around becoming mothers is exacerbated by a torrent of conflicting messages delivered by the media, which alternately warns them about waiting too long and advises them to put off pregnancy and childbirth until they have achieved a certain economic, professional, and emotional stability.

In my late twenties and early thirties, as I ping-ponged from one headline to another, I felt unsure of what or whom to believe. Marriage is an important institution in my family, and my parents' example hung over me, inspirational and daunting. My mother met her one true love at age seventeen, married him at twenty-one, and enjoyed five years of happily married life alone with him before having her first child at twenty-six. As far as I was concerned, she'd won the lottery. My dad was handsome, good-hearted, smart, successful, charming, and funny. Like any other couple, my parents fought, but it was clear that they were deeply in love.

It was also clear that theirs wasn't going to be my story. As the years ticked by and I hadn't found my own dreamboat, I started to worry that I was running out of time. Looking back, I realize how silly that seems. I was in my early thirties and there was no reason to believe I would have trouble getting pregnant. But I was scared by the statistic making headlines in the early 2000s: that a woman's fertility generally begins to ebb in her late twenties and drops substantially by her mid- to late thirties.[2] Scientists attributed these changes to the "decline in the quality of the oocyte" — which is to say, eggs do not age well.[3]

In 2005, I turned thirty-one. I was gainfully employed, owned my own home, and had a close circle of friends, but I was still single. The same year, a study came out that nearly lit my hair on fire. Women between the ages of thirty-five and thirty-nine are half as fertile as women between the ages of nineteen and twenty-six; on average, it takes them twice as long to get pregnant, it said.[4] Further, more than one in four women between the ages of thirty-five and forty fail to get pregnant after a year of trying — the marker at which doctors suspect fertility problems rather than simple bad luck[5] — compared with 13 percent of women ages thirty to thirty-four.[6] I vacillated between freaking out and drawing hope from regularly generated media hoopla around celebrity moms who gave birth to adorable cherubs when they were in their late forties.[7]

In retrospect, the headline-making news on both ends of the spectrum was equally misinforming. The chances of giving birth in one's late forties or early fifties are not zero, but they aren't high either. However, much-cited studies about women's diminished fertility were often misinterpreted, based on samples too small to be statistically significant, and used to fearmonger. Millions of women in their late thirties and early forties conceive babies naturally every year.[8] But this news doesn't generate clicks — outlier stories do. Some women, after anxiously scanning the headlines or listening to friends or relatives recount their fertility struggles, come away believing the same unforgiving timeline will apply to them. These external messages create a self-imposed pressure to nail it all down — the perfect partner, the kids, and the career — before it is "too late."

Economist Sylvia Ann Hewlett put an exclamation point on this fear in her 2002 book *Creating a Life: Professional Women and the Quest for Children* by proclaiming: "At mid-life, between a third and a half of all high-achieving women in America do not have children" despite wanting them desperately.[9] Hewlett, who focused her research on elite, high-earning, white-collar professionals, cited "career constraints and relationship difficulties" as the primary drivers of childlessness among these women.[10] Having suffered miscarriages and struggled for years to get pregnant after having her first child at thirty-one, she told her readers: "Learn to be as strategic with your personal life as you are with your career."[11]

The problem with that proffered wisdom is the inconvenient fact that falling in love and coupling up — which, for many women, is arguably the most important precondition of becoming a mother — are not life events that lend themselves to strategy. When, how, and if they happen is outside of our control. The heart wants what it wants, not what it is supposed to want, never mind the fact that the person on the other side of the equation has to feel the same way.

Hewlett was critiqued by many for inciting a "baby panic" while failing to take into account the reality that women's personal lives do not synchronize with ticking clocks. In 2002, a quartet of single female comedians on *Saturday Night Live* — Tina Fey, Amy Poehler, Maya Rudolph, and Rachel Dratch — took turns mocking her. Dratch, in a voice dripping with sarcasm, said: "Sylvia, thanks for reminding me to hurry up and have a baby. Me and my four cats will get right on that."[12] Three of these four female comedians went on to have children after the age of forty; the fourth, Amy Poehler, had a child just before turning thirty-nine.

More recently, other experts, including Dr. Jean Twenge, an author and psychologist at San Diego State University, have criticized Hewlett and others as relying on "questionable data." Writing in *The Atlantic* in 2013, Dr. Twenge countered Hewlett's claims with a study showing that European women over the age of thirty-five were nearly as fertile two days before ovulation as their twenty-something counterparts and a study of Dutch mothers who were nearly as fertile at forty as they had been at twenty. Twenge also included her own story. She and her husband naturally conceived three children when Twenge was in her late thirties.[13] Between the ages of forty and forty-five, however, the odds of getting pregnant without medical intervention decrease.[14] "By age 44, the chances of spontaneous pregnancy approach zero," Dr. Jane van Dis, an ob-gyn, told the *New York Times* in 2019.[15] Twenge advised: "Plan to have your last child by the time you turn 40. Beyond that, you're rolling the dice, though they may still come up in your favor."[16]

However, advances in science have increased the chances of becoming pregnant after forty with developments in assisted reproductive techniques (known as ART), mainly involving egg-freezing and in vitro fertilization (sometimes using donor eggs). How much store women should put in ART is a fraught question. These methods are expensive, usually not covered by health insurance, and far from foolproof. The chance that a woman over the age of thirty-five using ART will conceive and deliver a healthy baby is 22 percent, according to the Centers for Disease Control; after the age of forty-two, she has only a 6 percent chance.[17]

Further complicating matters is the anxiety about the health risks associated with childbearing after the age of thirty-five. These are "geriatric pregnancies," so called because of the heightened risk of complications, including miscarriage, stillbirth, genetic deformities, and low-weight and premature births.[18] (The first time I heard the words *geriatric pregnancy* applied to my thirty-six-year-old, newly knocked-up self, my mouth dropped open, but yes, that's the medical term.)

Dr. Laurie Green, the managing partner of Pacific Women's Obstetrics and Gynecology Group in San Francisco, has delivered more than seventeen thousand babies, including mine. She adds varicose veins, heightened risk of breast cancer, hemorrhages, gestational diabetes, hypertension, and high C-section rates to the geriatric-pregnancy-risks list. For women over forty, those risks increase. The chances that a woman under twenty-five will have a baby with Down syndrome is 1 in 1,200; at age thirty-five, it is 1 in 350; at forty, it is 1 in 100; and for a woman over the age of forty-five, it is 1 in 30.[19]

Studies show that fewer women are rushing to have children today because they want to establish their careers, pay off student debt, enjoy their independence, and find the right partner. A 2017 report issued by the U.S. Census compared the ages at which women marry and have children using two different cohorts. Members of the first cohort were, like my mother, between the ages of eighteen and twenty-four in 1975, spanning the baby boomer and silent generations. Those in the second cohort, contemporary young women, were eighteen to thirty-four in 2016, spanning the millennials and Generation Zers.

The differences were stark: "In the 1970s, 8 in 10 people married by the time they turned 30. Today, not until the age of 45 have 8 in 10 people married." Nearly 70 percent of the older cohort were mothers by the age of thirty; for the younger cohort that percentage had dropped to 46 percent.[20] These figures are not surprising. Far greater numbers of women today are finishing college and graduate school and entering the workforce, and they want to be on sound financial footing — loans paid off, a decent-paying job secured — before becoming spouses and parents.[21] Women in the second cohort have more professional opportunities than those in the preceding generations but also more burdens, including the rising cost of higher education, which can result in crippling student debt, and wages that have stagnated for all but the highest-paid, most elite workers.[22]

Which path is best, becoming a mother in one's late twenties to early thirties, which may mean putting a career on pause, or waiting until one's mid-thirties or early forties, when having a child might be harder?[23] It is helpful for women buffeted by waves of often conflicting information to orient themselves by keeping the shore firmly in view. Disputes about women's fertility are long-standing and heated, and while some general principles can be extrapolated, the individual characteristics of each case mean that every prediction is shadowed by uncertainty. Yes, women become less fertile as they get older. Which women, and to what degree, are impossible to predict with any certainty. Many women in their late thirties and early forties will have no trouble becoming pregnant. Others will succeed with ART. Still others will not be able to conceive either naturally or with technology. Fertility studies, which are based on limited samples, can speak only in generalities, probabilities, and debatable statistics. Stories like Hewlett's and Twenge's — stories like mine and yours and our friends' — can speak only in anecdotes. Every woman has her own fertility narrative, and it is unknowable unless and until she decides to write it.

We need to create space for more and different stories while fighting off the ingrained societal impulse to label women with a sell-by date at which they are expected to be partnered and pregnant. The fact remains that nearly a quarter of the way through the twenty-first century, women who pursue their professional ambitions and enjoy their independence well into their thirties are told that they are being too single-minded and shortsighted. Or, worse, that remaining single and childless isn't a choice, an accident, or irrelevant; it means something darker.

Sara Eckel, a freelance writer, wrote in a 2011 Modern Love essay in the *New York Times*,[24] about the dread she experienced when a new date asked her when she had last been in a relationship. "I didn't want him to know the truth: that I was 39 and hadn't had a serious boyfriend in eight years. I had seen men balk at this information before — even when the numbers were lower. They would look at me in a cool and curious way, as if I were a restaurant with too few customers, a house that had been listed for too long. One man actually said it: 'What's wrong with you?'"

Few people would ask that question if Sara were a thirty-nine-year-old man named Sam. Studies reflect this divide and also its impact on women's thinking and priorities. Young women are statistically more likely than young men to elevate the importance of parenthood by considering leaving a job or a city for a future partner with whom they envision having children, according to research presented in the 2005 journal article "I Can't Wait to Get Married: Gender Differences in Drive to Marry."[25] The authors did note, however, that women's interest in settling down and having children correlated with their stance on gender roles more generally: those who hewed to a more traditional view of women as subordinate partners and primary caregivers were more driven to make sacrifices to marry and become mothers.

In 2013, Scott Stanley, a psychology professor at the University of Denver, citing a study by the National Marriage Project, wrote that men, unlike women, "reported almost no societal pressures to marry."[26] This blasé attitude is rooted in the belief that there is no rush — a man in his forties or fifties can marry a younger woman and still expect to produce children.[27] For example, a 2018 study of twenty-one men between the ages of twenty-one and forty-six who were in fertility counseling with female partners found that not one of them was concerned about his ability to have biological children. At the same time, "many shared doubts about having children because they felt a sense of ambivalence about parenthood and/or did not feel 'ready' to do so." Readiness, to these men, was a psychological state. One participant, age forty, stated: "I have been a crazy teenager until I was about 38 or so, so I was much too irresponsible for that."[28]

Meanwhile, despite the celebration of some single women in popular culture and the fact that a record number of adults over the age of eighteen are unmarried — over 45 percent, according to U.S. Census data[29] — the stigma associated with being a single woman "of a certain age" remains embedded in society. This stigma has a long history. The phrase traces its roots to eighteenth-century England and, according to the late columnist William Safire, "suggested spinsterhood." Famous British writers used the term disparagingly. Lord Byron wrote: "A lady of a 'certain age' . . . means certainly aged." According to Charles Dickens, a woman "of a certain age" was just like "a very old house, perhaps as old as it claimed to be, and perhaps older."[30]

Twentieth-century single women continued to face condemnation and unrelenting pressure to marry, driven in part by their lack of access to well-paying jobs with the promise of stability or upward mobility. In a 1981 study published in the *American Journal of Psychiatry*, the authors noted that "an unmarried woman was seen as unattractive, unworthy, and unwanted."[31] A woman's diminished social status combined with her economic needs made her feel that partnering off was imperative.

Most single mothers were, like my grandmother, widowed or divorced — their situation was not of their choosing. Negative qualities were attributed to them; according to the same study, one in four people believed that single women were less emotionally stable and said that they were more likely to feel awkward around them. This, too, jibed with my mother's experience growing up in working-class Baltimore as a latchkey kid. She and her mother, she said, were looked down upon. "I didn't have an ordinary family so I didn't fit into any social group," she told me.

Beginning in the 1970s and coinciding with the women's liberation movement and the decision by many all-male colleges and universities to admit women, the numbers started to change.[32] The percentage of women attending college more than doubled from 1952 to 1979, rising from 6 percent to 12.2 percent.[33] By 1981, more women than men were earning bachelor's degrees. With the influx of women pursuing higher education came the promise of increased economic stability and a different take on marriage, family, and career.

In 1962, when my mother was a freshman in college, 98 percent of her contemporaries expressed a strong desire to get married. "Most women learned early in their lives that the choice of a husband, not a career or job, was the most important determinant of future status," the authors of the 1981 article wrote. By 1972, only 60 percent of college-educated women were firmly set on marriage, with fewer viewing it as necessary for economic security or a prerequisite for having children.[34] "College Women Want a Career, Marriage, and Children" was the title of an article published by psychologist Arline L. Bronzaft in 1974. Surveying 210 women on the cusp of graduating from the City University of New York, Dr. Bronzaft found that 79 percent "hope to have it all" and less than 10 percent viewed their identity as "centering upon home and family."[35] These women, it seemed, were leading a new trend, as the percentage of women with four-year college degrees jumped from just over 10 percent in 1974 to more than 38 percent in 2020.[36] With that level of education came greater opportunities and less economic incentive to marry as a way of assuring oneself of a secure financial future.

And yet.

Decades after Dr. Bronzaft's study was published, the same judgments continued to attach themselves to unpartnered women. In 2003, Phyllis Gordon published "The Decision to Remain Single: Implications for Women Across Cultures" in the *Journal of Mental Health Counseling*. Gordon found that, even in the twenty-first century, the terms *never-married* and *unmarried* were associated with "a state of lacking." Dr. Gordon urged mental-health professionals to "reexamine their own biases." She critiqued default thinking of marriage as "the norm" and the ingrained impulse to view all single women as lonely and unloved rather than as a diverse group that included many people who had made a deliberate choice. Those single women deserved validation, not pity, she argued.

High-profile single women, with and without children, have worked to dispel the stereotypes Dr. Gordon addressed in her research. Some of these women, including Kate Bolick in her 2015 memoir, *Spinster: Making a Life of One's Own,* take on a misogynistic trope directly and turn it into a battle cry of empowerment. Tellingly, though, the book begins this way: "Whom to marry, and when will it happen — these two questions define every woman's existence."

Verna Williams, who is the dean of the University of Cincinnati College of the Law, met her husband, David, in 1995, when she was thirty-four. Both were hard-charging public interest attorneys; Verna was living in Washington, DC, and David in New York. Verna found dating difficult. As a strong, successful Black woman, she was constantly being told, "You are too intimidating, you are too smart." Verna, who graduated from Harvard Law School, said she had expected to meet someone there. She hadn't. As the years went by, she said, "I am thinking, *Oh, gosh, my mom was twenty-five when she got married and had me.* And I didn't see marriage and kids happening anytime soon. In the back of my head, *When is it going to happen?* was playing on repeat." Verna and David got married two years after they met. She had their daughter, Allison, at the age of thirty-nine.

The pressure to conform to the nuclear-family model remains strong. Dr. Gordon noted that first-generation women from some immigrant groups faced particularly intense social pressure to marry and have children at a relatively young age due to cultural norms and familial definitions of respectability. I found this to be true among some of the women I interviewed.

Diana Luong came to the United States from Vietnam on August 29, 1994, with her parents and four siblings. She was fifteen. I asked her what she knew about America before they arrived and she said, laughing, "Nothing." Enrolled in a large public high school, Diana learned English by carrying a heavy dictionary in her backpack and looking up the words she didn't know. She also watched every episode of *Friends*. "It was funny and it helped me a lot with communication," she said. "My favorite character was Rachel. I loved her because she was so beautiful." But Diana's life looked nothing like the carefree singletons' on the show. After living briefly with her grandparents, her family moved to a cramped one-room apartment in the Tenderloin, a low-income, high-crime neighborhood in San Francisco.

Diana met the man who became her husband in tenth grade, shortly after immigrating. He, too, was Vietnamese, but he was two years older and seemed far more worldly. Diana said that her initial attraction was emotional: "He always took really good care of me." He would cut school, go home, make her the lunches she craved — eggs with rice and noodles, homemade sausage — and take the bus back to school to hand-deliver them. When the subject of sex came up, Diana was clear: "I told him I didn't want to be a bad girl who is having sex and gets dumped later on before I got married because I have very traditional ideas from Vietnam, so he said, 'Let's be husband and wife.'" His promise cemented the relationship. They became intimate, and he proposed a few years later. Diana, still a teenager, put him off to finish school. They got married after she completed her associate's degree. She was twenty-two. Her husband, she told me, had been her first and only boyfriend. Their children, Sarah and Brian, were born before Diana turned thirty.

Diana, although born more than three decades after my mother, made remarkably similar choices. Both of them married their first and only real boyfriends, whom they had met as teenagers. But while my mother's decisions blended in with the national culture at the time — and with the liberal coastal city where she lived[37] — Diana's conformed with the expectations of her immigrant community but were anomalous in the liberal coastal city where she lived. Today, there is a cultural and class divide, with poor, lower-middle-class, first-generation, and immigrant women getting married and having children at younger ages than middle- and upper-class American-born women, who are more likely to delay those decisions.[38]

The norm for women living in San Francisco is having multiple partners before marrying in their thirties. Fewer than 18 percent of women under the age of thirty-five have children. Today, younger mothers in the United States are more likely to be conservative and religious and hew to traditional gender norms, forgoing a career to stay at home. They are also likely to be less well-educated and less economically secure.[39] As a young wife and mother, Diana fit that mold in some ways, but when it came to her career and her role in the family, she smashed it. (More on that in chapter 5.)

There is also a geographic divide. The pressures on women who live in the South and the Midwest are different, pushing them toward earlier partnering and childbearing. Kenzie and her wife, Abbie, got married after a little over a year of dating. Abbie, who grew up in Minneapolis, had recently moved back to her hometown to take a job as a hospital chaplain after graduating from Harvard Divinity School. After attending college in Los Angeles, Kenzie, who grew up in nearby St. Paul, had also moved back to work as a policy director at a social services nonprofit.

Kenzie and Abbie met as they were emerging from long-term relationships. Both described feeling similar "panic moments." Abbie said, "I was thirty when my relationship dissolved and I realized I really wanted to have kids. Thirty here is like forty-eight somewhere else." Kenzie, then twenty-eight, described feeling as if she were "back to square one. Some of my close friends were starting to get married and have kids. Maybe it is the achiever in me, but I was looking at where am I in relation to my peers and the other piece of it too is that I have always felt called to pregnancy, to experience that and have a child."

In the Midwest, they both noted, earlier marriages and childbearing were common. Even then, they had watched some of their friends struggle with fertility issues. But there was another factor. Abbie put it succinctly: "Because we are queer, we have to be so intentional. Everything has to be planned out." Kenzie added, "We want to be realistic. Lesbian friends of ours had to go through multiple rounds of fertility treatments to get pregnant. We know we could be gearing up for a long fertility process. We can't count on the fact that we are going to try once and have a kid nine months later."

When Abbie discovered that her health insurance covered intra-uterine insemination, they decided to get started right away. They tied the knot over the Christmas holidays in 2019 and bought a house with a big backyard. COVID put their reproductive plans on hold for a few months, but in May 2020, Kenzie got pregnant after the first round of IUI and gave birth to their son, Dashiell, on February 25, 2021, when she was thirty.

Poring over the empirical data and competing narratives from my interviews with dozens of women, I thought about my own life choices and how much they were shaped by media-driven fears and a fervent desire to conform to my family's norms. In my twenties and early thirties, I had a thriving career as a trial lawyer in the Office of the Federal Public Defender in Los Angeles. My salary was in the low six figures; I did battle with the federal government in high-stakes trials where my clients faced years, even decades, in prison. I had a healthy social life; with friends and on dates, I went out to restaurants, movies, museums, and concerts. As a relatively new transplant to California, I traveled all over the state, wine-tasting on the central coast, hiking in Joshua Tree, and taking in the orange-red majesty of the Golden Gate Bridge as I walked across it, high as a kite. Looking back at pictures from that time, I see a young, vibrant, successful woman living her best life in the big city.

Still, that's not entirely how I felt. I was proud of myself, yes. I knew I was a good lawyer, a good daughter, a good friend. There was plenty of external validation to corroborate those feelings. But the drumbeat in my head starting in my late twenties often drowned out my accomplishments — the countdown to what I feared was a fast-approaching sell-by date. I enjoyed hanging out with my girl-friends and spending time by myself, but anxiety about the future tinged everything. Several long-term relationships ended in break-ups. The idea of remaining single well into my thirties scared me. Like Verna Williams, I heard the same when-is-it-going-to-happen drumbeat. In the game of musical chairs that was matching with a life partner, I feared I would have nowhere to land. I feared I wouldn't have children.

The implicit family comparison also nagged at me. There was my mother, of course, perfectly in keeping with her generation: married at twenty-one, a mother at twenty-six. Then there was my older sister, Emily, and my younger sister Jill — both were married at twenty-seven and had their first children before they turned thirty. In my early thirties and after a particularly bad breakup, I went to visit my parents in Philadelphia. When I confessed my fear that I would remain single and childless for the rest of my life, my mother observed: "Well, most people meet the person they are going to marry in college or in graduate school." When I pointed out the obvious — that those years were long past for me — she just nodded, looking thoughtful.

When my husband and I started dating seriously in late 2006 — after an earlier, failed attempt — we were both thirty-two. Looking back, that seems young, but at the time all I could picture was my diminishing supply of healthy eggs. Matt, who had gone to law school as an older student after working for eight years, graduated and landed a prestigious clerkship with a federal judge in San Francisco. He moved north in August of 2007. In January of 2008, I left my Los Angeles life behind — my job, my friends, my house — just like the women in the "I Can't Wait to Get Married" study. Matt was happy about the move — he had grown up in Marin just across the Golden Gate Bridge and his family still lived there.

For the next year, I struggled to transition to life as Matt's live-in girlfriend in a city where I had no friends and worked remotely on a death-penalty case I found hopeless and uninteresting. I was unhappy and at a professional crossroads. But here, I want to be careful about oversimplifying. The professional crossroads was entirely of my own choosing. After seven years as a public defender, I had crested a long, steep learning curve and was hungry for a change. Starting in 2006, I spent three semesters teaching once a week as an adjunct at LA's Loyola Law School, and I was hooked. I did some writing — a few op-eds about legal issues that mattered to me — and seeing my ideas out in the world gave me great joy and satisfaction.

I set my sights on what I secretly called "the Five-Million-Dollar Bet," a tenured job as a clinical law professor and what I estimated it was worth over a twenty-year period. This very particular kind of job would allow me to do what I loved — write, teach, and litigate — in precisely the way that I wanted. With tenure came job security, earning power, and almost complete autonomy; I could choose my own cases and speak my mind. Having tenure would let me set my own schedule, which meant I could parent on my own terms. The life of an academic allows for a crazy-quilt schedule; as long as I was productive, I could write from home on my nonteaching days and even take the day off to do whatever I wanted without raising any eyebrows. After years of 8:30 a.m. court appearances, ever at the mercy of mercurial judges whose rulings could destroy dinner plans and even entire vacations, I wanted out. And so, newly determined to transition to a career in academia, I spent my days home alone writing a law review article and scouring the internet for job postings.

I didn't say the words *Five-Million-Dollar Bet* aloud to Matt. I worried, perhaps unkindly, that if I did, he would shake his head at my grandiosity and foolhardiness in thinking I could pull it off. Tenure-track positions at law schools — really, anywhere in academia — are notoriously hard to get, and for clinicians, they are rarer still. Many law schools view clinical teaching, in which the professor operates a pro bono law firm within the school and litigates cases side by side with the students, to be less prestigious than "podium positions," where professors lecture to a large class and often interrogate students using the Socratic method. As a result, many law schools do not offer tenure to clinicians. And even for those that do, the climb to a secure permanent position takes years. I was not an established scholar and had very little teaching experience. The chances of a position coming open in Northern California and my getting it seemed unlikely. I worried, correctly, that if I insisted on leaving the Bay Area or even the state for one of these jobs, Matt would push back hard.

Matt and I were passionately, frantically in love, but our relationship was deeply problematic. Even during our happiest times, we fought constantly, seemingly over everything but in particular about my preoccupation with my career and my feeling that Matt failed to support me in my ambition or appreciate my success.

Couples who divorce always tell you that, looking back, there were red flags. Here is one of mine. Late in December 2007, several weeks before I moved to San Francisco, I tried my last criminal case in federal court. My father, who had never seen me in trial, flew across the country to surprise me. To this day, rounding the corner and seeing him sitting on a bench outside the courtroom remains one of the most joyful moments of my life.

The case, even by the generous standards of a public defender's office, was a dead-bang loser. My client, an elderly man suffering from mental illness, had walked into a bank in west Los Angeles and passed a note to the teller that read *This is a bank robery* [*sic*] *give me all of the money.* The teller, who was eight months pregnant, did as she was told. Her coworker pressed a safety alarm that was a direct line to the police. When they arrived, my client was in the lobby, crumpled bills in hand.

The incident was captured on surveillance cameras. Even the judge couldn't hide his disbelief when we rejected the prosecutor's offer to plead guilty in exchange for one hundred months in prison. When I proudly introduced the judge to my father, he jerked his head in my direction and told my dad, "I have no idea what she thinks she is doing here."

But I did know what I was doing. To convict my client, the jury had to find that he used force, fear, or intimidation. Otherwise, it was just plain old theft — a lowly charge the government had not bothered to bring. As witness after witness testified, the jury was left confronting a different kind of evidence: a frail old man, shaking and muttering at counsel table beside me and my trial partner. As I explained in my closing argument, the fact that my client thought he was committing a bank robbery didn't make it true. The only thing that mattered was whether the tellers were actually scared. And, despite their dramatic proclamations to the contrary, they weren't. The FBI agent who interviewed both of them was an honest guy and admitted as much when I made the gutsy choice to call him to the stand and question him as a hostile witness.

The gamble paid off; the jury acquitted. Afterward, my trial partner and I were ecstatic. Some people go their whole careers without a win in federal court. This was my third acquittal. I was going out on a high. But when I called Matt to tell him the news, his voice was flat. "That's great," he said in a tone that signaled he thought it was anything but great. I went from feeling like a conquering hero to feeling like a swatted fly in seconds. The contrast between Matt's indifference, my colleagues' hugs and high fives, and my dad's heartfelt congratulations felt extreme. For whatever reason — for many complicated reasons — Matt could not express happiness for my professional success. At least, that is how it seemed. It is important to point out here that there are two sides to every story. I write about my relationship with my ex-husband well aware that the reader is hearing only one side: mine. I am describing the way that I felt being on the receiving end of a communication that seemed dismissive and hurtful. That is not the same thing as claiming to know what Matt intended.

For a time — during which I mainly flailed in my pursuit of my academic dreams — that issue abated. Other problems quickly rose to fill the void. But I was far more invested in getting Matt to marry me than in facing up to that reality.

Matt proposed on Valentine's Day of 2008, the day I turned thirty-four. Equal parts ecstatic and relieved, I said yes. Ring on my finger, I turned my attention to my next goal: having a baby. I had read the studies and I was worried. I told Matt we needed to start trying immediately. I had irregular cycles and had been on birth control for months. All of these factors, I told him confidently, combined with my age meant that the process of getting pregnant would likely take at least a year.

I remember the conversation clearly. It was just after the Fourth of July and we were sitting in the backyard of the house we were renting in the Castro. It was unseasonably warm for San Francisco, which is often wet and miserable in the summer — balmy enough to forgo, briefly, the cardigan I never went anywhere without. As I made my case, I watched Matt's eyes widen. He protested. Couldn't we wait? We were planning our wedding in October. Meanwhile, both of our jobs were ending, and the recession had hit. A bright future had suddenly fogged over with uncertainty. "No," I told him firmly. "No, no, no."

In fact, getting pregnant took roughly eleven minutes.

I'm not joking. Later that month, we spent a long weekend with Matt's family in Tahoe. His mom snapped a picture of us during one of those days at the beach. I am wearing a floppy straw hat and a green-and-white-striped bikini. Matt's hair is blown upward by a sudden wind. We are in profile, my arms wrapped around his neck, our faces inches apart. Our son was with us already, inside of me, no bigger than a grain of rice. We had no idea how radically our lives were about to change.

When I told my parents, the first thing my mother said was "Oh my God, what about your dress!" She and my sister Jill had flown to San Francisco to help me pick it out, a process that had taken days and visits to at least five different boutiques. It was beautiful: satiny, off-white, floor-length. With a very unforgiving bodice. My father's reaction was, in retrospect, more unnerving, although at the time I dismissed it as dated and ridiculous. "Aren't you doing this in the wrong order?" he asked. "Have you really thought everything through?"

Looking back, I think I misunderstood what my father was trying to tell me. He did not mean it was a mistake to get pregnant before getting married. He meant it was a mistake to get pregnant and get married in an unplanned rush. He and my mother lived together for five years before having their first child. During that time, they established routines. They had discussions about who would do what. (In my opinion, my mother got the short end of the stick, but the point is that they agreed on the division of labor — she knew what she was getting into.)

In hindsight, I am struck by how much planning and preparation went into singular, onetime events — our wedding day and the birth of our son — and how little went into what our lives would look like afterward. I gave a great deal of thought and attention to the finer details of my wedding: invitations, guest lists, venue scouting, menu-tasting. I gave even more time and attention to preparing for the birth of my son. Together with Matt, I spent hours at weekly birthing classes learning how to breathe through labor, time my contractions, and swaddle our baby. But I gave almost no time and attention to thinking through the duller details of day-to-day life as a partnered, professionally striving parent, much less to figuring out whether Matt was on the same page as me.

The debates about the optimal time for women to get married, get pregnant, and have a baby while creating the minimum possible career disruption create a lot of heat and little light. They miss the point. Falling in love and having that love reciprocated, wanting to get married and having that desire reciprocated, trying to get pregnant and actually conceiving, are, to a large degree, beyond our control. There is no recipe to follow. There is no predicting what your heart or the heart you hope to win over will want. There is no predicting what your body will do.

What is in our control, however, is our vision of ourselves as spouses, partners, and professionals. It is important to understand, at the outset, whether this is a shared vision and if it isn't whether compromise is possible. The basic boring parts matter — they matter a great deal. Is your partner willing to take family leave, and if so, for how long? Is your partner willing to divide household chores, including childcare, fifty-fifty? Who will drive the kids to and from day care, elementary school, soccer practice, violin lessons? Will you have a nanny or a babysitter, and if so, how will you afford it? Is it important for one or both of you to live near your families? Most crucially, does your partner understand the importance of your career and support you in your ambition even and especially when it makes it hard and burdensome on him or her?

Matt and I never had these conversations. We should have. Because the hard truth is that if you don't, no amount of love can save your relationship.

CHAPTER TWO

THE CULT OF MOTHERHOOD

Damned if You Do, Damned if You Don't

THERE WAS A DRAWER IN A CABINET IN MY BEDROOM WHERE my mother kept the congratulatory cards she received after I was born. When I was little, I liked to take them out and look at them.

My favorite card was a drawing of a mother and child. The mother's soft white arms cradled the baby to her bosom. Her pretty profile — small delicate nose, long-lashed downturned eyes — was focused entirely on the small sleeping bundle. She had lustrous golden hair that rippled and encircled the baby. She had created a world just for the two of them.

In my senior year of college, I took a creative writing class taught by the author Mary Gordon. One day she asked us to do an impromptu in-class writing assignment. We were to spend fifteen minutes writing about what the word *mother* meant to us. My mind went instantly to the Mother on the Card. She wasn't even real, but she continued to hold the same power over me that she had since childhood.

My actual mother was nothing like this woman. My mother's hair was dark, almost black, cut short in the same no-nonsense style for decades. Her skin was olive, and her arms were naturally sinewy. She was short and thin, definitely not what anyone would describe as *bosomy*. Her embraces were usually quick and hard, her eyes often focused on the next task immediately in front of her. I was never in doubt that my mother loved me or that I was important to her, but I rarely felt the radiant force that I imagined the child on the card experiencing: undivided and all-encompassing maternal attention. It just wasn't possible. In addition to having three other children, my mother had a full-time job.

So why did the card hold such sway over me well into my teens and twenties? Why does it still, even as I, too, bear no resemblance, physical or otherwise, to this fictional mother? Four decades later, I can readily call up her image and the feelings it evoked: a nostalgic longing for something that never was but that I felt sure *could* and indeed did exist for other children.

In fact, I believed I knew such a mother growing up.

Gretchen Rossman was the mother of my best childhood friend, Tamara. In my child's-eye view, Gretchen was everything my mother was not. She was always home, it seemed, baking a pie or sewing an exquisite doll's dress on her sewing machine on the second floor of their large, comfortable home. Gretchen wasn't a doctor — she was married to one. Gretchen was beautiful in the same way that the Mother on the Card was beautiful. But she was also a bit aloof, not quite knowable.

Part of the aloofness was that Gretchen seemed impossibly perfect, and it was hard not to make invidious comparisons. Non-Jewish holidays at my house were often slapdash affairs, particularly the ones my father called "excuses for conspicuous consumption," like Mother's Day. (Once, when I asked my dad what he wanted for Father's Day, he told me, "For you to treat me with respect the other three hundred and sixty-four days of the year.") We did not celebrate present-heavy, decoration-laden Christmas, with its twinkling lights and lit-up, ceiling-high fir tree beside the mantel. But the Rossmans did. And every Easter, Gretchen handed out baskets with pink and green streamers before sending us off to hunt for eggs in the backyard.

Halloween was when the divide between my mother and Gretchen became a chasm. Interestingly, my mother remembered it that way too. "I liked Mary Feary, your kindergarten teacher," she told me, "but she always made me feel like I was doing something wrong." I asked what she meant. "Well, there was somebody in your kindergarten class who had a stay-at-home mom, and she made Halloween costumes, and not only did I hate Halloween, I could never get my act together. I couldn't figure out how to do it and I just thought it was so stupid. I remember Mrs. Feary saying to me, 'So-and-so's mother made her the nicest Halloween costume,' and then looking at me as if to say, *What's your problem?*"

I was pretty sure I knew which mother Mrs. Feary was talking about. Tamara's Halloween costumes were always perfect; everyone exclaimed over them. Gretchen could do anything, it seemed, with her sewing machine.

The year Tamara and I were in Mrs. Feary's class, I wanted to be a tiger for Halloween, in honor of the stuffed animal I carried everywhere to sniff and shred while I vigorously sucked my thumb. When I asked my mom about the possibility of her making me that costume, we were standing in my little sister's room, which was in the process of being redone as she transitioned from a crib to a bed. My mother gestured to a roll of yellow-and-white-striped wallpaper that was lying on the ground. "Why don't you just wrap yourself up in some of that?" she suggested. "I can make it stick together with Scotch tape."

The idea of walking into Mrs. Feary's classroom with my head and feet sticking out of a Scotch-taped roll of leftover wallpaper — arms presumably pinned to my sides — filled me with dismay, which was quickly followed by outrage. Could my mother possibly be serious? She was. She didn't have time. And she didn't care. Halloween wasn't an occasion my mother looked forward to as a chance to showcase her domestic skills. It was a day that she dreaded because it made her feel overwhelmed and inadequate.

But if that was true for my mother, was the opposite true for Gretchen Rossman? Did she see holidays and celebrations as joyous and meaningful exercises in creativity? Was Gretchen Rossman the icon of motherhood I had always believed her to be — the ever-nurturing, always-present Mother on the Card?

My friendship with Tamara fell apart in elementary school, and she moved away by eighth grade. We did not keep in touch, and I was not remotely prepared for what I found when I googled her mother. Gretchen Rossman was a professor emerita of international education at the University of Massachusetts Amherst, the coauthor of nine books, and an internationally recognized expert on education reform involving something called "qualitative research design and methods." I stared at the photograph next to the biographical information. It was definitely her.

With some trepidation, I cut-and-pasted her e-mail address and started writing. "Dear Gretchen," I wrote, then paused, my finger hovering over the cursor. Should I call her *Professor Rossman?* It also occurred to me that Gretchen might have no memory of who I was, so I wrote a few explanatory sentences. After describing the book I was working on, I got to the point: "This request may seem bizarre, but I am writing to see if I can interview you." She wrote back a kind note, assuring me that yes, she did remember me, and asking that I send her a list of the topics I wanted to cover. I responded with a long list, like a lawyer probing a mystery witness. "I have very particular memories of you," I wrote, "but I don't know if they are real."

My memories, as it turned out, were both real and not real. The whole time I had known Gretchen, she was pursuing a PhD in education. She came from a family of academics; her father was a well-known economist at MIT. Her mother had a BA in economics but stayed at home. "That's where I learned all the crafty stuff," she told me. "She was always knitting and jamming and preserving and making cookies. But I think she was very frustrated with that life."

Gretchen got her undergraduate and master's degrees from the University of Pennsylvania. Afterward, she taught at a school in North Philadelphia. All of her students were Black and poor. She vividly remembered one boy who had been held back for two years and could not read. The school had no funding for special-needs children, so Gretchen started experimenting to create her own curriculum, one that was tailored to fit his needs and those of some of her other struggling students. The educational tools the school provided had failed, and it was up to her to figure out an alternative. "I was fascinated with epistemologies. I would try to explore the root assumptions that were driving particular learning methods to test what the experts assumed they knew about how we acquire knowledge. Because often, they were wrong."

In 1968, during the second year of her master's program, Gretchen met her husband, Milt, who was a medical student. They were married the following year. Gretchen was twenty-four. "That was my internalized path, and that was the societal narrative." Gretchen gave birth to their first daughter, Dara, in 1971, and Tamara followed in 1974. Those years revolved around child-rearing, and the family followed Milt as his career took them to the Texas-Mexico border, then to Cleveland, and then, when Tamara was a year old, back to Philadelphia. Gretchen protested against the final move because the family had put down roots and she loved her community, but ultimately she gave in. "Milt's career was the most important thing," she said.

Back in Philadelphia, Gretchen was lonely and at loose ends. "I think I was a pretty good stay-at-home mom," she said. "I did what was expected of me, but it wasn't enough. I needed to do something for myself." In 1977, when Dara was six and Tamara was three, she returned to the University of Pennsylvania to get a PhD in education.

Gretchen loved graduate school, which connected her with professors and students who shared her passion for addressing deep-seated racial inequities in the educational system. "It was my world, not Milt's world." Sometimes, she said, she would go out drinking with friends after class and come home at 1:00 a.m., leaving Milt to make dinner and put the girls to bed. "He tolerated it," she said. While in graduate school, she began working part-time at a federally funded program called Research for Better Schools. There, together with three colleagues, she published her first academic paper. More papers followed, with Gretchen as the lead author. After a stint as an adjunct professor at Penn, Gretchen decided she wanted to teach full-time at a university.

When Gretchen learned that the University of Massachusetts Amherst was hiring for a tenure-track position in its graduate department of education, "it sent shivers up and down my spine. It was like they wrote the position for me." (When I realized that throughout the time I worshipped her as the perfect stay-at-home mother, Gretchen had been in avid pursuit of her own Five-Million-Dollar Bet, it sent shivers up and down *my* spine.) But Milt had a thriving career as a professor of medicine at the University of Pennsylvania. He had no intention of moving.

Gretchen said that, over the years, "Our marriage slowly unraveled. There wasn't fighting. We were just growing further and further apart. When I applied for the UMass job, I think I knew on some level that it was over." She was hired and started in 1987. Gretchen spent the first semester splitting her week between the two cities in an attempt to make things work. Then she gave up. "It was all very rational," she said. "We did the divorce ourselves and divided everything up equally. I didn't get alimony because I didn't want it. At that point, I was making good money."

Tamara moved to Amherst with Gretchen after seventh grade, and Dara, a junior in high school, stayed behind with Milt. Two years later, Dara moved north, too, to go to Amherst College. Now minutes from her mother, Dara set firm boundaries. "I had to call or make an appointment to see her," Gretchen told me, laughing. "She didn't want me just dropping by her dorm." Several years after that, Tamara moved back to Philadelphia to go to her mother's alma mater. She was now a fifteen-minute drive from her dad. Of the zigzagging trajectories that separated and reconnected the family, Gretchen said, "People don't believe me when I tell them that. It's wild."

Saying goodbye to Gretchen Rossman at the end of our first Zoom call, I found myself blinking back tears. Seeing her again after so many years was moving, and hearing her story was both a surprise and a relief. Gretchen wasn't the Mother on the Card. My vision of her was skewed by my child's eye and sliver of access to her life. When I spoke to Dara and Tamara, both told me that they regularly took the bus home from school and entertained themselves until Gretchen came back from her classes at Penn or the fieldwork she was doing for her dissertation. Some nights, their dad cooked dinner and put them to bed. With Gretchen, I saw what I wanted to see — or maybe I simply saw the image she projected.

She was, in fact, more like my own mother than I ever would have guessed. They were both conflicted strivers, acceding to and struggling against convention. Gretchen's ambition, what she preferred to call her "longing for achievement," made her even more of an outlier. She had left her marriage, her home, a daughter, and a settled life for something entirely different. She did it out of love for her job and a desire to be independent. Her choice was extremely unusual for a married mother in the 1980s.

The next generation of women — my generation and the millennials who followed — did not face the kind of explicit choices and societal norms that presented themselves so starkly to baby boomers like Gretchen and my mother. We were told we could have it all, with the explicit proviso that "having it all" meant remaining modest about our achievements at work while loudly proclaiming that we were putting our children first. This message, it turns out, is its own kind of trap.

Since the Victorian era, motherhood has been held up as the pinnacle of a woman's happiness and touted as her ultimate achievement. In her groundbreaking book *The Cultural Contradictions of Motherhood,* sociologist Sharon Hays coined the term *intensive mothering* to describe an impossibly high standard that professional mothers were measured against: not only must they be the primary caregivers, they must be laser-focused and utterly absorbed by their children to the exclusion of anyone and anything else.[1]

These unrealistic expectations need not even be explicitly stated anymore because the rise of social media has created a way of disseminating the message through exquisitely filtered content.[2] "Consider the Instagram image of the pregnant and postpartum supermom: a nurturing, organized, sexy-but-modest multitasker who glows during prenatal yoga and seems unfazed by the challenges of leaking breasts, dirty laundry, and sleep training," wrote Dr. Alexandra Sacks, the coauthor of a parenting book called *What No One Tells You,* in her viral *New York Times* essay "The Birth of a Mother." "This woman is a fiction. She's an unrealistic example of perfection that makes other women feel inadequate when they pursue and can't achieve that impossible standard."[3]

Unlike the women of my mother's and Gretchen Rossman's generation, twenty-first-century women are encouraged and often financially compelled to have professional careers. When women try to perform the hat trick of holding down a full-time job while parenting and looking fantastic doing both, they find themselves overwhelmed and under-resourced often to the breaking point. Meanwhile, they are surrounded by carefully curated social media stories featuring beautiful, svelte, successful celebrities touting their 24/7 devotion to their children while professing that motherhood has come at no cost to their careers. This impossible-to-live-up-to illusion makes mere mortal women feel that much worse.

Women with small children are bombarded by messages that mothering is a joyous, almost ecstatic experience. Motherhood is glorified and fetishized.[4] Nearly every celebrity mom, from Princess Kate to Drew Barrymore to Jennifer Garner, describes her parenting style as "hands-on," claiming to rely on little if any outside help. Again and again, we hear from these glamorous, famous, professionally accomplished women that their "number-one priority" is being a mother even as they jet off to faraway locations to film their latest movie or embark on worldwide concert tours.

The multiplatinum singer Adele, the mother of a six-year-old, was described in a March 2, 2020, *People* article as "very involved with his school. She loves her mom life." Her son, we were told, was the inspiration for her slimmed-down physique, which was contrasted with "before" shots of her plumper self. After a paragraph describing her fitness regimen and her forthcoming, much-anticipated album, the piece concluded: "She's an artist and a mom. She needs to make sure she's able to handle both flawlessly. She just wants it all to be perfect."

In the December 2019 issue of *People,* Jennifer Lopez, then fifty, discussed her hit movie *Hustlers,* her upcoming Super Bowl halftime show, and her yearlong, sold-out music tour in a six-page spread naming her one of the magazine's People of the Year. These accomplishments, however, paled by comparison to her most important work: "Being a mom to her 11-year-old twins, Emme and Max." Motherhood, said Lopez, was her "number 1 job." According to a January 2020 article in *People,* actress Kate Hudson is busy "building an empire" that includes writing books, creating a clothing line, a podcast, and a vodka brand, and starring in three upcoming films. But the mother of three made it clear to readers that "I can have a balanced life." In the final paragraph, under the heading "Family First," Hudson's children were described as "her top priority." Quoting an unnamed source, the piece concluded: "She loves to cook and chill and have family and friends over. Her door's always open, and she loves throwing theme parties and having her nieces and nephews over for sleepovers. They're all one big happy family."[5]

The takeaway is that it is possible — and optimal — for mothers to have wildly successful careers while always being present, all five senses attuned to the needs of their children as they transition effortlessly from movie sets to yoga pants on a run to the grocery store, all while managing to look picture-perfect. And if a conflict arises, celebrities are quick to say that they forgo tantalizing job opportunities to tend to their children. The rap star Cardi B dropped out of a world tour with Bruno Mars after giving birth to her daughter. "I can't leave my baby at night," she said, dispensing with the idea of having anyone else look after her daughter — "not for one second."[6] Salma Hayek, the mother of a young daughter, told *People* magazine, "If later on [acting] gets in the way of her development, I'll just stop working."[7]

For more than twenty years, I have subscribed to three magazines: *People, Us Weekly,* and *The New Yorker* — two of which I read religiously. My habit was to save *People* and *Us Weekly* for trips to the gym, where the best-dressed lists, true-crime exposés, and breathless gossip proved a welcome distraction from the tedium and agony of the elliptical machine. These weekly binges seemed like a harmless indulgence. It wasn't until I started writing this book that I realized how fast and furious the Message of Magical Motherhood was coming at me in these pages. The stories — really, the same story — were in every issue. Beautiful women on set and at home, talking excitedly about their most recent project with a suitable level of humility, careful to place it squarely within a larger context: only one role mattered, and that role was being a mother.

Cole Valley, the picturesque San Francisco neighborhood where Matt and I settled after our son was born, reflected a similarly happy tableau. Young professional mothers were everywhere, all of them lithe, loving, purposeful. Or so it seemed. Like my own mother, I had no close friends at the time. I continued to long for my life in Los Angeles, where Katie and Lauren, two of my closest girlfriends, both extremely hardworking and ambitious, lived with their new babies.

Had I been able to spend time with close female friends who were new mothers, I think I would have felt less miserably inferior, because the scaffolding that made their working lives possible — babysitters, nannies, and, in Katie's case, a stay-at-home husband — would have been visible to me. So, too, their messes: their insecurities and struggles — financial, marital, professional. Together we would have laughed at these celebrities and their blithe assertions of self-less motherhood, which required, among other things, financial re-sources unavailable to most people, including us, and in any event did not seem credible. But no one in my immediate orbit was in on the joke, and laughing to myself just made me feel lonelier, skirting the edge of crazy.

Motherhood first was the mantra that rang in my ears. It was socially unacceptable, even politically perilous, to say otherwise.

Perhaps the most prominent example was former First Lady Michelle Obama. It is hard to think of a more accomplished woman: a graduate of Princeton and Harvard Law School, former partner at a major law firm, former associate dean at the University of Chicago, and former vice president of Community and External Affairs for the University of Chicago Medical Center. For most of her marriage, including when her two daughters were young, she outearned her husband.

But in 2012, while giving a speech at the Democratic National Convention following Barack Obama's nomination for a second term as president, Michelle Obama wanted her millions of listeners to know that "at the end of the day, my most important title is still 'mom in chief.'"[8] Jessica Valenti, a feminist author and mother of a young daughter, tweeted in response, "I long for the day when powerful women don't need to assure Americans that they are moms above all else."

Contrast the steady drumbeat of "mom-first" messaging with what some dads have to say. Consider the late Larry King, who retired from CNN in 2010 after twenty-five years of hosting his eponymous talk show. In his anchor chair, King interviewed more than fifty thousand people, including numerous U.S. presidents, heads of state, Academy Award winners, humanitarians, and religious leaders. Asked about his work-life balance, King, who had five children, was blunt: "My career always came first. I used to say, if CNN called with an emergency or my wife called with an emergency, I'd call CNN back first."[9]

If a celebrity mom spoke those words, she would be skewered on social media. To baldly admit to prioritizing one's career over motherhood — and it is likely that most successful women, famous or not, have done just that — is a social death sentence. As San Francisco State University researcher Melissa Seelye wrote, "Motherhood, unlike fatherhood, is presented as a sacred, self-sacrificial mission that defines all women and to insult or make light of that holy task would be akin to questioning the very essence of woman-hood. If she is not an adequately devoted mother, what is she?"[10]

Left unstated in these stories and underlying expectations is that a mom-first, career-second stance is a luxury available only to women who can afford to take substantial time off from work because they have flexible jobs and high-earning partners. Most women have neither. When Diana Luong had her daughter, Sarah, she was working full-time at a nail salon as an esthetician after going to a trade school to get her cosmetology license. Her husband was a maintenance worker at a hotel. "I worked and worked," she said, "double- and triple-booked sometimes, and even if a client came in fifteen minutes before closing, my boss would say, 'Take them,' so I was always coming home late." The hourly pay was poor, but the tips made up for it; Diana earned about $130 a day.

The salon did not pay for maternity leave, but California law provided postpartum women with state disability for eight weeks. Diana and her husband were able to scrape by on that meager sup-plement, but when it ended, she returned to work. Her schedule left no time to pump milk, but even if it had, there was nowhere to do it, so she stopped breastfeeding abruptly. "That was hard," she said. Every day, Diana used her thirty-minute lunch break to drive home and spend a few minutes with her baby before she had to leave again, shutting her ears to the sound of Sarah crying. But she feared overstaying and getting in trouble with her boss. "I would drive back panicking and in a rush."

Hely Harris is in a similarly unforgiving business. She has spent the past twenty-five years working in restaurants, beginning at eigh-teen as a hostess at TGI Fridays in Orlando. Over the years, Hely worked her way up from a server and bartender in chain restaurants and small bistros to become floor manager for Cookshop, a longtime staple in New York's trendy Chelsea neighborhood. But although the restaurant had a corporate owner — the Bowery Group — and had been profitable for years, it offered no paid time off.

Hely's husband, Tim, is also in the industry; until 2018, he co-owned several restaurants in Manhattan. After the restaurants closed, Tim took a job at the Bowery Group as the beverage director. In 2013, they had their son, Jack. Hely's pregnancy was difficult; at thirty-two weeks, she had to be hospitalized and put on bedrest. Jack was delivered by cesarean section two weeks later, weighing only four pounds, two ounces. He spent three weeks in the neonatal intensive care unit (NICU). Hely took an additional twelve weeks off to heal and take care of her son. During that time, she applied for short-term disability, which amounted to $130 a week, and used up her two weeks of paid vacation. (In 2016, New York State passed a law mandating paid parental leave, and Hely told me that Cookshop now has much better policies, offering its employees three months of leave at 75 percent pay.) In total, Hely was out for four months, either on bedrest or caring for a premature baby, without a salary.

In the absence of formal benefits, sometimes lower-income women can stitch together a community to make it work — barely. Nicole DeVon was twenty-four and working at an electronics store in a mall in Spokane, Washington, when she met a guy "who was really cool until he wasn't." When she found out she was pregnant, she broke up with him. "I thought about the kind of parent I wanted to be," she said. "I didn't want to be with this guy, working a low-wage retail job the rest of my life." Raised by her adoptive father, who came from what she described as a "very white, conservative, immigrant family that was all about 'pull yourself up by your bootstraps,'" Nicole struggled with issues of race and identity. She knew little about her birth parents other than that her mother was Black and that she had been raped by Nicole's father, who was white. (Nicole later learned she also had Native parentage.) Nicole and her adoptive father lived on the Yakama Reservation near the Canadian border, where he worked as a guidance counselor. Nicole always sensed she was different and at times was made to feel that difference. "A lot of things did not compute for me. I had no vocabulary to deal with bias and discrimination. I did not understand these concepts even though I experienced the feelings." She also struggled academically. "I was a horrible student," she said.

Growing up among the children who lived on the reservation, though, Nicole felt relatively privileged. And she was a star athlete who had plenty of friends; she got her sense of self-worth from sports. But while her father's job was to help kids get into college, he was not helpful to Nicole. "I was a tough girl who raised myself, and asking for help was a sign of weakness, so I didn't. It was going to ruin my badass image." She flunked out of three different community colleges.

But once Nicole learned she was going to be a mother, she told me, "I got my shit together." With some financial help from her father, Nicole enrolled in Eastern Washington University when her daughter, Peighton, was two. For the next three years, mom and daughter lived together in a small off-campus apartment. "I had this great circle of friends from all different backgrounds: Mexican, Native American, African American. There was a bunch of us in school who were single moms. So we helped each other." Relying on this small community and a few relatives for childcare, Nicole was able to get her bachelor's degree and graduate at thirty. She had been working part-time at an Early Childhood Education and Assistance Program run by Spokane Community College, which offered free partial day care and prekindergarten to underserved children. "I was lucky to have a job where I could take my daughter to work." The early years trying to take care of her daughter as a single mother while getting an education and earning money were difficult. "When I tell my origin story, people always say, 'Oh my God, look at what you've been through.' But from my point of view, I was blessed, and yet I was always one degree away from a large amount of trauma."

Even women who do have the luxury of paid time off don't always take it, worrying that they are signaling to their colleagues and bosses that they are not going to be as reliably present, focused, and high-achieving moving forward. Asked if she took maternity leave when her first child was born, Amanda Renteria, who is now the CEO of Code for America, smiled ruefully. "I sort of did." Amanda, who was born in 1974 to Mexican farmworkers in the poorest county in California, always prided herself on breaking barriers with her no-holds-barred, work-hard, play-hard ethic. She was the first woman and first Latina from her small rural high school to get into Stanford. The class valedictorian, she also lettered in three varsity sports.

At Stanford, Amanda double-majored in economics and political science and graduated with honors. Her senior thesis focused on the dearth of women of color in politics. After several years working for Goldman Sachs on Wall Street, she went to Harvard Business School, where she met her husband, Pat. "That is where I fell in love," she told me, "with him and with public service." She decided that she wanted to go into politics.

In 2004, during the fourth inning of a Red Sox game, Amanda proposed to Pat on the jumbotron in front of his mother, father, and siblings. Wearing a baseball jersey that said *Branneria* on the back — a combination of her last name and his, Branelly — she got down on one knee and handed Pat a baseball inscribed with the words *Will you marry me?* The following year, they moved to Washington, DC, so that Amanda could take a job working as an economic adviser to Dianne Feinstein, California's senior senator, a Democrat.

Several years later, a position as chief of staff to Feinstein's colleague Senator Debbie Stabenow, a Democrat from Michigan, opened up. Going into the interview, Amanda knew she was an underdog; she was aiming to become the first Latina chief of staff on Capitol Hill while still in her early thirties. And she wasn't even from Michigan. She said her thinking was "*Damn it, the difference is good. I was prepared to name it and give it value.*" To her surprise, Stabenow was already sold. "I want you," she said. Hearing those words, Amanda said, "I was startled. Because I have always felt like I had to prove myself and she validated me. She knew me and my work."

Having children had not been a focus for Amanda. "I thought I couldn't because there were fertility problems in my family." But at thirty-five, she got pregnant. She was overjoyed and also concerned with how her pregnancy would be received and "the realities that you cannot do the kind of stuff you used to do." Every Friday at 6:00 a.m., Amanda played in an invitation-only basketball league with reporters and staffers on the Hill. All the other players were men. When she started her second trimester, one of them told her, "We can't play with you anymore."

Sports for Amanda had always been a way to excel — an athletic scholarship had paid her way through Stanford — and in her job as chief of staff, the weekly basketball game helped her "navigate the guys' world." The Senate, both members and staff, was dominated by white men. Being "one of the guys" — even if it was just for an hour once a week — gave Amanda an insider's connection that other women didn't have. Suddenly it was gone. "I wanted to be treated normally," she said, "but I was going through this major transformation."

For the most part, Amanda tried to pretend nothing was different. When she was overcome with morning sickness, she would quietly run down the corridor to an unoccupied bathroom to throw up. "I didn't want anyone to know." When the details of what became the Affordable Care Act were being hammered out at midnight, Amanda was there, nine months pregnant. The morning of the day she gave birth to her son, she attended a fundraiser. "Walking out, I told the senator, 'I think I need to go home.' That was the first day I left work early."

Initially, Amanda told the human resources department she intended to "ease into returning to work." But after a few weeks, she was back full-time. "I wasn't a baby mom," she said. She hired a babysitter, who brought her son, Diego, to work so that she could breastfeed. "I was lucky," she said. "I had an office where I could close the door." Amanda did not go back to work because she needed the money; she had paid maternity leave, and Pat earned a good salary at a nonprofit. She went back in part because she missed the fast-paced work environment but also because she continually felt that she had to "make a case for myself." Paradoxically, the higher she rose, the more pressure she felt.

"I was better when I had my second," she told me about her son who was born in 2012. "But that was only because one of the female assistants told me, 'When you were pregnant with Diego you made it look really easy and that makes it hard for other women.'" It had not been easy. Between her first and second child, Amanda had a miscarriage in Senator Stabenow's bathroom. The conversation with her aide and the miscarriage, she said, "shaped my thinking and I realized, I do have to talk more openly about these things." By pretending that nothing was different and hiding her own struggles, Amanda realized, she was presenting a facade that made it more difficult for the women in her workplace to ask for what they needed or even to take what was rightfully theirs — paid time off after having their babies.

Running through all these very different stories and so many others I encountered is a common thread: Each of these women felt that her situation was uniquely her own. With the exception of Nicole, they confronted the challenges of having a baby without feeling as if they could share their struggles or ask for additional support in the workplace. Their pregnancies and first few months with their babies were suffused with stress, partly because they all felt on some level that to rise higher — or simply keep their jobs — they were expected to act as if they had never given birth.

So many of the women I interviewed spoke of learning to suppress the physical and emotional pain they experienced from miscarriage, birth complications, or the abrupt discontinuation of breastfeeding with a smile and a can-do attitude. It was the emotional equivalent of a celebrity mom posing in her skinny jeans weeks after giving birth, an image I saw repeatedly in the glossy magazines I rabidly consumed. What was required of these women — of so many working mothers in the United States — was a public-facing denial of the deprivation that went into making their work personas possible.

There is a flip side to the Mother on the Card, equally powerful, equally illusory. She is the Mother in the Workplace, smiling and soldiering on as if nothing has changed. Together, they are the twin faces of the cult of motherhood.

What about the women who can afford to stay home for months or even a full year to bond with their newborns? Unexpectedly, with my first child, I was one of them. Complaining about this luxurious situation seems absurd, like the famous story of the princess who could feel the dig of a pea in her back despite lying on a stack of downy mattresses. Yet for some women, including me, being a stay-at-home mother can, at times, feel like a poor fit. But voicing anything other than gratitude and joy for this privilege sounds obnoxious, obtuse, and ungrateful in the extreme.

My son, Carter, was born on April 18, 2009. The months that led up to his birth — which were also the first months of my marriage — were awful. The recession was in full swing and Matt had been unable to find a job. Shortly before Carter was born, I landed a position as an associate at a boutique law firm in Los Angeles, which required us to leave San Francisco and move back to my house, which I had been renting out. Matt was angry and upset — about his circumstances, about the move, about me. He wanted to stay in the Bay Area, close to his parents and his brother. Moving away for my job, knowing there was nothing in LA for him, was maddening. This fight — over where to live and whose career mattered more — continued throughout the duration of our marriage.

The relationship deteriorated to the point where I considered moving to LA alone. But I didn't do that or even bring up the possibility with Matt. Declaring our marriage a failure less than six months after the wedding and going it alone with an infant was too shameful and frightening to contemplate. And I was still in love with him.

We moved to Los Angeles in January, and I started work at the law firm, heavily pregnant. Matt spent the days alone in my house, applying for jobs and not getting any. He grew colder and more distant. The tables had turned since my previous move to San Francisco for him, and now he was the one adrift. He resented me in the same way that I had resented him, only more.

I became increasingly anxious and clingy, which predictably made Matt retreat further. I started sinking into depression — something I had experienced in college and had no desire to relive. I went on Prozac and took medication to sleep. Studies could not rule out negative impacts on a developing fetus,[11] but on balance and in consultation with my ob-gyn, my therapist thought it was safer than me trying to white-knuckle it. The drugs helped me sleep and remain calm, but they also made me feel guilty and fearful. What if I was hurting my baby? Crying one night, I promised Matt that if he got a job in San Francisco, I would quit mine and move back.

It was a relatively easy promise to make. Our life at home was miserable and my life at work was not much better. Unlike my job at the federal public defender's office, I was rarely in court, had no autonomy, and found much of the work delegated to junior associates like myself dull. I was still focused on pursuing my dream of a life in academia. I didn't want to sell my house and leave LA for good, but I was willing to do it to save the marriage, provided I had opportunities too. A friend sent me a job posting for a two-year clinical fellowship at UC Hastings College of the Law in San Francisco. The pay was execrable — less than a third of my law firm salary. In fact, it was less money than I had made since graduating from law school eight years earlier, but the experience could prove invaluable. Fellowships like these were often stepping-stones to full-time academic positions. I applied.

And then, several weeks before Carter was born, our luck suddenly changed. Matt got an offer from a large firm in San Francisco, a job that came with a hefty salary and excellent benefits. Days later, I got the job at Hastings, with an agreement to stagger the fellowship with another applicant. She would start immediately, and I would begin one year later. In the meantime, I could stay home with my baby. Suddenly, a months-long nightmare was over. It felt like magic.

Carter felt like magic too. Somehow, despite everything, he was completely normal. More than that, he was beautiful in a way that few newborns are: born with a full head of blond hair, Matt's ocean-blue eyes, and delicious pink and white skin. He took instantly to breastfeeding, latching on and holding tight, his cheek muscles working furiously. Holding his little body in my arms in the hospital, I felt my heart smash to pieces.

The first year of Carter's life was the closest I ever came to being the wife and mother that Matt — and our society — envisioned. Matt moved north in July of 2009, while Carter and I stayed behind for several months to get my house ready for sale and give Matt time to find us a new place to live. I quit my law firm job, not wanting to take maternity leave I didn't feel I had earned. My days were filled with errands, pediatrician appointments, visits with friends, and sleeping when I could.

Carter and I moved to San Francisco in October. Matt found us a one-floor flat in a hundred-year-old Edwardian building with a back garden that looked distinctly French: stone pathways, wildflowers, hedgerows, and a burbling fountain. The neighborhood felt like a little village. There was a main street within walking distance that had a grocery store, a dry cleaner's, a hardware store, and several very good restaurants.

Matt worked long hours, and I continued my daily routine with Carter, who hit every milestone and seemed to be thriving. I should have been overjoyed with this idyllic life. I thought again of the Mother on the Card. Now, finally, was my chance to be just like her. But I wasn't. At times I was deliriously happy with my delicious baby, but I was also bored. And it would be a stretch to say that Carter got my undivided attention. I have no memory of his first word or first steps — probably I was reading or on the phone. I dutifully joined a mothers' group, then wondered what the point was. I liked the other women, but we had nothing in common other than the fact that we had all recently given birth. I felt lonely, adrift, and mortified by those feelings — what the hell was wrong with me? When Carter was six months old, I signed him up for a part-time day care. I justified the decision to Matt by explaining that I needed those uninterrupted hours to write; when the fellowship was over, I would have to go on the job market, and I needed to produce and publish scholarship.

I had other reasons too — reasons that were harder to admit. The full truth is that I had always valued my independence and enjoyed spending time alone. Being married and being a mother eviscerated that part of my identity, and I wanted it back. Sometimes,

I used my time away from Carter in ways that felt selfish: I got my nails done or went on a long run, appreciating the fact that the only needs requiring attention were my own.

I didn't talk about my feelings with anyone because they seemed so abnormal. I worried that I would be judged. Other women I've interviewed since confided having similar feelings — and fear of judgment. Lyn Dexheimer and Caroline Halstead met through their church in Hoboken, New Jersey, and bonded over their shared frustration at being stay-at-home mothers, Caroline with two-year-old twins and Lyn with a two-year-old and an infant. It was 2002, and Caroline had recently quit her job as a marketing manager at Pfizer. She and her husband agreed that someone should stay home and that that someone should be her because he made more money. "I was not always happy because I didn't have anything of my own. I found it really difficult to have honest conversations with other mothers. I was supposed to be happy and excited all the time. Lyn was receptive to my need to say, 'This is really hard' a lot, and 'I am not a bad person for saying that I am tired,' and 'This is often not fun.'"

Lyn, who had dropped out of her PhD program at the London School of Economics to move back to the United States for her husband's job, said, "I was disappointed with myself and felt like a failure. Caroline was my friend who I didn't have to talk constantly with about our kids' activities. We talked about books and movies." Lyn, who said she was "a super-ambitious weird kid — I wrote novels and had publishing parties for myself," wondered where the old Lyn had gone. Caroline understood. It was as if she had gone from driving a hundred miles per hour to a full stop. They became closer; Lyn said, "We realized that we were on parallel tracks trying to figure out how to get back to work. Our conversations evolved into *This is important to how our daughters think about us.*"

Relying on each other, their husbands, and a small group of supportive mothers, Caroline and Lyn rejoined the workforce, Caroline when her twins were finishing preschool and Lyn when her younger daughter entered preschool. Lyn began teaching at Rutgers as an adjunct professor in writing composition and went back to pursuing her doctorate. Caroline got a teaching certificate, taking classes on nights and weekends. Today, Caroline teaches part-time at a two-year college, and Lyn is the executive director of the writing program at Rutgers. Over the years, they have repeatedly turned to each other. "I would leave a sick kid with Caroline," Lyn told me, "so I could go teach. If it was spring break for her kids but not for Rutgers, she would look after my kids. It was a lot of patching things together and relying on each other."

Both Caroline and Lyn are happily married. Nevertheless, they both said that they would give their daughters different advice than what they absorbed as young mothers and make some different decisions. Caroline said, "I would be careful about this need to be all things to all people. Because the person who gets shortchanged is you." Lyn said, "Let go of this idea that by default, the kids and the home are your responsibility. Sometimes I would erupt and say, 'We have to be more equal!' and I would get buy-in from my husband." But years of ingrained habits and learned behavior meant that, inevitably, "we would slide back."

I did not take Caroline and Lyn's path and step back when my children were very young. To do so, I reasoned, would be to imperil the Five-Million-Dollar Bet. When Carter was two, I had my second child, a daughter named Ella. At this point, I was working full-time as a teaching fellow at UC Hastings. The school gave me only twelve weeks of unpaid leave — the minimum required by federal law. I was told that if I asked for more, I would lose my job. I was resentful because as the person with the lowest status, I was being treated differently and worse than the women above me in the pecking order although I was doing essentially the same job. At the same time, I also wanted to go back — I understood the importance of this job in the big picture of my career ambitions.

But the transition back to work after Ella's birth was difficult. For the first few weeks, I cried leaving Ella for a full day at the infant-toddler center. And I told myself I had to work harder than ever, figuring, like Amanda Renteria, I had to prove to my colleagues, my supervisors, and my students that having another baby hadn't fundamentally changed me. My marriage, which had improved significantly after Carter was born, got rocky again. Matt did not understand my choice, particularly when my job paid so poorly, barely enough to cover the cost of the kids' day care. He couldn't understand why I continued to be consumed by work the same way I had always been even though the rest of my life had changed so profoundly.

It was not that Matt wanted me to be a stay-at-home mother. He didn't. It was that he wanted me to be less single-mindedly focused on my career when our children were so young. He wanted, as he often said, for me to be more "present," physically and emotionally. And often I wasn't because I was either at work or because I was home with my children but distracted by my work.

The concern about how a mother's focus on her career might negatively affect her young children is reflected in the larger culture. In 2008, more than 60 percent of women with a child under the age of six worked outside the home. But a 2013 study by the Pew Research Center found that only 16 percent of those surveyed thought that a mother working full-time was good for her children, less than half approved of part-time work, and one-third thought she should stay at home altogether.[12]

Sociologists Jerry A. Jacobs and Kathleen Gerson, analyzing a wealth of similar data in 2016, wrote: "One consequence of the ambivalence surrounding mothers' employment is the rise of intensifying conflict between the norm of 'intensive mothering,' especially among the middle class, and pressure on women to bring in income and build strong workplace ties." Consistently across studies in the United States over the past thirty years, "a considerable minority [of the population] remains hostile or ambivalent to women's labor force participation, particularly in the case of mothers with young children."[13]

The bottom line is that many mothers, particularly mothers of young children, are expected to prioritize children over career. They are told that caring for a baby — breastfeeding, diaper-changing, sleep-training — will fulfill them. It's true that babies are miraculous and adorable, but for many women, including me, much of the labor involved in nurturing them is repetitive and exhausting. *Who wants to be present for this?* I often asked myself as I performed the daily ritual of crawling on the kitchen floor, picking up smashed Honey Nut Cheerios with a wet paper towel to the soundtrack of enraged toddler howls.

New mothers are often tired and lonely. They miss the stimulation of work and being around other like-minded adults. But when new mothers do go back to work — because they have to or want to or both — they may be looked at askance. Even if explicit condemnation is rare, the subtle slights and judgments are real.

Leah Nelson, a thirty-nine-year-old mother of two who works at a small nonprofit in Alabama, told me,

> Sometimes [my work] takes me away from my kids. In a town that is built for stay-at-home-moms despite having an extraordinarily high number of single moms (I am married), I often feel like a terrible mom. When I have to choose between a kid non-emergency and a real actual emergency involving a person's safety or liberty, it's not a hard choice. What can be difficult

is feeling inadequate in the eyes of other moms, even though of course no one ever says anything.

Research shows that the children of full-time working mothers fare no worse than children of stay-at-home mothers when poverty is not an issue.[14] In fact, a 2018 study of more than a hundred thousand people across twenty-nine countries found that the daughters of working mothers were happier and more successful in their own careers than daughters of stay-at-home mothers.[15] For sons, there was no discernible effect, although sons of working moms did perform more housework in their own marriages. (More on this in chapter 8.) Those who criticize the cult of motherhood as "over-parenting" or "helicopter parenting" or even "bulldozer parenting" make the point that the children of busy working moms might be better off because these children understand that their needs aren't always paramount and that work and parenting are compatible, not antagonistic.

Michele Combs, an archivist at Syracuse University, put it this way: "It's long past time that we got over this worship of motherhood as some kind of sacred calling that should absorb one hundred percent of a woman's time and energy. Too much parenting can be as bad as too little, and besides, it's quality that matters, not quantity!"

Interestingly, though, empirical data showing that children are not harmed when their mothers work full-time outside the home has done little to reduce the anxiety and shame their mothers experience. Some experts believe the pressure has ratcheted up now that mothers are also expected to revert back to their pre-baby bodies within weeks of giving birth and display every other outward sign of having fully rebounded from pregnancy and childbirth. In the 2005 book *The Mommy Myth,* coauthors Susan Douglas and Meredith Michaels posit that perpetuating the ideal of the perfect mother is intimately linked to marketing a slew of products and services aimed at making women strive continually for the physical and emotional impossible.[16]

Many new mothers experience a constant tension between what the world expects of them and what they want for themselves. Often, their partners assume that they will fundamentally change their attitude toward work. Some women do, but many don't. Those of us in the latter category — those who remain as passionate and dogged as ever in our pursuit of professional success — are often judged as "bad mothers" by our partners, our families, and a society that makes no accommodations for us.

When a working mother strikes a hard blow against the "bad mother" trope, it can feel shocking. Here is how the award-winning novelist Lauren Groff, the mother of two young sons, responded to a question about motherhood in an interview with *The New Yorker:*

> I'd made the decision before the boys were born that I was going to feel no guilt or shame about my parenting. I'm a good mother and want to spend as much time as possible with my kids, but I travel a lot, I shut myself away from my family to work every day, I do not do birthday parties, and I went to one play-date in my life and wanted to break the Perrier bottle on the floor and stab myself with it. We have intense conversations in my house about apportioning responsibility, because neither my husband nor I wants to assume roles based on messed-up collective assumptions about gender dynamics. I think that, in our society, the idea of motherhood is pathologically ill, and even well-meaning people assume martyrdom in a mother. Guilt and shame are the tools used to keep people in line; the questions I get most at readings or in interviews are about being a mother and writer, when I'm expected to do this sort of tap dance of humility that I have no desire or ability to dance.[17]

Reading Groff's assessment, I nearly gasped at the boldness of her diagnosis and the brutal truth of her words. It wasn't ambitious mothers who were doing something wrong. It was society, for putting so many obstacles in their path.

CHAPTER THREE

LEARNING FIRSTHAND
ABOUT THE SECOND SHIFT

TO FIGURE OUT HOW WOMEN GET STUCK IN THIS UNTENABLE situation, we need to back up and consider how we were raised.

Beginning in the 1970s, a mantra took hold. Women were told that they could be whatever they wanted to be professionally and still get married and have children.[1] "Having it all" was the phrase popularized by *Cosmopolitan* founder Helen Gurley Brown; it was the title of her 1982 bestselling book wherein she promised women that financial success, professional fulfillment, marriage, children, and great sex were all on the buffet table — a feast that could be consumed in a single all-you-can-eat sitting.[2]

According to the feminist historian Ruth Rosen, the trope of "having it all" took root and has sprouted poisonous leaves ever since. Women's magazines, she wrote, "turned a feminist into a superhero, hair flying as she rushed around, attaché case in one arm, a baby in the other."[3] With the right clothes, hair, and makeup, and the right blend of modesty and self-reliance, having it all was made to seem entirely within reach.

This ideal was popularized in more progressive parts of the culture too, although the emphasis was not on physical appearance, much less hot sex, but on the celebration of women who pursued careers outside of the home. *Free to Be . . . You and Me,* Marlo Thomas's star-studded breakthrough album released in 1972, was an anthem for working women like my mother and for daughters like me.[4] In my favorite song, "Mommies Are People," Thomas paired up with Harry Belafonte to list, in verse, the endless professional opportunities open to women with children. "Mommies," they sang, could be "almost anything they want to be." The list included ranchers, doctors, poets, taxi drivers, chefs, and famous singers. Nothing was off the table, they said, except for becoming a father.

I knew every word to the *Free to Be . . . You and Me* album, which my parents played on an eight-track cassette tape throughout the 1970s and '80s whenever we hit the road in the family station wagon for our annual two-week summer vacation. Each song challenged gender stereotypes and advocated — often in a whimsical or hilarious way — for gender equality. Millions of people responded positively to its message. I was one of them, a fervent and inspired believer.

In some ways, my parents lived it. My mom was a successful physician who was respected by her colleagues, her patients, and the medical residents she supervised. And my parents drove home the message that my sisters and I could do anything we wanted. "I absolutely believed in equality," my father told me. "It never occurred to me that my kids would be limited by their gender. Because of Mom and because it was true of a number of our friends." I asked him which of their women friends had high-powered jobs like my mother's. He paused, then laughed. "I don't know, not so many. The fact that it wasn't true of our friends didn't necessarily mean that they didn't think it would be true for their children."

In elementary school, my older sister, Emily, went on a class field trip to a hospital. The girls were given nurses' caps, and the boys were given doctors' stethoscopes. In my father's telling of the story, Emily announced that she wanted a stethoscope, and she brought one home. My father loved that story. Of course his daughter refused to go along with the traditional gender-stereotyped roles. Dr. Bazelon was her mother.

But inside her own home, Dr. Bazelon found herself in a setup not so different from those of past generations. She was responsible for cooking, cleaning, and ferrying us to and from appointments, activities, and events and for hiring the babysitters and housekeepers who provided crucial support. Despite significant help — my sisters and I had a longtime beloved babysitter who took care of us when we were babies, picked us up from school a few days a week when we got older, did light housework, helped with the grocery shopping, oversaw our homework, and started dinner preparations before my mom came home — my mother had what was in effect a second job. I never saw my father make a bed, use a vacuum cleaner, do the laundry, or give any consideration to how those things got accomplished.

It was also clear that my father's career came first and that a different standard applied to him. It was not unusual for my dad to come home late, to take work calls during dinner, or to hole up inside a telephone booth for hours during those annual summer vacations. As an associate in a major Philadelphia law firm, he was determined to make partner, and he did, in 1976. But after that, if anything, he got busier and worked harder. In the late 1970s, my father became lead counsel in a complicated civil case that took him to Florida for depositions one week out of every month. This punishing schedule went on for years.

My dad's trips to Florida made me furious. When he called to say good night from his hotel room at the Hyatt Inn in Sarasota, I routinely hung up on him. I missed him terribly and felt his absence every day. But my anger evaporated as soon as he got home, and it never occurred to me to question his decision to prioritize his job. That may be because when my dad was around, he made it count, and because, paradoxically, his chronic absences made my time with him feel precious, whereas the time with my mother was something I took for granted and valued less.

My dad was the irreverent, devilish parent. He chased my sisters and me around the house, swatting our butts with kitchen towels, and tossed us upside down while we giggled and screamed. He was so tall — six foot four — that when he held me up, I could touch the ceiling. Being with my dad often meant having fun; he liked to organize and play games like hide-and-seek. (Once, when we played with another family, my dad hid on our garage roof. To this day, I have no idea how he got up there. More than an hour went by and no one could find him. I remember hearing his booming laugh and looking up in wonderment to see him standing triumphantly high above us.) Occasionally, he would even take the kids' side, like when we begged to stay up to watch the last half of *The Sound of Music* on TV or asked for two toppings on our ice cream at Hillary's.

My mother was the parent who made the rules and enforced them, nagging us to brush our teeth and pick up our wet towels from the floor and becoming incensed if we took food out of the kitchen. "Do you have any idea how many ants you will attract?" she would yell as we rolled our eyes. (Now, of course, I find myself saying exactly the same thing to my kids, and I am met with the exact same eye-rolls.) When her efforts at getting us to behave failed, she would issue the warning that inevitably left me terror-stricken: *Just wait until your father gets home.* My father imposed the harsh punishments, usually with a verbal lashing that left me in a puddle of tears, but those were reserved for the worst kinds of trespasses. Mostly, I associated my father with fun and games, my mother with homework and chores. I heard similar stories from other women I interviewed. Inevitably, the father was the "fun" parent, leaving the mother to bring down the hammer.

In my dad's absence, my mother was on her own. Sometimes, one of my grandmothers would come and stay with us, although I don't remember either of them being particularly helpful. I have no memory of my mom complaining about it or resenting my dad. Instead, she powered through. With three small children — and, later, four — when he wasn't around, she seemed more harried than usual and took a few shortcuts. We often ate breakfast food for dinner — scrambled eggs or pancakes with maple syrup. It was easier for me to be naughty, knowing she was too distracted to discipline me if I hit my little sister or ran away screaming as she approached with the nail clippers. Those were the upsides, although there was also less attention to go around. But I never felt unsafe or doubted my mother's competence. She was endlessly, thoroughly, tirelessly competent. She never fell apart. She never even cried. Looking back, I have no idea how she held it together night after night, month after month, year after year.

Imagining the reverse — my mother leaving us to go hundreds of miles away for work for days at a time — was unfathomable. My father simply would not have put up with it and, in any event, would have had no way to cope. Other than going to the hospital to give birth and taking her medical board exams in Minneapolis and, later, in Houston, my mother never spent a night away from us.

What I did not realize until I started interviewing my mother for this book was how many career sacrifices she made, although she was emphatic that she did so willingly. Initially, she wanted to be a nephrologist — a kidney doctor. But, she said, "there was too little flexibility, too many nights and emergencies. It just wasn't going to work out with my life." She became a psychiatrist instead. At the time, she told me, psychiatry was considered the redheaded stepchild in her field; other physicians thought it was beneath them because "it wasn't real medicine." But as doctor jobs went, it was a family-friendly choice. She could control her hours and choose her own workplace; she picked an office less than a quarter mile from our house.

My mother is adamant that she loved her specialty from the beginning and never regretted her career choices. But it wasn't until her youngest child went to college that she was able to capitalize on her earning power. While we were growing up, she made far less money than my father and worked fewer hours than he did, in part because her availability was limited. Many patients want to see their therapist at night, after regular business hours. For a few years, one night a week, my mother would make dinner, leave my dad at home to give us baths, and squeeze in an appointment or two. "But then came Florida," she said, "and that was the end of that." I asked if she was disappointed at the lost opportunity to expand her private practice. "No," she said, "it was exhausting and it wasn't worth it." She pointed out that having a smaller practice allowed her to do other work that she loved, including teaching at the Medical College of Pennsylvania and being the head psychiatrist at the health center of her alma mater, Bryn Mawr. These other jobs paid poorly, but she enjoyed them, and the diversity of her professional experiences made her career more interesting than it otherwise would have been.

I was surprised to hear that my mother was underpaid, and while it was true that she worked fewer hours than my dad, it was also true that she always seemed busier. I have no memory of my mother just sitting still. Even when she was supposed to be relaxing — for example, watching her beloved *Masterpiece Theatre* on PBS every Sunday night — she was still multitasking: paying the bills, writing thank-you cards, or knitting a sweater. She never just *stopped*, probably because she felt like she couldn't.

My mother's story is not unique. The percentage of female baby boomers working outside the home increased steadily beginning in the 1960s. By 1970, women made up 43 percent of the workforce. Ten years later, the percentage of women ages twenty-five to forty-four working outside the home had jumped to 71 percent.[5] Women were also pushing their way into professions typically dominated by men, such as law and medicine; their numbers climbed from 20 percent to 36 percent in jobs involving management skills. The same held true for blue-collar work. According to *The Atlantic*, "From 1970 to 1984 the number of female butchers in packinghouses had risen by more than a third and . . . by 1984 nearly 80 percent of new bartending jobs were going to women." But that story went on to caution that most women worked only part-time at jobs that allowed them to take on the primary childcare responsibilities at home and did not compensate them commensurate with their earning power. As of 1986, "married men [were] more than twice as successful in realizing their financial potential as married women."[6]

It is hard for a working mother to reach her full potential in her profession when a second unpaid job awaits her at home, much of it repetitive, menial, and thankless. In 1989, sociologist and University of California Berkeley professor Arlie Hochschild published *The Second Shift*, a seminal book that explored this reality. Yes, working women had escaped the fate of their own mothers, famously chronicled by Betty Friedan in *The Feminine Mystique*. Those women — white and middle class — were "1950s housewives" whether they wanted to be or not. That was what society expected and promoted. Pervasive sexism limited their professional opportunities largely to teaching and nursing, while poor women and women of color were generally confined to domestic work, cleaning other people's houses and taking care of their children.

But, as Hochschild noted, many of the trailblazing women who rejected the stay-at-home lifestyle had unwittingly walked into another trap. Yes, they could have it all — but only if they did it all. Bookending women's professional working days were the hours consumed by labor-intensive domestic chores: cooking, cleaning, shopping, laundry. A handful of women I interviewed made a series of deliberate choices designed to escape that predicament, including hiring full-time help and marrying partners who were willing to take on a primary caregiving role, but they were the exception.

Decades after the publication of Hochschild's seminal book, the second shift has shortened considerably but remains stubbornly persistent. Controlling for race, ethnicity, class, employment status, marital status, and geography, a woman's unpaid domestic labor in the home exceeds a man's by two hours a day according to a 2020 study conducted by the Institute for Women's Policy Research.[7] Another researcher studying this issue attributed the stubborn gap among married heterosexual dual-earner couples in part to "the simple fact that modern men do not adjust the amount of time they dedicate to housework based on their wives' employment status."[8]

Growing up, I often heard people describe my mother with an admiration bordering on incredulity. Inevitably, they would ask some version of this question: How does she do it all? The answer was threefold: with a significant amount of paid help, by scaling back her own career ambitions, and by nevertheless doing paid and unpaid labor around the clock. I didn't give that answer, though. Instead, I just shrugged. I was a kid. I took for granted the exquisitely complicated mechanics that made the family train run on time. It was only once I married and had children of my own that my mother's labor became visible to me, and I recoiled.

I wish I had been more introspective and clearer in my own mind and in talking to Matt about how I wanted and needed my own life to be different as a working mother. I had no intention of sacrificing any significant professional opportunity and no interest in taking primary responsibility for household tasks. I blithely and naively assumed that because I had picked a partner who seemed perfectly progressive on paper, he would intuitively understand, and the division of labor would naturally fall equally to both of us.

This kind of confidence often proves misplaced. Verna Williams's daughter, Allison, was eighteen months old when Verna joined University of Cincinnati College of the Law as a tenure-track junior faculty member. Her husband, David, was building a nonprofit organization from the ground up. Though both were extremely busy and focused on their careers, Verna expected David to be the "feminist guy" she fell in love with and married. Instead, "he just assumed I would do everything. It was so incongruous. Suddenly I was doing all the grocery shopping, the laundry, the errands." After what she described as "very difficult times," they went to couples' counseling. But the dynamic did not change much and Verna hired a housekeeper to outsource some of the chores. "We had that gendered thing that a lot of couples experience. David worked constantly, and Allison and I had our own routine. I have happy memories of those times. Sometimes he is a part of them and sometimes he's not. I look at my friends and it is all the same."

Samantha, thirty-nine, expressed similar frustration. She had her son David in 2010 when she was living with her husband in Costa Rica, where he was born and raised. In 2012, the family moved to Queens, New York, where Samantha got a full-time job as a business manager for a lighting-design company; her husband, who spoke little English, worked as a busboy for a bakery. Though he received a series of promotions, eventually becoming the operations manager, Samantha always outearned him and worked longer hours. Nevertheless, she was the primary caregiver, particularly after David was diagnosed with ADHD in kindergarten. "[My husband's] always been an involved parent," she told me, "but I am the one managing all of the parts and pieces. Anything related to schoolwork, doctors' appointments, [David's] IEP [Individualized Education Plan] plan, educating myself to know what to ask for with my child. My husband didn't make any effort to understand it, so it was up to me to figure it out."

Vanessa,[9] thirty-two, grew up in a middle-class family in Minneapolis, where her father owned a small office-cleaning business. Her mother, who had a high-school diploma, stayed home but also helped with the administrative side of the business. Later, she worked in the cafeteria at the public school Vanessa and her brothers attended. Devoutly religious, her mother was raised to be submissive to her father. Vanessa, determined to push back against her upbringing, which she called "exclusive and patriarchal," went to a small private college on a full scholarship.

In 2019, Vanessa got a job in local government in Minneapolis as a consultant, helping to bring better health care, education, and housing to communities of color in the region. She was also getting a graduate degree in education in nearby St. Paul, taking classes part-time. Her partner, Travis, who did not have a college degree, worked with adults and children struggling with mental-health issues. After five years of dating, they got engaged in 2018, one year after their son was born. Vanessa described the biggest challenges in their relationship as centering on money — she made more and thought Travis could do better managing his finances — and the unequal distribution of labor at home. "I don't feel that there is reciprocity," she said, "or the initiative on his part to share labor. Just constantly having to verbalize that I need help and reminding him to wash the dishes or clean the bathroom is labor in and of itself I don't think I should have to do." Travis agreed in principle, she said, "that we need to redesign our roles to make them more gender-neutral," but the reality of their day-to-day lives had not caught up to their aspirations.

Again and again, I heard from Gen X women and older millennials that they went into their relationships with the idea that domestic labor would be equally divided, only to be rapidly disabused of that notion once their babies arrived. The data supports this finding. As I dug more deeply into the research, I began to wonder: To what degree is this idea of inherent female competence in all things home and children simply a stereotype? To what degree are women my age and younger operating under an outdated instruction manual we received from our own mothers, either because they told us explicitly or because they normalized it by soldiering on, always on double duty? On the one hand, there was having it all and *Free to Be . . . You and Me*. On the other hand, many women were also told both *Yes! Go for it professionally* and *No! Don't drop the ball at home*.

Why is this so? In large part, it's because our country perpetuates an unequal division of labor in the home by continuing to insist that mothers are better suited to be the primary caregiver and perform domestic tasks. Also missing from the equation is the refusal by our politicians — overwhelmingly men — to put in place a social safety net that would greatly alleviate the burden on working women who don't want to give up their jobs. The United States stands alone among industrialized countries in refusing to provide subsidized childcare and paid maternity leave, for example, despite employers stressing a path to success at work that requires long hours spent at the office.[10]

As we enter the third decade of the twenty-first century, surprisingly little has changed. Even in those heterosexual households where couples initially split the household chores, many report the parity vanishing after they have children.[11] More than 75 percent of mothers assume responsibility for their children's medical appointments, and they are four times more likely to miss work to care for sick children than fathers, according to a study published by the

Kaiser Family Foundation in 2018.[12] The numbers have remained static since Kaiser first began studying the issue in 2001.

Journalist and psychologist Darcy Lockman interviewed fifty mothers as part of the research for her 2019 book, *All the Rage: Mothers, Fathers, and the Myth of Equal Partnership,* and she counts herself among these women who, despite their determination not to repeat the past, became the default primary caregiver and household manager.[13] The COVID-19 pandemic exacerbated this inequality. During quarantine, it was usually the mothers, not the fathers, who took on additional burdens that made the previous reality of working a second shift seem positively dreamy by comparison.[14] "I feel like I have five jobs: mom, teacher, C.C.O., house cleaner, chef," one full-time-employed mother who was now also a homeschooler told a *New York Times* reporter, adding, "My kids also call me 'Principal mommy' and the 'lunch lady.' It's exhausting."[15]

A study released by McKinsey in the spring of 2021 noted the dire impact of the pandemic on working mothers. Nearly one in four women with a child under the age of ten was considering leaving the workforce in part because vital support systems — schools, after-school care, babysitters, grandparents, and nannies — were no longer available.[16] By contrast, only 13 percent of fathers were contemplating a similar decision. For women who could not afford to leave their jobs — often the sole breadwinners, single mothers, and women of color — the stress, burnout, and anxiety escalated with no available off-ramp.[17] And these were the mothers who were lucky enough to have jobs.

Same-sex couples fared somewhat better, but the empirical data showed that they, too, had a tendency to allocate a larger share of unpaid domestic labor to one person in the relationship once they had children, moving from parity[18] to a model that ceded primary responsibility on the home front to the spouse with the less demanding and lower-paying job.[19] Interestingly, though, same-sex couples reported less friction about the issue "because they communicated; because the parent not doing the bulk of the childcare took on other chores; or because the division of labor didn't carry the baggage of gender."[20]

When I interviewed Abbie and Kenzie eight months after the birth of their son, Dashiell, on a hot summer day in late July 2021, I saw a same-sex couple that fit that mold. Both had been working full-time in demanding jobs before Kenzie gave birth. But when it came time to return to work, Kenzie could do so remotely, with flexible hours, and Abbie, a hospital chaplain, could not: her fixed hours were 7:30 a.m. to 5:00 p.m. Pre-baby, they divided the domestic labor fifty-fifty. Despite their conscious intention to keep it that way, post-baby life has made it impossible. In describing this change, Kenzie was matter-of-fact: "There have been moments where I have gotten overwhelmed and looked at Abbie and said, 'I need help carrying this load, and my brain feels fried,' but if I honestly reflect on that, it doesn't stem from division of labor, it more stems from my wanting to multitask and involve [my baby] in my life." For her part, Abbie sounded wistful: "I still appreciate what I do, it is extremely fulfilling, but I wish the ratio was different so I had more family time, less time inside the walls of a hospital."

Before, during, and after the pandemic, working mothers tried their damnedest to be all things to everyone, creating a level of stress that can lead to the breaking point. My interview with thirty-nine-year-old Daphne LaSalle Jackson, an Alabama-based air force lieutenant colonel and JAG instructor, began on FaceTime when she was in the middle of changing her daughter's diaper. She answered my steady stream of questions as she finished up, kissed her husband and two sons goodbye, got into her minivan, drove twenty minutes to the Maxwell Air Force Base in Montgomery, went through security, and headed to her office, where she changed from sweats into her military uniform, pausing periodically to respond to a text.

She never once lost her train of thought, her friendly, cheerful demeanor, or the cell phone connection. When I commented on this remarkably fast and apparently seamless transformation, Daphne noted that her own mother had set the bar high following her divorce from Daphne's father.

"In elementary school when I brought home a paper with a ninety-seven on it, she was like, 'Great! What did you miss?'" Growing up in Patterson, Louisiana, near the Gulf of Mexico, a small town with one blinking yellow traffic light, Daphne excelled in the gifted and talented program at the local high school. She was all-state in track. "I got one B," she told me, "and it broke my heart." At Louisiana State University, Daphne signed up for the ROTC program. After the first year, she was the number-one cadet on a full scholarship. In 2003, she became the first African American female corps commander of the corps of cadets at LSU as well as the president of the school's Black Student Union.

Having watched her parents go through an ugly divorce that had sent her mother into an emotional tailspin, Daphne was hesitant about settling down. But in 2008 she met Jared Jackson at a Walmart parking lot near the Altus Air Force Base in Oklahoma, where they were both stationed at the time, and she fell in love. Jared separated from the air force a few months later to become a private defense contractor, and they got married in 2010. When Daphne had her first son, Jett, in 2013, she was part of the team of defense lawyers representing Abd al-Rahim al-Nashiri, a Guantánamo Bay detainee accused of bombing the USS *Cole*. The military refused to let her bring her son to Cuba, but Daphne did bring her breast pump, determined not to give up the case.

"I pumped in the detention facility, I pumped on airplanes, I pumped in between client meetings, I pumped at midnight and again at three a.m. and I had an ice chest with me so I could freeze the milk. And I was super-super-proud of myself because here I was, a first-time mom, and I was handling it. But it was so hard." When Daphne became pregnant with her second child eighteen months later, she said, "I thought, *I cannot do this again. I can't.*" Daphne was granted a release from the legal team and given a new assignment that brought even more responsibility: chief of military justice at the Air Force District of Washington with oversight of forty thousand military members worldwide.

The new position did not diminish Daphne's stress or domestic load. Her second child, also a boy, was born prematurely at thirty-two weeks and spent his first twelve days in the NICU. At five months, he had difficulty breathing and had to be placed on a ventilator. Crucial to Daphne's ability to cope and take care of both children was the support of leadership in the military. "They bent over backwards to find additional leave that was available to me so I didn't have to burn through my personal time. They were great."

Two years later, she was offered a position as a JAG instructor at Maxwell Air Force Base. It was yet another promotion, but Daphne hesitated, unsure about destabilizing an already challenging domestic situation. Jared was a loving and supportive partner, but Daphne was still the primary caregiver. She had given the military ten years of her life and was considering leaving now that she had satisfied her service commitment. In many ways that made sense, particularly because they planned to have a third child. It was Jared who posed the hard question: "Are you done?" he asked.

Daphne thought about her trajectory within the military hierarchy and about what she could do with the status she had worked so hard to attain. "It is about using how far you have gotten to reach down and pull somebody up; that is how I feel about the African-American community in the JAG Corps," she explained. "I wanted to be that mentor, that Black face in a sea of white faces, a female face in a sea of nonfemale faces. I wanted to be that person who would motivate and inspire and propel all these people who feel like maybe 'I don't belong.'"

She answered, "I don't feel like I am done," and Jared said, "Well, we'll stay, it's that simple."

It was not simple. Following the move to Montgomery, Daphne gave birth to their third child, a daughter, in 2018. Jared's work took him to Huntsville, three hours north. Every week for two and a half years, he left the house at 4:30 a.m. on Monday and arrived home late at night on Thursday. It was Daphne's job to get the kids out the door by 6:45 a.m. and off to preschool and day care so that she could be at work by 7:30. On Sundays, she cooked meals for the entire week because there was no time to make dinner when she got home. Jared was staying in a single room with no kitchen, so Daphne packed up half the food and sent it off with him. Ironically, the pandemic brought more, not less, equality to their domestic life by forcing Jared to work from home, which allowed him to be more engaged in caregiving and chores. "Up until COVID hit, I felt like a single mom," Daphne said.

Ashton Clemmons described her husband, Bryan, as "a guy's guy, a Republican who drives a pickup truck and likes to hunt and fish." He is also, she said, unconditionally supportive of her career aspirations. They met in 2006, shortly after Ashton's father became seriously ill with cancer. Ashton, who grew up in a small town in Alamance County, North Carolina, and graduated from UNC Chapel Hill in 2005, had been accepted to Harvard's master's in education program. "I told Bryan I was going and he said, 'I am going with you.' I told him no, not unless we get married first. This is very much a Southern tradition and I knew it would have put my mom over the edge for us to move in together not being married."

Three weeks before Ashton's father died, Bryan asked for his permission to marry his daughter. They wed in 2008, when Ashton was twenty-four. Bryan, twenty-seven, quit his job in construction to follow her to Cambridge, Massachusetts. While Ashton got her graduate degree, he worked as a waiter in a Mexican restaurant in Harvard Square. "He never complained once," she said. "I remember saying, 'You must be miserable,' and him saying, 'I don't want you to worry because this is the happiest you have ever been.'"

She told me, "It has been a blessing for our life because he is willing to say at pivotal transitions, 'I don't know what this is going to look like, but we can make it work.'" A major transition came after the 2016 presidential election. The family was living a comfortable if hectic life in Greensboro, North Carolina, with a six-year-old daughter and three-year-old twin boys. Ashton had become an assistant superintendent of education and Bryan had started his own construction business. They were working and patching together childcare with some help from Ashton's mother and a nanny.

"I was dismayed by how many white women had voted for Donald Trump," said Ashton. In North Carolina, a swing state, Trump won by nearly 175,000 votes, and the Republicans held supermajorities in the state legislature. Although Ashton's father had been the head of the Democratic Party in Alamance County, she had never seen politics as her calling. But within a few weeks of the election, Ashton and some close friends started Onward, an organization that encouraged women who also felt unnerved by the country's sharp rightward turn to become politically active. The group swelled to five hundred members.

In the spring of 2017, Ashton went out to lunch with Tammy, a recruiter for LEAD NC who worked to find candidates for state-level races. Ashton brought with her a list of women she had identified as potential candidates. Tammy told her, "I think it should be you."

"My gut response was *No way,*" Ashton told me. In addition to having three children under the age of six, she had just started in her assistant-superintendent position and was writing her dissertation for her second graduate degree, an EdD from UNC Greensboro. "But then I thought, *How can I not do this?*" Ashton was particularly concerned with how the current Republican leadership had starved public schools of funding, undermining what she had striven to do throughout her career: improve the quality of public-school education for underserved communities. She was tired of watching helplessly as her state's Democratic governor vetoed pieces of legislation only to have Republicans override him. "I felt like I had to bring balance and decency back."

When Ashton told Bryan she wanted to run for office, she said, "He was great. He knew the timing was bad but also that it was a unique opportunity, and we would make it work." Ashton announced her candidacy for the state assembly in November 2017 and left her job to campaign full-time. Her schedule was grueling; six nights out of seven, she didn't make it home for dinner. Bryan stepped up every day after the babysitter left, picking up groceries, feeding their children, and giving them baths. One year later, he celebrated with Ashton when she won her district of eighty thousand people with 69 percent of the vote.

But once Ashton started her job in 2019, commuting ninety minutes each way from their home in Greensboro to Raleigh, they quickly returned to past roles. "I am still the go-to parent in almost every situation. Whether it is the pediatrician, the dentist, teachers, or the babysitter, the calls come to me." When Ashton had a meeting at night, Bryan helped by coming home early from work, but Ashton was still, in her words, "orchestrating what the night is going to look like." Ashton paused. "I don't know. Maybe I am just better at the day-to-day stuff at home. Or maybe it is the socialization of mothers. Just knowing that I have to give up control and have him do the mom stuff when I am gone is hard for me because I know it won't be done the same way."

Many mothers whom I interviewed echoed Ashton. While they often felt overwhelmed by the second shift, they also believed that they were naturally better at those tasks; ceding authority over the domestic sphere to their male partners would mean accepting that everything would be done differently and, they felt, worse. Some women did not want to make that compromise even if it meant doing additional work.[21]

When Matt and I were married, I felt similarly. It was more acceptable, somehow, for me to be professionally ambitious if I was also doing the bulk of the domestic work. And like Ashton, Daphne, and so many other mothers, I told myself I was just naturally better at it. Making small talk for hours on playdates with other parents (almost always moms) — or even for a few minutes at day-care pickup and drop-off — was not in Matt's wheelhouse. I, meanwhile, derived great satisfaction from feeling competent. My kids were making friends (if that's what social interactions between toddlers can be called); they were getting their medical checkups; and I gave them a bath every night. One of my most cherished compliments came from Carter's preschool teacher, who told me, "Your son always smells so good." She then lowered her voice. "Not all of them do, you know."

But the second shift was also grueling, stressful, and lonesome. I felt like a hamster in endless frenzied motion on an ever-churning wheel. To stop was to fall off. When Carter was three and Ella was one, I did stop, in rather dramatic fashion; I accepted an academic job in Los Angeles that meant commuting from our home in San Francisco. From Monday to Thursday, I was gone, just like my father. In fact, it was more extreme — his out-of-town trips were monthly; mine were every week, including the summers. I abruptly let go of the idea that I was the "better" nurturer. As it turns out, it wasn't true. Matt in some ways is more present, observant, and levelheaded than I am. He is also better at imposing structure and discipline. I have my strengths as a parent, but I lack Matt's calm, unflappable demeanor, his aura of competence, and his keen attention to detail.

Some women — younger than my mother and older than I — whose children grew up in the 1990s and early 2000s described their husbands as responsible for the majority of the domestic labor and childcare. Elizabeth Gleicher, a court of appeals judge in Michigan and the mother of three sons, was one of them. She traveled around the country and internationally as a trial lawyer; her husband, Mark, had a lower-key appellate law practice. "I was definitely an atypical mom," she said. "I didn't go to a lot of their events. Mark went. He had total flexibility." Elizabeth, meanwhile, made most of the money, paying for the boys to go to private school and college. "I had multimillion-dollar verdicts and settlements," she said. "I made a lot of money."

Beth Fouhy, a public affairs consultant who spent decades as a political reporter and editor, most recently with NBC News and MSNBC, said her husband often served as the primary caregiver for their son, Jonathan, who was born in 1996, when Beth was thirty-four. "My husband doesn't fit the stereotype of 'I come home, crack open a beer, and watch sports.' He does a ton at home, always has, and never acted like it was a big deal." His parental duties increased substantially in 2008 after he was laid off from his job in high tech and Beth, who was then working for the Associated Press, temporarily became the family's sole breadwinner. She was assigned to cover Hillary Clinton's first presidential campaign, and she estimates that from September 2007 to January 2009, she spent 250 nights away from home, living out of a suitcase as she hopscotched all over the country to every rally and fundraiser.

But the truth is that these relationships are outliers. Few fathers in heterosexual partnerships participate equally. Nor are they judged equally. Fathers are praised for mundane tasks such as taking their children grocery shopping, to the doctor, or on a playdate.[22] When mothers do the same, no one bats an eyelash, because, well, that's what mothers do. The mothers who forgo the midday potlucks or leave town for days-long business trips often feel they are getting the stink-eye. Their choices are judged differently.

What does all of this mean for the next generation of ambitious women who are deciding whether they want to become mothers? I talked to Jill Filipovic, a feminist author and journalist who got married in 2018. At thirty-seven, she was profoundly ambivalent about having children. "I am a freelancer and my husband is not. He goes to an office all day and I work from home. I think that existing distinction of where we are and whose time is flexible would likely result in me picking up more of the childcare duties than I would want to." They could not afford full-time help and wouldn't be able to live the way they currently did. Jill vacillated between worrying that if she did not become a mother she would regret it and wondering whether she was reacting to a culture that told women "your life matters more if you have children" and that "motherhood is the entrée into adulthood and the primary place from which women should derive meaning and purpose" — a conceit she had devoted her professional life to dismantling.

Sarah Corning, twenty-two, graduated in May 2020 from the University of Virginia and told me that she has struggled to figure out how she can do things differently. By her own description, her childhood was unique and wonderful. Her father's job as an executive at blue-chip companies like Whirlpool and Nike took their family all over the globe. Born in Japan, Sarah went on to live with her parents and older sister in Chile, Switzerland, Thailand, and Brazil before they finally settled in Atlanta. "Our life," she said, "was one big international adventure." But with the family uprooted every few years, Sarah's mother was never able to have stable work completely on her own terms. What her mother wanted, Sarah said, was a college-level teaching position, but those plans were perennially on pause.

"I wish I didn't want kids so badly," she told me. "Because even though you can have the most progressive, hands-on partner in the world, the onus always falls on the woman." She continued, "I am steeped in this feminist theory that empowers me to stray from the conventional path. And while those ideas have led me to a more self-determined life, they don't neatly fix everything. I will marry a man and I want children. Then there is reality: We can't all go around pretending we are something else. Or that our partners will be. So I'm left to worry about how I can be unconventional in my conventional relationship. How I can have kids, expect more from my partner, and pursue my career."

Listening to Sarah, I thought of my interview with Mashal, who was just a few years older and a married working mother. Mashal, whose parents are refugees from Afghanistan, was one of four children raised in a strict Muslim household. Growing up, Mashal knew she was poor — "Once when I was going through some paperwork I found an envelope full of money and it was colorful. I asked what it was and my mother said it was food stamps" — but her family, determined that she get a good education, moved to a Northern California suburb with excellent public schools. Both of Mashal's parents worked, her mother as a preschool teacher, her dad as a dishwasher and, later, a bus driver. Still, she said, "My mom was the kind of mom who would sacrifice her job for her kids. She would work part-time even though we needed the money."

Mashal went to community college while working part-time at a local deli. That's where she met Dave, who went to the same school. "I guess he liked the sandwich I made him," she told me. Unlike Mashal, Dave came from a middle-class family and was a fifth-generation Californian. Mashal's family disapproved of Mashal dating anyone, especially a Christian; the only way to even partly mollify them was to get married. Six months after they met, they did. Mashal was nineteen, Dave twenty-two. Mashal transferred to a four-year college and graduated with a BA in writing and communications. She got a job with Catholic Charities working with clients who had chronic illnesses and substance-abuse disorders and quickly rose through the ranks to become a site manager overseeing a staff of her own. In the midst of this upward trajectory, when she was twenty-four, she gave birth to their son.

Mashal told me, "I thought in my head that I would be like my mom and sacrifice everything for my son, but I don't feel that way. I love my son and want to give him everything but I have learned to change my expectations. If I give him even eighty percent after a crazy day at work, I think I am doing an okay job." Dave makes a good living as a senior art director for a marketing company, and Mashal knows they can afford for her to step back or stay home. But she doesn't want to. "I never imagined not working. I come from a family that works to survive. But I also love my job and I love my career. I am the youngest site manager at our agency and I think I can only go up from there. It motivates me; it fuels me."

Dave and Mashal pay her nineteen-year-old brother to watch their son while they are at work, dropping him off and picking him up at Mashal's parents' house, where her brother lives. They work roughly equal hours and split the domestic labor equally. "No one has specific roles," she told me. "People do what needs to get done. But there is no gender to the roles." Interestingly, despite her conservative upbringing, that was true in Mashal's house when she was growing up too. "My dad would make dinner every night. They were a team and we are a team."

Millennial fathers like Dave are generally more progressive than the men of my parents' generation, more willing to reconceive traditional gender roles. Most do at least some housework and childcare. And there are a growing number of families in which the primary caregiver is the father, who sometimes chooses to stay home full-time. When I was growing up, the term *stay-at-home dad* did not exist. In 1989, when the Pew Research Center first started tracking stay-at-home dads, 4 percent of men put themselves in that category, and 25 percent of those men said they were looking for work. By 2014, the percentage of stay-at-home dads had doubled. While exact figures are hard to come by, there is no disputing that the number of fathers who are the primary caregivers for their children has ticked steadily upward. According to the National At-Home Dad Network, it may be as high as seven million.[23]

For women whose husbands also work outside the home, what needs to happen to chip away at the default assumption that the second shift is primarily the mothers' burden to bear? First, a decoupling of gender from domestic work. Men are equally capable of making the bed, shopping for groceries, cleaning the bathroom, and fixing dinner. This isn't "women's work," any more than running a small business, performing open-heart surgery, or operating heavy machinery is "men's work." The fact that, as Sarah Corning put it, "the onus always falls on the woman" is a diagnosis of a problem. It is not an inevitable prognosis.

Second, and more controversially, we need to decouple gender from childcare. It is true that pregnancy, childbirth, and breast-feeding — mind- and body-bending experiences — are unique to women. But after those first six to twelve months, male partners can and should participate equally. There is nothing to suggest that women are inherently better at sleep-training, butt-wiping, bath-giving, bedtime-story-reading, Lego-building, hand-holding, spoon-feeding, and otherwise nurturing their young children. As kids get older, the tasks remain gender-neutral: school pickup and drop-off, ferrying to and from sports and other activities, and helping with homework. The historical feminizing of these tasks is just that — a relic of history. As more and more fathers engage, their fitness for such chores will be taken for granted rather than gawked at. Normalizing the genderless nature of this labor makes it easier to split and maintain that split under stress — the stress of additional children, additional burdens at work, and other pressures.

Third, and finally, mothers need to let go of the concern that, as Ashton put it, their male partners won't do "the mom stuff" the way they want it done. There is no doubt that frustration and dissatisfaction inevitably arise as you watch your partner do a job less than perfectly, or even poorly, knowing that you could do it twice as well in half the time. But sheer repetition tends to improve performance with all skills, including childcare and housework. Gritting one's teeth through one's partner's learning curve is worth the thousands of hours of "found time" for a working mother and the countless resentments that never accrue as a result.

Of course, there will be times in many relationships when one partner's job takes priority over the other's or when one partner's work schedule is far more flexible — for example, the years when Daphne had to do most of the childcare because Jared had a job that required him to live in another city during the week. The key is reciprocity; as we will see later with Daphne and Jared, the pendulum swung dramatically. There is no way to predict the precise contours of your career or your partner's, but there is a way to predict whether the person you marry will give you the same consideration you gave him or her when it's time for your career to take center stage.

Falling in love can be as blinding as staring into the sun. It is better to bask in the warmth while keeping your gaze closer to the earth. Ask yourself: *What am I signing up for with this person? Is he truly happy for me in my professional success? Does he understand the importance of my work? Will he take the laboring oar at home when it is his turn to paddle against the current?*

It is true, as Sarah said, that "we can't all go around pretending we are something else." But we can reimagine our roles. We can hand our male partners an apron, a crying baby, or a shopping list knowing that they are not doing us a favor; they are doing their part. The second shift will never disappear, but when it is a shared burden, it is half as long, half as hard, and half as draining. I liked the way that Mashal put it: "People do what needs to get done." If male and female partners in heterosexual relationships go into the wild experiment that is love, marriage, and parenting with the expectation that the onus is on both of them, the paradigm will change. Slowly, and in fits and starts, at times with white knuckles. But for ambitious working mothers, the up-front investment and effort that goes into changing dysfunctional gender dynamics in the home will pay huge dividends in their ability to thrive professionally, emotionally, and in their relationships with their children.

CHAPTER FOUR

THE TOXICITY OF FEMALE AMBITION

T HE DOZENS OF WOMEN I INTERVIEWED FOR THIS BOOK were diverse across racial, ethnic, and geographic lines. They were cisgender women, LGBTQ, single, divorced, and widowed and worked in an array of professions: small-business owner, politician, restaurant manager, chaplain, esthetician, law school dean, appellate court judge, prize-winning author, librarian, grassroots activist, ob-gyn, opera singer, lieutenant colonel in the air force. Ranging in age from their early twenties to their mid-eighties, they lived in small towns and big cities, in red states and blue states. What they shared was motherhood and professional ambition. And that was it. Or so I thought.

In fact, most of the women I interviewed shared something else: a reflexive rejection of the "ambition" label and a deep-seated reluctance to acknowledge that ambition fueled their drive to succeed. Nearly all of them expressed deep skepticism that they were a good fit for the book when I described it. Mimi Hu said, "When I first read the title of your project, I am like, *No, no, no, that's not me. I am just . . . I don't think I am that ambitious.*" This from a woman raised in an agricultural province in China who graduated first in a high-school class of more than four hundred people and was one of only twenty teenagers selected by a private foundation to go to college in the United States on a full scholarship.[1] She came alone, speaking little English, never having flown on an airplane before.

More than a few suggested that I interview someone else instead — a friend who, they insisted, was truly an ambitious mother, while they were merely "lucky" and "fortunate." I heard those words over and over again, along with "I was in the right place at the right time," offered as a complete explanation for what was in fact years of striving, determination, and demonstrated excellence. "Oh God," my mother said, making a face when I asked her if she was ambitious. Finally she said, the reluctance clear in her voice, "You didn't go to medical school then or even now without being ambitious, so yes, I guess." I imagined interviewing high-achieving men for a book on ambitious fathers. Their overwhelming response, I guessed, would be a greeting along the lines of "So glad you found me!"

Ambition, according to the *Oxford English Dictionary,* means "having or showing a strong desire to succeed." When I asked the author Mary Gordon to define *ambition,* she answered, "You would like to be very, very good at something and be recognized for what you do and get rewards for it." Why do women find the term viscerally repugnant when applied to themselves? The writer Robin Romm, who edited the essay collection *Double Bind: Women on Ambition,* wrote that women's hesitancy to apply the word *ambition* to themselves stems from "the pervasive sense that striving and achieving had to be approached delicately or you risked the negative judgment of others."[2] Roughly translated: Women fear that if they say they are ambitious, other people will think they are cold, ruthless, self-aggrandizing bitches.

They're right. In our culture, when men are driven and relentless in pursuit of success, those traits are seen as positive. But studies show that when women exhibit those same qualities, they are often viewed as overly aggressive and calculating. Women with children, particularly young children, are judged even more harshly. Prioritizing work over family is expected of fathers. But mothers who make the same choices to pursue recognition and success are "roundly condemned" for leaving their children to suffer as the result of their selfishness, according to the scholars Robin J. Ely and Irene Padavic, who study gender in the workplace. "One could imagine their being held up as exemplars, but we routinely heard them described as bad mothers — 'horrible' women who were not 'positive role models for working moms,'" they wrote in the *Harvard Business Review* in 2020. The message to younger working mothers coming up behind them? This is a lose-lose situation. "If they respond to the pull of family by taking accommodations, they undermine their status at work, but if they refuse accommodations in favor of their professional ambitions, they undermine their status as good mothers."[3]

Consider Hillary Clinton. For years, she was the primary breadwinner for her family, working as a partner at an elite law firm while her husband pursued a career in politics. When Bill Clinton first ran for president, in 1992, Hillary defended herself from an opponent's political attack by saying, "I suppose I could have stayed home and baked cookies and had teas, but what I decided to do was pursue my profession."[4]

The backlash was instant, intense, and — apparently — everlasting. Clinton spent weeks trying to walk back her remarks, apologizing repeatedly and even submitting a chocolate chip cookie recipe to *Family Circle* for a baking contest with First Lady Barbara Bush, who had stayed home to raise her six children. The "cookies" remark shadowed Clinton for years, as did the pervasive sense among many voters that her seemingly endless ambition — to overhaul health care as First Lady, to run for the Senate after leaving the White House, and to embrace her high-profile role as secretary of state — made her grasping and unlikable. Her first bid for the presidency was dashed when she lost the Democratic nomination to Barack Obama. Throughout their hard-fought primary, questions swirled around Clinton's "likability," addressed head-on in one debate when Obama said, infamously, "You're likable enough, Hillary," in a tone that implied the opposite.[5] Obama's own ambition was obvious and even breathtaking — he decided to seek the presidency after serving less than one term in the Senate. But in Obama, that ambition translated as a sunny self-confidence that assured voters with doubts that he had the necessary experience to do the job.

During her second run for the presidency, in 2016, Clinton was still striving to soften her image as what *New York Times* reporter Amy Chozick called "a radical feminist in her critics' imagination, the Lady Macbeth who was an affront to the choices so many other women had made."[6] Chozick's piece, written days before voters went to the polls, was titled "Hillary Clinton and the Return of the (Unbaked) Cookies."

As we all know, Hillary Clinton lost on November 8, 2016, in a shocking upset to Donald J. Trump, a real estate developer, reality-TV star, and political novice who repeatedly expressed contempt for women, famously bragging that he could "grab them by the pussy" and using gendered language to deride Clinton herself, including calling her "a nasty woman" in the final debate.[7] While there were many reasons for Clinton's defeat, her gender — and the coded messaging around it, including *overprepared, calculating, ruthless* — was undoubtedly among them.[8] In her concession speech, Clinton acknowledged as much. After thanking the millions of women who supported her campaign, she said, "I know we have not shattered that highest and hardest glass ceiling but someday, someone will."[9]

More recently, it has been interesting to watch this dynamic play out on the political stage as increasing numbers of mothers run for office and are nominated for powerful government positions. In 2020, Kamala Harris and Amy Coney Barrett, two high-profile women from opposite ends of the political spectrum, took pains to deflect the ambition label. Each emphasized her devotion to her family as a way of seeming relatable and taking the edge off the perception that she was too career-driven.[10] When Harris, a U.S. senator, was the perceived front-runner for the vice presidential selection, some in Biden's inner circle were not subtle in their critique. Days before Biden announced his choice, they waged a "shadow campaign" against Harris, who had challenged Biden for the Democratic presidential nomination before dropping out of the race. Their concern? "That she's too ambitious and that she will be solely focused on becoming president herself."[11]

Let's unpack that critique, starting by removing the word *solely*. There was nothing in Harris's history to suggest she would neglect the traditional duties of vice president and "be solely focused" on taking Biden's job. Indeed, her running-mate persona was entirely traditional; she attacked Trump in sharper, more pointed ways than Biden so he could stay above the fray, and she sang Biden's praises. What remains is a warning that Harris will entertain the desire of "becoming president herself." Of course she will! And in that desire, she is no different than any vice president in recent memory, with the exception of Dick Cheney.[12] Barack Obama selected Joe Biden as vice president after Biden's own failed campaign, then Biden ran for the top job again. George H. W. Bush followed the same model after losing to Ronald Reagan in the Republican presidential primaries. So did Al Gore, Bill Clinton's second in command. In other words, this particular type of ambition is a feature, not a bug, of the vice presidency. It is only because Harris is a woman — and a woman of color — that her ambition is viewed by many as disqualifying.[13]

In mid-August 2020, Biden, apparently unmoved by the ambition critique, picked Harris, making her the first woman of color ever nominated for the post. On the campaign trail, Harris touted her domestic bona fides, repeatedly stressed the importance of her role as a stepmother of two, and emphasized her commitment to cooking dinner every Sunday night come hell or high water.[14] Harris, who broke barrier after barrier as the first Black woman to became San Francisco's district attorney, California's attorney general, California's junior senator, and vice president of the United States, told interviewers that "there is one title she treasures even more" — "Momala," the name her husband's children bestowed on her.[15]

In September 2020, President Donald Trump announced federal appellate judge Amy Coney Barrett as his pick to replace Ruth Bader Ginsburg on the U.S. Supreme Court. In his public remarks from the Rose Garden, Trump exulted that Barrett would "make history as the first mother of school-aged children ever to serve on the U.S. Supreme Court." What does motherhood have to do with judging? Everything, apparently. Barrett, who has seven children — one of them with Down syndrome — was commended as much for her skill at parenting her "sizable American family"[16] as for her intellectual acumen. The admiration for this judicial "supermom" was bipartisan and continuous throughout Barrett's days-long testimony, with Democrat Diane Feinstein, the senior senator from California, asking if Barrett had a "magic formula"[17] for a perfect-motherhood-plus-career equation and North Carolina senator Thom Tillis joining a Republican chorus in praising Barrett's mothering skills as "remarkable."

Clearly, no one — man or woman — could have risen to the dizzying professional heights that Barrett had without a healthy dose of ambition. But that key ingredient of the recipe went unmentioned by everyone, including Barrett herself. She, too, carefully adhered to the motherhood-first script, telling the Senate Judiciary

Committee at her confirmation hearing, "While I am a judge, I am better known back home as a room-parent, carpool driver, and birthday party planner."[18]

The women of my generation, girls who grew up in the 1970s and 1980s, were educated to believe they could be anything they wanted to be, a message that was also given to millennials and girls who are part of Generation Z. The message was one of equality: Boys and girls would be judged by the same metric in a meritocracy designed to reward intelligence, hard work, and raw talent. But it didn't turn out to be true, not for the women of my generation and not for the women who came after me. We are held to a different standard than our male peers, a metric that does not allow for a candid acknowledgment — by us or anyone else — that our success was due to anything other than luck, good fortune, mentoring.

The simple truth — "I am here because I deserve it" or "I got the job because I was the best candidate" — rarely comes out of a woman's mouth because she knows it will read as prideful, arrogant, and distinctly unfeminine. Men brag; women bow their heads in humble gratitude. When we became mothers, the standard became still more exacting; never, *ever* could we admit that — even once — we had put our careers first. Doing so would have invited a torrent of judgment. Not only would such a woman be perceived as self-aggrandizing, she would also be branded a Bad Mother.

Over the past fifty years, women have made great strides on the education front. On August 4, 2019, *Inside Higher Ed* reported, "Today, women earn 57.4 percent of Bachelor degrees, 58.4 percent of Master's degrees, and 52.8 percent of Doctoral degrees.[19] Taking Associate's, Bachelor's, Master's, and Doctorate's together, women have earned 13 million more degrees than men since 1982."[20] But in school and in the workforce, men and women are judged differently and expected to present themselves to the world in profoundly different ways. Boys are rewarded for being boisterous, unapologetic, and confident. Girls are expected to be modest, self-effacing, and averse to taking credit. This duality in expectation continues into adulthood.

Perhaps no celebrity, on or off the screen, reflects the knife's edge that ambitious women must navigate more powerfully than the Academy Award–winning actor Reese Witherspoon. Reflected in the characters Witherspoon has played over the course of her career, in her turn to producing films, and in her frank public comments are not only the maddening stereotypes but also her determination, using her ambition, to turn them on their head.

In 1999, at the age of twenty-three, Witherspoon starred in the indie classic film *Election,* where she played the lead, Tracy Flick, a straight-A striver competing for class president against a likable but dim-witted jock and, later, his rebellious gay sister, who ran as a lark but ended up with a significant fan base. Flick's naked, unapologetic ambition — "You can't interfere with destiny, that's why it's destiny," she proclaims about her soon-to-be-storied career — was viewed by peers and teachers alike as off-putting and threatening. So threatening, in fact, that Mr. McAllister, a beloved social studies teacher played by Matthew Broderick, goes to elaborate lengths to ensure her defeat.

Election is a dark comedy. Mr. McAllister's ham-handed scheming and blatant hypocrisy are played for laughs. (Even as he cheats on his wife, McAllister judges Tracy for having an affair with his married coworker, who gets fired as a result. It never occurs to McAllister to question the age imbalance or gross abuse of authority that student-teacher relationship necessarily involves, essentially what we now all recognize as a form of sexual abuse.) In the end, McAllister and the jock end up on the losing side, but few people watching the movie walk away thinking, *Gee, I want to be just like Tracy.*

Early on, women are socialized to explain away or diminish their accomplishments so as not to threaten men, who have no such behavioral limitations. In a widely reported 2003 experiment, Frank Flynn, a Columbia Business School professor, presented half his students with the professional biography of Heidi Roizen, a successful venture capitalist in Silicon Valley.[21] The other half of the class received the identical materials, but Flynn changed Heidi's name to Howard. All of the students then filled out a survey with their impressions of Howard or Heidi.

Flynn reported that "students were much harsher on Heidi than Howard across the board. Although they think she is just as competent and effective as Howard, they don't like her, they wouldn't hire her, and they wouldn't want to work with her."[22] The fictional Howard wore his "aggressive personality" and "assertiveness" like a fine cologne; attributed to real-life Heidi, these same qualities stank like skunk spray.

Likable ambitious women are women who don't appear to be ambitious at all. In a November 2020 *New York Times* profile of rising CNN star Abby Phillip, a thirty-one-year-old Black woman, John Harris, her former boss at *Politico,* described her approvingly as "very quiet and ambitious, but she doesn't present in a flamboyant way like some ambitious people do." While Harris used gender-neutral language — "some ambitious people" — it isn't the kind of qualified praise typically used to describe men looking to advance in the same profession.[23]

Two years after *Election,* Witherspoon demonstrated this "quiet" type of ambition in the box-office smash *Legally Blonde.* She played Elle Woods, perhaps the most unlikely admit in the storied three-hundred-year history of Harvard Law School. Elle, who loves nothing more than primping, preening, and shopping, astounds her sorority sisters by acing the LSAT and getting into law school on her own merit. But her purpose isn't to get a prestigious graduate degree; it is to win back the cad who unceremoniously dumped her on the night she thought he would propose.

Throughout Elle's sojourn at Harvard, we watch as she is continually humiliated and dismissed as an empty-headed fool by professors and classmates, only to prove everyone wrong with her razor-sharp intellect and canny insights. But all of Elle's rhetorical blows are delivered with a sweet smile and profession of humility; even in triumph, she never abandons her Easter egg–colored outfits, perfectly blown-out blond hair, and adorable demeanor. Her sharp-wittedness, cloaked in eyelash-batting winsomeness, is the punch line. Indeed, Elle's skill in the courtroom is so unexpected that it provides much of the fodder for the comedy. By hiding her smarts behind a veneer of coquettishness and inanity, Elle Woods was far more desirable and less threatening — to men and women alike — than Tracy Flick, who climbed the ladder to success with a dogged single-minded determination, utterly convinced of her deservedness. Just like a man.

Legally Blonde was playing in movie theaters when I was in my second year at NYU School of Law. I was no Elle Woods by any stretch of the imagination, but I shared her reticence about proclaiming my intelligence. I had always excelled in school; I attended an Ivy League college and graduated with honors. NYU is an elite law school, consistently ranking in the top five in the nation.

I went to law school to become a great lawyer. In pursuit of that goal, I racked up coveted prizes: top grades, a spot on the *Law Review,* a federal clerkship. But publicly, I instinctively shrank from owning any of it. I was so intimidated by the interrogation methods of my professors, almost all of whom were white men, and the humiliations heaped upon students who got the answer wrong that I remained silent for the entire first year unless I was "cold-called," in which case I had no choice but to answer. I noticed that many of my female classmates felt similarly, while our male classmates generally shrugged it off. Being wrong and shamed for it didn't stop them from trying again and again. I was also afraid that other people — particularly the men I wanted to like me — would think I was full of myself. Who would want to date, much less marry, someone who proudly owned these achievements?

It is embarrassing to admit that I worried being outwardly ambitious would have a negative effect on my dating life, but the data bears out my concern. Just pause for a moment and consider this present-day statistic: More than a quarter of all Americans believe that the children of full-time working mothers are worse off than the children of mothers who stay at home, according to an analysis by the AP-NORC Center at the University of Chicago.[24]

"Even in the 21st century, men prefer female partners who are less professionally ambitious than they are," wrote economics professors Leonardo Bursztyn, Thomas Fujiwara, and Amanda Pallais in their 2017 empirical study "'Acting Wife': Marriage Market Incentives and Labor Market Investments." They continued, "Men tend to avoid female partners with characteristics usually associated with professional ambition, such as high levels of education. It is relatively unlikely that a woman will earn more than her husband, and when she does, marital satisfaction is lower and divorce is more likely."[25]

Women who are loud and proud about what psychiatrist Anna Fels calls their "mastery of a special skill" and the professional status they have attained as a result of it risk the perception that they are less "feminine" and therefore less attractive to potential male partners. Studies have demonstrated that "the daily texture of women's lives from childhood on is infiltrated with microencounters in which quiet withdrawal, the ceding of available attention to others, is expected, particularly in the presence of men," she wrote. "They refuse to claim a central, purposeful place in their own stories, eagerly shifting the credit elsewhere and shunning recognition."[26]

Instinctive self-diminishment isn't a biologically determined female trait; it is a learned and rewarded behavior.

Subconsciously, I was always aware that owning my ambition could be toxic. After graduating from law school with honors, I moved to California for my clerkship with the Honorable Harry Pregerson on the U.S. Court of Appeals for the Ninth Circuit. Inside, I was bursting with pride; externally, I made sure to remain modest and self-deprecating whenever I was congratulated. That year was wonderful. Judge Pregerson was a fervent feminist and my three co-clerks were women; two of them remain my closest friends. But we labored in the background, working to support the judge. I remember the feeling of pride when, during oral arguments, Judge Pregerson would ask the lawyers one of my questions. But the words were coming out of his mouth, not mine.

The following year, I got my dream job as a trial lawyer in the federal public defender's office in Los Angeles. Now all the words were mine. But to be a trial lawyer as a young woman, particularly in one's early years, is to exist under a harsh spotlight: my stumbles were glaringly public and everything I said, wore, and did was examined under a microscope. Suddenly, the implicit was explicit. It was a rude awakening to what the late scholar Deborah Rhode famously characterized as "the double standard and the double bind." Professional women, she warned, had to be careful not to come across as "too 'soft' or too 'strident,' too 'aggressive' or 'not aggressive enough.'"[27]

The double standard and the double bind are not solely enforced by men. Later in my career, after I had had two children and barely had time to sleep, much less drop by a salon for a regular blowout, I had a female supervisor who told me in no uncertain terms that I should wear makeup and color my hair when it started turning gray. In fact, she told me I needed a total makeover and offered to pay for it, leading to my first trip to Sephora. "Do you need help with anything?" the sales assistant inquired politely. "I need help with *everything*," I told her.

Now I'm a rewards member.

I have given a lot of thought to the demand that professional women cultivate a certain kind of appearance. My feelings about it are conflicted. On the one hand, it is unfair that I pay these costs while my male colleagues do not. On the other hand, there is a part of me that enjoys turning into a more polished and stylish version of my actual self. It can feel empowering.[28] And I associate the fashion piece of it with my mother, who loves to take me shopping when I come back to Philadelphia once a year with my children. She always encourages me to pick bolder colors and edgier designs than I ever would on my own. I treasure those yearly afternoons; we have so much fun and always have lunch together afterward. Inevitably, when someone compliments me on what I am wearing — a leopard-print wrap dress, a sweater with a keyhole cutout, a turquoise blouse — I smile sheepishly and say, "Thank you, my mom got it for me."

But my positive associations are a happy coincidence, not an endorsement of the mandate that women must invest time, money, and energy in the pursuit of a certain look, especially after they reach a certain age. And when I add up the time, money, and energy I have spent on "upkeep" — cosmetics, skin-care products, manicures, pedicures, eyebrow waxing, hair coloring — the cost is significant, not only to my wallet, but to my time. The gendered nature of societal expectations around appearance can be jarring. Recently, I watched a Netflix documentary featuring an older, quite famous male attorney. When the camera zoomed in, his nose hair stood out. How many women in his position would ever "let themselves go" to the point where a shot like that would even be possible? I am guessing the number is close to zero. And yet, in a man, this laissez-faire attitude toward physical appearance is a given.

The costs — economic and psychological — of maintaining a certain kind of appearance should not be a tax ambitious women must pay. Yet for many, it is, and it grows more arduous and expensive as we age. Sometimes it feels like chasing an ever-receding horizon line on a highway with exorbitant tolls and no off-ramp. Debora L. Spar, then the president of Barnard College, articulated this problem when she wrote in the *New York Times* that "if [a] woman ignores the process of aging and eases more honestly into her inevitable wrinkles, belly fat and gray hair, she is liable to stand out as an anomaly within her personal and professional circles."[29]

The pursuit of a very particular feminine-yet-professional look could be better spent on substantive achievements, and to play the game is to accept the message that if women embrace their femininity in this traditional way, they will appear less threatening to the power structures dominated by men. Then there is the issue of further marginalizing women who are not white and cisgender. In 2019, California passed the CROWN Act,[30] which bans discrimination against employees because of hairstyles traditionally associated with being Black, including dreadlocks, braids, and natural hair. The preface to the statute notes that the law was necessary to combat the ingrained prejudice that "professionalism was, and still is, closely linked to European features and mannerisms, which entails that those who do not naturally fall into Eurocentric norms must alter their appearances, sometimes drastically and permanently, in order to be deemed professional."[31]

The same is true for demeanor; a canny woman masks her ambition by modulating her voice and cultivating facial expressions meant to evoke the girl next door or, for middle-aged women like me, her equally wholesome mother. Women who raise their voices, point with their index fingers, or look angry are viewed as pushy, aggressive, and mean. These are not qualities that translate into future professional opportunities.

When I transitioned to academia, I found a larger platform for my ideas. Articles and books that I wrote led to requests for me to appear on television and give public speeches. The advice poured in, much of it the same as when I was interviewing for jobs: smile more to counteract the impression that I had "resting-bitch face."[32] In the jobs themselves, I have been called out more than once for being "too shrill" — in the courtroom, in faculty meetings — when I argue my points. Whether it is challenging a hostile witness, pushing back against a legal argument by opposing counsel, or responding to an offensive comment by a colleague, no matter how disrespectful or dishonest the speaker or how meritless the position, I've learned to take a "more in sorrow than in anger" approach. Failure to follow those rules makes me unlikable and unreasonable, and unlikable, unreasonable women get fewer opportunities. It is that depressingly simple.

I found these gender-based rules of the road difficult to follow at times. I was not raised to smile if I didn't feel like it, never mind to police my tone of voice. My mother is a clotheshorse, yes, but when I was growing up, neither she nor my father ever told me I had to be pretty — or that I was. The best my father could summon was a gruff "You look appropriate" when I cleaned up for a special occasion like a Broadway play. And getting visibly and verbally angry? That was part of life in my roiling, intellectually combative Jewish family. I yelled constantly, often in self-righteous outrage, and didn't hesitate to use my sharp elbows to get what I thought I deserved: the front seat, the last doughnut hole in the box, the last word in an argument.

But in the courtroom, in the classroom, in radio interviews and on television sets, when I feel a rising tide of outrage, I fight as hard as I can not to slide into its undertow. I fear coming across as strident — or, worse, as a bitch. When I succeed, I feel as if I am betraying my feminist principles. But when anecdotal and empirical

evidence tells me that approach will deliver a more favorable outcome — whether for a client or for myself — not taking it seems
like an unforced error. In pursuing my ambition, I have striven to be
one of the "quiet and ambitious" women whom powerful men like
Politico's John Harris praise and reward.

I am an excellent trial lawyer. I am an excellent law professor. I
am very, very good at the multiple aspects of my job: writing, public
speaking, fundraising, teaching, and, most important, getting people out of prison. It shouldn't be difficult to write these sentences,
but it is. Women aren't supposed to say "I'm talented." We are supposed to play down our accomplishments by saying "I got lucky" or
"I was fortunate to have the opportunity and such a great mentor."
Luck and mentors have a big role to play. So do skill, drive, and
raw ambition. When you hang a jury or get an acquittal in federal court — and I have, multiple times — it means you beat the
most powerful government on the face of the earth. When you raise
$250,000 in three months to double the staff of your law clinic,
when you create the idea for a commission to exonerate wrongfully
convicted prisoners that the district attorney then makes a reality
and puts you in charge of, that's not luck, and it's not because of
your mentor.

Nor are eternal modesty and self-effacement necessarily a winning strategy — not if you want to be out in front and in charge.
Men are only too happy to co-opt and take credit for women's
ideas, seamlessly integrating them into their own achievements.
Until women own their work, they won't get the credit and, with
it, the opportunities they deserve. It is long past time to recognize
that encouraging women to "go for it" at work only if they do so
in a modest, "feminine" manner throws up obstacles in the path to
women's success. The knife's edge to walk — be attractive but not
too attractive; be hardworking, but not in a "look-at-me" way; be
assertive but unthreatening — will end, inevitably, in a fall. Keep-

ing to the prototype isn't just impossible; it is unwise because it tells women to metabolize rather than push back against setbacks that range from gendered and belittling comments to harassment to getting passed over for plum assignments and promotions.

Ann Marie Sheehy, forty-six, got her bachelor's degree from Stanford and her medical degree from the Mayo Medical School in Rochester, Minnesota. In the years since, she has gotten a divorce, raised two daughters, and risen through the ranks of the University of Wisconsin School of Medicine and Public Health to become the division chief of hospital medicine. Today, her duties include overseeing a department of sixty and representing student-athletes' interests in the Big Ten Conference, which in 2020 involved a fraught decision about whether to allow athletics to go forward in the midst of the COVID-19 outbreak. Yet she responded to my request for an interview by insisting that I talk to Amanda Renteria, her Stanford roommate, instead — "She's the really ambitious one." (My response was to interview both of them.)

"I think part of it is cultural," Ann Marie told me about her instinctive urge to flinch when she hears the word *ambition* applied to herself. Part of it she attributes to impostor syndrome. "I am constantly asking myself, *Am I good enough? Am I the right person?*" That feeling is reinforced when, even after she has spent two decades of steadily rising through the ranks, her own coworkers cannot quite fathom the powerful position she holds. "Now that I have to wear PPE, with the face shields and the gown and the gloves, the number of people who assume I am a nurse has skyrocketed." It is all too easy to feel like an impostor when the people who surround you in your own workplace do not recognize you for who you are.

When Ashton Clemmons arrived in the North Carolina state assembly to start her first term, she found only four other women with school-aged children out of her 120 colleagues. She described "frequent belittling — some intentional and some not," ranging from constantly being addressed by her older white male colleagues as "sweetheart" to having them visit her office "and ask me to my face, 'Where is Representative Clemmons?' then do a double take when I say, 'You're talking to her.'"

Ashton was determined to be as effective as she could for the people of her district and state. To accomplish that goal, she made sure to work across the aisle, produce substantive policy proposals, and, crucially, let much of the sexism and bias roll off her back. Calling it out, she knew, would only alienate the people whom she needed to offer her a seat at the table. It worked. As a freshman lawmaker, Ashton was named cochair of the COVID Education Working Group, one of the first times in ten years, she said, that a Democrat was named the cochair of any committee. At one meeting, she noticed, "Everybody calls me Madam Chairman. No one could just say 'Madam Chair.' I sit there thinking, *This should be the title of a book.* It's crazy. But here I am doing budget negotiations and it is mostly older white Republican men and me and one staff member who is the only Black person in the room. So I say every tenth or fifteenth thing I want to say because I know if I talk too much or I push back too much they won't let me back in the room."

Sheila, thirty-six,[33] was born in the Midwest and later moved with her parents to a small town in northern Florida. I asked how small. "If you go to the Walmart, everyone knows what you bought before you get home," she told me. Sheila's mother, who was seventeen when Sheila was born and never completed high school, "carried this expectation that I was going to be the person in the family who was going to be successful." Church and school were paramount. After graduating from a state college, Sheila decided to go to law school — though she knew no lawyers personally, the profession appealed to her. Naturally an introvert, Sheila shone when asked to make a speech in church. She thought her innate talent might be a good fit for the courtroom — what she was doing resembled the lyrical monologues delivered by the attorneys on one of her favorite TV shows, *Law & Order*. Sheila's first job out of law school was working for the local district attorney's office. She hit the ground running, starting with low-level misdemeanor cases and moving on to prosecute serious felonies with a focus on sex crimes.

Sheila worked long hours, always arriving at 9:00 a.m., rarely leaving before 8:00 p.m., and sometimes staying until the wee hours of the morning. Her work ethic stemmed from her devotion to her cases and also because, as a Black woman, she felt an additional need to prove herself. The defense lawyers she faced off against were often older white men. They were more comfortable, she said, communicating with attorneys who looked like them. At times, some of them seemed to question her authority, going over her head to her male supervisor rather than negotiating with her directly when she offered plea agreements they thought were too harsh.

In 2018, a judge on the local trial court retired unexpectedly, creating an opening. State law required that the governor appoint an interim replacement recommended by a nominating commission. Sheila decided to apply, knowing it was a long shot: "I questioned whether they would give it to me because of who I was, a Black woman, plus at that time I was only thirty-three." These facts, she thought, would count against her and she wondered if the selection committee would balk at her presumption.

After several rounds of interviews, Sheila got a call from the governor's office. She had been selected. She started in 2019 and had her first child the following year. Of her success — she has since run for election to the same seat and won — Sheila gives credit to God and also to her own quiet persistence and deep understanding of the community she serves. She also knows that she is an anomaly. The ability to forge relationships with white male powerbrokers and maintain a hyper-competent nonthreatening persona proved to be essential job skills.

In 2013, when her second child was eight months old, Amanda Renteria decided to leave her job as chief of staff to Senator Debbie Stabenow in Washington, DC, move back to her hometown in California's Central Valley, and run for Congress against the Republican incumbent, David Valadao. Campaigning was grueling. Amanda raised nearly $2 million by doing fundraisers up and down the state. She missed plenty of family dinners, but her husband and children joined her for local parades and community nights. "The kids loved that," she said.

Selling herself as a viable candidate was an uphill climb, however. The district was Republican and conservative. Amanda was a young Latina mother running as a Democrat. "The racial dynamics are pretty tough around there. Being a person of color from farm country, I got told a couple of times, 'I love you, Amanda, but you are not supposed to be running.'" Her gender and the fact that she had young children also raised some eyebrows. When her husband, Pat, stepped in to pick up and drop off the kids at various activities, the response coming from the other parents — overwhelmingly mothers — was "We are so sorry you have to do this." Amanda told me, "He would get kudos and apologies because the thinking was *Where is your wife?*" Amanda knew that her candidacy would be a hard sell to many in her district, but she said, "What was frustrating to me was that there wasn't anything I could say or do to change this mindset."

Amanda lost to Valadao. Shortly afterward, she got a call from Hillary Clinton's presidential campaign. Did she want to come on board as the national campaign director? She did. In February 2015, Amanda and her family moved to Brooklyn. Once again, she was campaigning at a breakneck pace, traveling across the country and going several weeks without seeing her family. "I had to be on all the time," she said. "I was so exhausted when I got home,

I could not form sentences." But Amanda was also proud to be in the inner circle, crafting strategies and collecting endorsements that she hoped would propel the first woman to the presidency.

Amanda and I discussed the second presidential debate, when Donald Trump stalked Hillary Clinton around the stage, at times coming within inches of her. Clinton recounted it in her postelection memoir, *What Happened:*

> It was one of those moments where you wish you could hit Pause and ask everyone watching, "Well, what would *you* do?"
>
> Do you stay calm, keep smiling, and carry on as if he weren't repeatedly invading your space?
>
> Or do you turn, look him in the eye, and say loudly and clearly, "Back up, you creep, get away from me."

Clinton chose the path so many women do, "biting my tongue, digging my fingernails into a clenched fist, smiling all the while, determined to present a composed face to the world."

I asked Amanda what she was thinking at that moment as someone who had just lost her own hard-fought campaign in no small part because conservative voters could not see past her gender or the validity of the ambition that drove her to run. "Did I want her to just instinctively yell at him?" Amanda let the question hang in the air unanswered. "The feeling was, she cannot lose credibility. There was so much fear around how do you define the first female leader of the free world in a way that will be acceptable? She was stuck. People hold women to a different standard."

Should Joe Biden decline to seek a second term, Kamala Harris will likely run for president. If she does, she will almost certainly face the revival of the race-and-gender-laced "she's too ambitious" trope. Rather than bat away the label, maybe she should embrace it. Which brings me back to Reese Witherspoon. After she won an Oscar for Best Actress in 2005 for her role as June Carter Cash in *Walk the Line,* her professional and personal life took a turn for the worse. A year later, she had separated from her husband, the actor Ryan Phillippe, with whom she had two children. The end of her marriage, which she called "very humiliating and very isolating," coincided with a career slump that seemed to signal the dead end faced by so many former ingenues as they segued into their thirties and beyond.

In 2012, Witherspoon decided that she needed to make a radical change. Rather than accept the dwindling number of roles offered to her (at the ripe old age of thirty-six), she started her own production company with the goal of developing projects with strong female leads. This imperative grew, she said, from meetings with studio bigwigs who had worked with her in the past. The meetings, she reported, all went the same way: questions about her kids, and remarks about how long it had been since her Oscar-winning role, a not-so-subtle hint that her career was on the wane. When Witherspoon asked about auditioning for roles with a strong female lead, she said, "I was met with nothing, blank stares, excessive blinking, uncomfortable shifting."

Witherspoon formed her production company, Pacific Standard Films, around a central idea: to make films featuring fierce, flawed, independent women, betting that there was a significant audience for them. And she was right. Over the past eight years, Witherspoon has produced (and, in some cases, starred in) one hit after another, all of them based on books written by women: *Wild,* adapted from Cheryl Strayed's bestselling memoir; *Gone Girl,* which Gillian Flynn wrote for the screen based on her bestselling thriller; *Big Little Lies,* Lianne Moriarty's blockbuster drama; and *Little Fires Everywhere,* based on the acclaimed novel by Celeste Ng.

Reese Witherspoon is now more powerful than she has ever been. For that, she credits her ambition. In 2015, *Glamour* named Witherspoon one of its women of the year for her achievements. Accepting the award, she took the A-word by the horns, proudly proclaiming that she had been driven by ambition since the age of fourteen. "Let's talk about ambition," she said, acknowledging that "people have prejudiced opinions about women who accomplish things," even to the point of "feelings of disgust." Then she exhorted her audience to push back hard, using her own experiences as an example. She concluded her remarks by saying, "I believe ambition is not a dirty word. It's believing in yourself and your abilities. Imagine this: What if we were all brave enough to be a little more ambitious? I think the world would change."[34]

Of course, Witherspoon is a white, cisgender, multimillionaire celebrity. (And she has also said repeatedly that motherhood is her greatest achievement.) Her story isn't the story of most working mothers. But her example points to a way forward that all of us would do well to embrace. Every loud and proud ambitious mother creates a wake, much like the bicyclist who is in the lead in a race. Those who follow in her path face fewer headwinds. As more women come out of the ambition closet, an ever-larger community will materialize, providing not only individual support but collective power. The normalization of ambition in women of different races, ages, and sexual orientation and across professional spheres is a vital milestone in the long march to gender equality, particularly for working mothers.

Ambitious mothers number in the tens of millions. They vote and pay taxes. Their labor contributes billions of dollars to the U.S. economy. United in a common cause, they can exert the political pressure necessary to enact long-overdue policies at the state, local, and federal level to make workplaces and home lives more equitable.

But first, they have to own their drive and their deservedness to themselves and to the rest of the world. Until *ambition* is no longer the A-word that women must wear like a scarlet letter, we will never be free to shoot for the moon and be our true selves — flawed, fierce, fantastic — in the process.

CHAPTER FIVE

I'M IN LOVE . . . WITH MY JOB

W HEN WORKING WOMEN BECOME MOTHERS, THEY FACE vexing choices and harsh judgments. Most women can't afford to stay home for the first few months, never mind the first few years of their child's life. But the truth is that many women would not choose to. They are passionate about their work because it gives them identity, purpose, and money in the bank. That passion and need don't magically disappear with the arrival of a baby.

Consider Dr. Laurie Green. She took five weeks off when she had her son, Ross, and three weeks off when she had her daughter, Monica, eighteen months later. That was 1988, and Laurie was about to start her own practice with another female ob-gyn. There were few women ob-gyns in those days and fewer still out on their own, but Laurie and her partner, Joanne Hom, were determined to make it after establishing a strong track record in a specialty dominated by older men. "Our trajectories had shot up. We started outpacing them in earning and patients, but the compensation was not keeping up."

Laurie's goal was to practice medicine in a different way than her male counterparts did. "Medicine was very patriarchal and I was into shared decision-making. I wanted to empower my patients to make their own choices. *Doctor* means 'teacher,' not 'dictator.' But that's not the way it was done back then." She and Joanne hung out their shingle on the theory that there were a significant number of female patients who wanted a different kind of experience with their doctors, particularly when it came to the intimate and life-altering decisions surrounding pregnancy and childbirth.

Laurie poured herself into building the business and outsourced the care of her infant daughter and toddler son to her nanny and her daughter's father, Tim. "I never changed an overnight diaper [with Monica], I never burped her," she said. "I cut every corner I could." Laurie breastfed, then followed each feeding with formula so her baby would sleep longer. "That was to save time," she told me. "I couldn't mess around. I was out the door by seven a.m."

Obstetrics and gynecology was one of the medical specialties my mother rejected. To be fair, it was not her particular passion, but she also reasoned that delivering babies at all hours of the day and night was not compatible with her marriage or family plans. My mother was busy, but she was never out the door by seven a.m., and my father was no Tim. We counted on her to keep the refrigerator stocked with the specific items each of us demanded (there were always, at a minimum, six different kinds of breakfast cereal), to provide us with home-cooked dinners every night (yes, sometimes she made them on weekends and froze them, but they were still whipped up from scratch), and to be home every weekend to ferry us to sports events and friends' houses. I pictured my sisters and me living under Laurie's regime and slowly turning into feral animals. I wondered what Laurie's children thought. (My interview with her son, Ross, is in chapter 8.)

Still, my mother, too, had taken very short maternity leaves. With each of her first two children — Emily, born during her internship, and me, born during her residency — she got six weeks by cobbling together sick leave and vacation time. With each child she had after that — Jill and then Dana — her part-time job at Bryn Mawr gave her only four weeks, and her private practice evaporated, so twice she had to start all over again. Each time, she said, "I was unhappy to go back," but she felt she had no choice. To buck the medical establishment during her training as a physician would have set her career back months or years; to demand more time from Bryn Mawr would likely have resulted in her losing her job. She did, however, make it a point to go home for lunch every day for the first year of each of our lives so that she could continue to breastfeed.

When I asked my mother if she considered pumping, she told me that the models available at the time were smaller versions of the machines used to milk cows. Enough said. When I asked if my dad took any time off, she noted that paternity leave did not exist. It was not until the 1990s and the passage of the Family and Medical Leave Act that parents were allowed to take time off following a child's birth. Even then, it was unpaid and, for many fathers, frowned upon. "You knew the expectation was that you would just keep working. You had to come back," she said. "You had to do your job if you wanted to keep your job."

Three decades later, when I became a mother myself, I had more options; the law and society's expectations had changed, and I wasn't a medical intern. And yet. I thought of my mother's words: "The expectation was that you would just keep working." But now the expectation was one I had put on myself. I thought back to the work e-mails I'd made sure to answer even as I lay in my hospital bed recovering from delivering my daughter. I'd felt like I had something to prove — that motherhood hadn't changed me — but I was also afraid that I was going to be complicit in my own professional erasure. Looking back, I can see that this fear was overblown, but at the time I worried that being a new mother meant that the world would perceive me as less capable of doing my job, which in turn would lead to fewer opportunities. And I wanted those opportunities just as fiercely as I had before I became a mother.

Something Laurie Green said resonated with me: "It is important to have an identity other than being someone's mother or spouse." Who would I be if I weren't a lawyer, a writer, and an aspiring law professor? No one I recognized or wanted to be. "When you are in a purposeful profession, you never have to ask why you are getting up in the morning," Laurie said. "You read these books about happiness, and the conclusion — whatever the genre — is that people who are happy have a purpose. It is about an outward-facing life."

Most women take more time off than Laurie and my mother did after having their babies. The Family and Medical Leave Act guarantees twelve weeks of unpaid time off, and some employers and states provide partial subsidies.[1] But it is the rare employer or government entity that will pay once that time is up.[2] For some women, twelve weeks feels stingy and insufficient; their bodies are not healed or their infants have birth complications. Even for "easy" deliveries of healthy babies, some new mothers find it disorienting and traumatic to finally establish a routine only to have it abruptly taken away.

Other women, though, are ready to go back. They appreciated the time to bond and recover but are looking forward to resuming their outside-facing lives. These mothers are often made to feel bad about their decisions and about their feelings about those decisions. Having a baby is a transformational event, women are told, not only for their bodies but for their brain chemistry. The changes can be profound, turning their passion and desire to work into a passion and desire to nurture. While that is true for some women, it is not the reality for others. Mothers who do not experience that magical transformation are made to feel that something about them is unnatural. A woman's continued devotion to professional success — a forbidden desire that poses an existential threat to the family — makes work her mistress. A working mother's unabated ambition in the professional sphere can come at the expense of her marriage; if the partnership survives, it may require a profound change in the relationship, particularly if her partner is a man who also works outside the home.

This zero-sum game does not allow for the possibility that a good mother can have different priorities. It does not allow for the simple truth that loving one's baby is not fundamentally incompatible with finding — and needing — pleasure and satisfaction in work outside the home. In her book *Get to Work,* the author and cultural historian Linda Hirshman wrote of the numerous young women graduating from college: "'Modern' society puts roadblock after roadblock in their path. It will take a laser focus for women to reach their ambitions for a full human life. They must even resort to the love that dares not speak its name: love of work."[3] Hirshman's book came out in 2006, but her words still resonate today.

Then there is the framing problem. The debate about the merits of the stay-at-home versus back-to-work mother is often portrayed as a woman's personal choice — as if the options are available on demand and it comes down simply to a matter of personal taste, no more controversial than picking strawberry ice cream over mint chocolate chip. In fact, most women don't get to choose; they have to work to support their families. The "choice" framing reflects a picture of the fortunate few perched at the top of the financial pyramid. "'Choice,'" Hirshman wrote, "is the weasel word, and it is legitimated, especially for women who consider themselves liberals, because it's been adopted by the feminist movement."[4] In pursuing the goal of inclusivity, she argued, the feminist movement had

watered itself down. "A movement that stands for everything ultimately stands for nothing," she wrote.[5]

When new mothers return to work, they are often made to feel
that they are harming their children and compared unfavorably with
images of self-sacrificing, child-first supermoms. The message is that
their primary focus should be on motherhood because it is vital
to their children's physical well-being and moral development. Let's
take the choice framing out of it for a moment. The theory itself is
fundamentally flawed. It operates from the premise that a certain
kind of all-encompassing, child-first mothering — *intensive mothering*, to use a term coined by sociology professor Sharon Hays in
The Cultural Contradictions of Motherhood — is integral to a child's
healthy development, as unique to women as breast milk.[6]

Notably, there is no such parallel theory of "intensive fathering"
that men must push back against when they return to work, often
within weeks of a child's birth. Nor should there be. The idea that
one parent — that one individual — bears a unique caregiving role
elides the reality that children benefit immensely from the love and
care of both parents as well as grandparents, babysitters, teachers,
and other extended family members. "I don't think it is good for any
human being to have a singularly focused life on any one relationship, marriage relationship, a work relationship, a parenting relationship," the journalist and feminist Jill Filipovic told me. "Human
beings need a lot of resources, we need love from multiple people
and connection with multiple people, and we need to find purpose
in multiple places."

I put Jill Filipovic's theory to the test in 2012, when my son was
three and my daughter was one. I was offered my dream job: direct-
ing a small innocence project at Loyola Law School.

But the offer came with an asterisk. The job was in Los Angeles;
we lived in San Francisco, and Matt did not want to leave his job
or move away. Matt's position made sense. The salary Loyola was

offering me, while double what I had made as a clinical teaching fellow at UC Hastings, was still only half of what he earned. Not only was he the primary breadwinner, his parents lived nearby and were loving and involved grandparents. We had no family in Los Angeles, and Matt had no obvious job prospects there. But I wasn't willing to give up a once-in-a-lifetime opportunity to help free wrongfully convicted people who were languishing in prison. So I said yes to Loyola and to a 384-mile commute. It was a decision that proved to be a defining moment in my professional and personal life.

For the next three years, I regularly spent three nights a week away from my family. Monday morning, I drove across the Bay Bridge to Oakland, took a Southwest flight to Burbank, got into my Hertz rental car, and headed downtown to the law school. Late Thursday afternoon, I repeated the process in reverse. Door to door, it was a four-and-a-half-hour journey, during which I also worked, drafting pleadings on the plane and making work calls in the car. As weeks turned into months, then years, I got to know the flight attendants and the people behind the rental-car counter on a first-name basis.

I was living the life my father had lived when my sisters and I were small children — because I had made the same choice. Just like him, I took a professional opportunity that made me an often absent parent. I did not ask for his blessing or his advice because it did not occur to me to make the connection at the time. The peculiar parallel hit me only when I began writing this book.

Matt and I hired a full-time nanny, Celeste, to take care of baby Ella and drive our son to and from preschool. Celeste, who was loving and devoted to our children, also made them dinner and did the laundry. Matt stepped in and stepped up, spending more time with our children. So did his parents. I let go of the idea that I had to be present for every special moment of my children's lives or even that I had to be home for dinner.

Almost no one thought what I was doing was a good idea, and a few people candidly told me it would harm my family. How would two toddlers adjust to having a "part-time" mom? Think of all I would miss: family dinners, bath time, bedtime. When my children looked back on so many occasions, I would, quite literally, not be in the picture. Then there were the practicalities. How would my husband, with his law firm associate's hours, adjust to being the full-time parent half of every week without seething with resentment and questioning my priorities on a near-daily basis?

In many ways, I was simply in denial. *We will make it work. We are making it work,* I stubbornly insisted to anyone who asked. Yet I felt guilt and shame. When Carter's and Ella's sweet baby faces popped up on my phone when it was time to say good night, my heart ached. Sometimes, lying alone in the bedroom I was renting from my close friends, I cried. I was spending as much time with their children as I was with mine. My marriage was suffering. But I also believed fervently in the importance of the work that I was doing.

I don't want to let myself off the hook. An ambitious mother of young children doesn't need a wrongfully imprisoned client to justify her decisions. Reflecting on what I did and why I did it is painful, not because I believe I made the wrong choices but because I was not honest with myself or my husband about what those choices revealed. Growing up in my parents' house, I learned that the life I wanted was my father's, not my mother's. I was not willing to make her sacrifices. I wanted his ambition, not her constraints. My denial about desires that in hindsight seem blindingly obvious stemmed from a deep-seated fear that what I wanted was not only unmotherly, it made me a Bad Mother. So I didn't admit it — not even to myself.

Shortly before he died, in 2012 at the age of eighty-three, the famed children's book author Maurice Sendak spoke with NPR's

Terry Gross for her *Fresh Air* program. Sendak talked about his childhood and the importance of his brother, Jack, in inspiring him to reject the pressure from their parents to live a "prosaic life." Instead, Jack "took his time with me to draw pictures and to read and to live a fantastical life" — Jack, too, was an artist and writer. They also had a sister, "but mostly, after all, she was a girl," Sendak said. "All that was expected of her was that she should grow up and be very pretty and marry a decent man. So she had to concentrate on what my parents expected of her. And she didn't have the creative insanity that existed between me and my brother to go further than that. I wished she had."

Sendak spoke with evident pain and sadness about those he had lost — his life partner and his closest friends. But he was also at peace, if wistful. "Oh God, there are so many beautiful things in the world which I will have to leave when I die but I'm ready, I'm ready, I'm ready." He described the richness of his career, one in which he took the time to see and listen and think and create. His professional arc, he told Terry Gross, was one "of the deepest pain and the wondrous feeling of coming into my own." Sendak ended the interview with these words of advice: "Live your life, live your life, live your life."

I remember when I heard that interview. It was 2011, six months before I started at Loyola, and I was on my daily run in Golden Gate Park. Sendak's words stopped me in my tracks. I was overcome with emotion. More recently, I listened to the interview again, and again I found myself crying. Mentally, I fast-forwarded four decades, picturing myself, like Sendak, elderly, frail, nearing the end. Would I be able to say that I had lived my life? Without the opportunity to do the work I wanted — the writing, the advocacy, the teaching — the answer was no. If those vital parts of me were smothered, I would die having been only half alive. Dozens of mothers whom I interviewed, all of them doing very different kinds of work, told me they felt the same way. Every time I heard one of them describe a stretch in her life where her work took priority or the simple joy she derived from kicking ass in her job, I felt a thrill of mutual recognition and also relief. I wasn't freakish, or alone.

In the fall of 2012, I was given the case of a lifetime: fighting to free an innocent man, improbably named Kash Register, who had been convicted thirty-four years earlier of a murder he did not commit. Kash had been incarcerated since April 1979, when Los Angeles Police Department detectives snatched him from the small apartment where he lived with his mother, Wilma. A devout Christian, she had remained there ever since, praying that her son would come home. When the Loyola Law School Project for the Innocent got involved, she told me she believed it was divine intervention; after more than three decades of Wilma begging someone, anyone, to listen, her son had a small but mighty army behind him. But the Los Angeles district attorney's office was fighting back, using every tool and resource at its disposal.

There is no pressure like the pressure of fighting to free an innocent client. For the next twelve months, Kash Register's case took over my life. It was the last thing I thought about when I went to bed at night and the first thing I thought about when I woke up in the morning. Interestingly, though, the face I saw most often when I lay wide awake in bed was Wilma's. What happened to her child amounted to a legally sanctioned kidnapping. Every time I thought about the continual anguish she experienced as Kash's mother, I felt not only visceral pain but also a renewed determination to bring her son home. When I kept Wilma in the front of my mind, I felt more clear-eyed and purposeful.

Good litigators think like surgeons: coolheaded, exacting, precise. Decimating the prosecution's case against Kash wasn't about wildly swinging a hammer; it was about exposing and removing the cancerous tumors with careful, preplanned incisions. The most reasonable person in the room usually wins, I told my students. And so I set out to be that person. Running my daily five miles, standing under the spray of the hot shower afterward, waiting in line at Trader Joe's, I thought and rethought how to tell the story — the story of the case that the jury never heard.

There was only so much, though, that I could compartmentalize, and there was a limit to my ability to hold my outrage, fear, and stress in check. An innocent client is a fire in the brain. It crackles and consumes. Sometimes when I was with my children or my husband, I was unable to track what they were saying or pay close attention to what they were doing. It was difficult for me to focus on anyone or anything else, including the three of them — the most important people in my life.

"Mom, you look blurry," my son said to me once at dinner, jolting me out of yet another Kash-related thought. He had a phrase for my inattention: "When Mom goes away." But he used it to describe the times I was actually at home, often right next to him. At least, my body was.

In July of 2013, Los Angeles Superior Court judge Katherine Mader granted Kash an evidentiary hearing, which is the equivalent of a retrial in front of a judge rather than a jury. That legal battle began that October. As lead counsel, I opened, closed, presented our crucial witnesses, and cross-examined most of the witnesses put up by the State. When I questioned Kash about the series of horrific events that led to his incarceration and what he had lost in the decades that followed, the pain and loss were so acute, I nearly cried myself.

Every minute of the retrial absorbed me, body and soul. It was as if my entire professional life had led up to that moment. I had a mission and I was in my element. I love the courtroom the way other people love drugs or sex or money — the pulsing adrenaline, the roller-coaster highs and lows, the anything-can-happen feeling that is both terror and exhilaration, the way that I am completely present and in the moment.

When I was in the thick of it, I was absent from home. A month before the retrial began, I rented a small apartment near the courthouse and lived there during the weeks it took to prepare and present all of the witnesses and evidence. Occasionally, I took breaks to fly north to see Matt and my children, but only for a few days at a time. I missed them, but I did not dwell on their absence from my life or mine from theirs. I had one singular, all-consuming goal: to walk Kash out of prison and into Wilma's arms.

My son, then four, had a lot of questions. "Why are you gone so much?" he would ask me. "Why are you always talking on the phone about the guy with the funny name?" At the time, my son was obsessed with superheroes. He ran around the house in T-shirts emblazoned with their pictures — Superman, Batman, Iron Man — and a red cape Velcroed to his tiny shoulders. On the nights I was home, we read the stories of their adventures out loud. In speaking about my work, I used the language of those stories. I talked about the case's superheroes — Kash, Wilma, the dogged law students. I described its villains — the prosecutors and police who lied and cheated to steal Kash's life. Casting the case as the ultimate battle of good versus evil, I explained to my son that I needed to be away so that I could bring Kash home to his mommy, who was waiting for him.

Kash is at home now with Wilma. They live in a beautiful house in west Los Angeles. After the verdict, Kash sued the City and County of Los Angeles and won a $16.9 million settlement, the largest in Los Angeles County history. The exoneration of Kash Register was a group effort that involved my students, my colleagues, and Kash himself. But at the end of the day, Kash is home because I fought like hell. He is home because I was his lawyer.

I am not a religious person like Wilma, but if I were, I would say that the fight for Kash's freedom was God's work and that I used every skill and ounce of energy I possessed to rectify the worst kind of wrong. I hoped that my husband would understand, that in the end the resentment would be replaced or at least tempered by the appreciation of how much I loved what I was doing and how important it was. Caught up as I was, I failed to comprehend how much I was asking — or that my marriage was fast approaching the breaking point.

Seven years later, in December 2020, I was invited to be a guest on the Emmy Award–winning *Tamron Hall Show* to defend this particular set of decisions and others that followed. The topic was modern motherhood. Tamron Hall, fifty, who debuted her eponymous talk show shortly after giving birth to her son, Moses, started off by telling her audience, "The ongoing conversation about women who work inside the home versus women who work outside is divisive, it is sometimes hard; at the end of the day some of these women sound just like you."

Tamron had some hard questions for me. After quoting from a *New York Times* op-ed I had written a year earlier in which I had admitted to missing birthday and school events, she asked, "Why did you go down this path of having children if you weren't going to be there?" My first impulse was to be defensive. Then I thought better of it. "I think what you have to understand is what I was doing instead," I responded. I talked about Kash's case, the stakes, and the imperative to free him. "And I think that is something that my kids get, which is what I am doing when I am away from them is incredibly important." I continued, "It doesn't mean that they're not sad or hurt or that they don't resent me sometimes, but they know

Mom is out there making the world a better place." The all-female audience applauded.

But there is no denying that my children routinely express frustration at my distractedness and unavailability; there is no denying that the fracturing of our family took a psychological toll. My marriage did not survive, and even though Matt and I do our best to co-parent and remain friends, divorce is hard on the children. I admitted all of this, believing it was important to tell the full story. When Tamron Hall asked me, only half jokingly, if my kids would be scarred for life, I wanted to respond, *Of course not!* Instead, I answered honestly: "The jury is out." As mothers, we make choices, some instinctive, some well thought out, some grossly mistaken. Some are more consequential than others. In the moment, it is difficult to discern which decisions will slot into which category. The truth is that with children, the jury is always out.

Some women are more prescient than I was. Before making that final commitment to a romantic partner, they see that what they want for themselves professionally lies at the core of their identity and that compromising it for a relationship will prove ruinous. One young woman told me that she had recently ended her engagement "because I wasn't able to align my ambitions with the relationship I was in." She explained that her fiancé would not be supportive of her having children unless she agreed to "lower [her] ambitions." She was unwilling to do so.[7]

Others have been able to renegotiate with their partners and come out the other side. Diana Luong — the woman who had immigrated to the United States from Vietnam as a teenager — told me that in 2016, when her son and daughter were ten and twelve, her job at the nail salon had become untenable. Her ambition — to go out on her own — started to seem not just plausible but necessary, both for her family's financial well-being and her emotional health. Diana was an esthetician, but her boss told her that she had to work as a receptionist two days a week as well as open and close the salon. For this additional labor, which meant longer hours and fewer clients, Diana was paid forty dollars extra per week. Her boss also started to deduct money from Diana's tips, which were her main source of income. She was working nine- and ten-hour days with only thirty minutes for lunch while making less than she had a year earlier. She was the family's sole breadwinner, and her dwindling income meant that she was barely able to pay the bills and put food on the table. "Every day when I came home, I was so tired I was like a dead body," she told me. "I am thinking: *I have to do something to find a way out. I cannot be stuck like this and put up with this.* So the energy in me to get out was strong."

The following year, Diana went back to school part-time to get certified in eyelash extensions and micro-braiding. It was a three-month program that was quite expensive; she went one day a week and worked the other six, paying for the classes with the tip money she had saved over the years. She saw it as an investment in her future. "I thought, *If I have a better education, I will have better chances.* After I finished the courses, I started to look for another job." Her focus was on taking the steps necessary to start her own esthetician business.

An opportunity arose in mid-2018. One of Diana's customers was a woman who owned a hair salon just a block away. She told Diana that the esthetician who had rented the back room had recently retired after eighteen years. The space was now empty, and the woman was wondering aloud what to do with it. Diana, mindful that her coworkers were within eavesdropping distance, bent down and whispered in her ear, "Can I go there and take a look?"

The same day, on her short lunch break, Diana rushed over. "Everyone is so welcoming and they know exactly who I am and they are expecting me. And I am like, Wow, this is welcoming energy. It is convenient for my clients and a beautiful space."

When Diana came home from work that night, she was bubbling with enthusiasm; the rent the salon owner was asking, $200 a week, seemed reasonable. "I just knew that this was my opportunity and I know my clients are loyal and they will come with me." But her husband, she said, saw only risk. "He keeps saying to me, what if I fail? I told him, 'I am confident, I feel like I can do it.'" He responded by telling Diana to try to negotiate better terms with her boss at the nail salon. "I am like, No, I know her, and anyway I am done." They argued. "At one point I think, *Shut up, I am going to do this but I am not going to let you know. Because you are being a chicken and not supportive.*"

Diana felt that after so many years of concessions and the downsizing of her own dreams, it was time to make a radical break. "Maybe just this once in a lifetime I will take a chance." Her husband continued to discourage her, but Diana held firm, figuring that if she waited to tell him until after she had quit and set up her own shop, it would be too late to stop her. In the end, though, Diana won the argument. "A few days later," she said, "he is thinking it over and he says, 'You know what? If that makes you happy you can just go for it.' And I said, 'Thank you. Finally.'"

Breegan Jane also found herself at a crossroads as her twenties came to an end and she realized that she had settled for too little for too long. Breegan's career began when she was two years old, and she has the Screen Actors Guild card to prove it. Her mother owned a children's clothing store in Hermosa Beach, California. She loved to take pictures of her adorable daughter in an outfit that was part of her inventory, frame the pictures, and use them to decorate the walls of her store. Breegan was a natural in front of the camera, bright-eyed with a sunny smile that conveyed joy and mischief; inevitably, her mother sold out of whatever Breegan wore in the pictures. Professional modeling gigs with name brands followed. OshKosh, the Limited, Talbots, even Clorox flew Breegan and her mother all over the country for photo shoots. "The trend in marketing at that time was one white girl, one black girl, and one Asian girl," she told me. Breegan's biological father is Black (she was adopted as a baby). "I had the look they wanted," she said.

Breegan modeled until she was fifteen years old. "I loved every minute of it," she said. What she loved most was watching the stylists work to assemble the full picture — from the snowcapped mountains behind her to the color of the barrette in her hair — meant to conjure a life experience that came with purchasing a product. Breegan's parents put her earnings into a savings account, hoping to use it to pay for college. But when the time came, Breegan, an indifferent student, did not want to go. Instead, at eighteen, she used the money to open her own clothing store. Within the first couple of years, however, she suffered a traumatic event that sent her into a tailspin.

Breegan closed her store and moved from Hermosa Beach to Los Angeles. "I partied and was self-destructive." Slowly, she regained her emotional footing. What followed were years of working as an executive assistant to powerful older men: the CEO of a yacht-building company and, later, the head of a movie production studio. In those roles, Breegan took on more and more responsibility. She overhauled the yacht owner's brand, became his marketing director, and worked on his advertising campaigns. She oversaw the renovation of the studio executive's properties down to the smallest details, picking out the tile and the fabrics.

When she was twenty-seven, Breegan began dating a longtime friend; *When Harry Met Sally*, she called it. They married, and after becoming pregnant, she quit her job with the studio executive and devoted herself to helping her husband succeed both financially and professionally. Together, they opened a restaurant. "I thought supporting CEOs would translate into my life as a mom. I would help this man become more successful. I will work, but I don't need to be the outward-facing person. I told myself that I was okay with traditional gender roles."

Breegan took a hands-on approach to the restaurant: picking out the decor and doing the manual labor, including scrubbing the floors while her baby napped in the stroller. At this point, she was pregnant again. During this time, the family was living in a home that Breegan's parents bought for them. But her husband did not acknowledge Breegan's hard work or her parents' contributions — quite the opposite. He told their friends he had purchased their home with his own money. He gave the impression, she said, "that I was his spoiled wife" and he was the brains behind their business. She remembers listening as he created this false impression during get-togethers with friends and thinking that "his ego as a man could not handle it" — not her family's help and not her crucial role in his business. The restaurant began to fail, as did the marriage. Less than three years after they tied the knot, Breegan filed for divorce.

As a single mother with two toddlers, Breegan decided it was time to go her own way. She started a design firm and began flipping homes. "I buy the ugliest one and I sell it as the prettiest one. Of course, you learn things, and I work a ton but I have a natural visual ability to walk in and see what it can be." Breegan began branching out, expanding her business as a designer, lifestyle guru, and entrepreneur. Her clients were looking for change — in their homes, their businesses, or themselves — and they wanted her to provide the vision.

With the collapse of her marriage came Breegan's realization that she did not want to continue using her talents to support a powerful man. She wanted to run her own business. To promote it, she started a blog, posting personal content about her divorce and her remade family in addition to beautifully shot pictures of the houses she had renovated. She mixed the personal and professional; these remodels often featured pictures of Breegan herself having a glass of wine, embracing her children, throwing back her head in laughter. Traffic on her website increased. In 2019, she was contacted by a production company and asked to audition as a host for *Extreme Makeover: Home Edition.* After several rounds of grueling auditions, she got the job. When she got the news in July 2019, Breegan was ecstatic. "I was excited that as a Black woman in a very Caucasian, male space, I could inspire others."

From July to October, Breegan spent weeks at a time away from her sons, filming ten episodes in ten weeks in locations all over California and Utah. On and off camera, she and her cohosts oversaw the demolition and rebuilding of houses for families in need, including three siblings who had fled from Uganda after their parents and baby sister were murdered in front of them.

"My parents are an amazing help and resource," she said, noting that her kids had gone to stay with them while she was away. Before she left, Breegan explained the importance of her work to her sons, who were three and five. "They are already aware that I build houses and it was awesome to be able to tell them that Mommy was helping people who don't have a place to live." It was not the first time she had gone away. "I left them to go to Kenya for ten days to do philanthropic work when they were two and four. I said, 'Mommy is going to help other people. [My son] ran into his room to grab toys — I had ordered tons of school supplies to bring with me — and as I am filling the bag he runs in with three toys and says, 'I don't need these, Mommy, will you give them to someone else?' And I was like, 'Oh, he gets it.'"

Hely Harris, the Cookshop restaurant's floor manager, told me, "Working mothers deserve to be honored." Her career in the restaurant industry, which she loves, requires her to work ten hours a day, five days a week. At the same time, she said, "Being a mom is really important to me." Hely makes the most of the time she and

her son, Jack, have together; every morning she makes him breakfast while he reads aloud to her. Before the pandemic struck, she
dropped him off at school in their Queens neighborhood before
boarding the E train to head into Manhattan. "I do have that tinge
of guilt that I work so much, but I see the little man he is becoming
and I know I am doing a good job."

Hely, whose mother emigrated from Indonesia by way of Hol-
land, grew up understanding the importance of work as a financial lifeline. Her mother, who had an associate's degree, worked as
a bank loan underwriter; her father, a truck driver, did not finish
high school. The family was able to climb into the middle-class life
by relying on two incomes. But when Hely was seven and her sister was four, their parents divorced. Afterward, she watched her
mother struggle as the sole breadwinner; her father, she said, "paid
child support but not all the time and I never wanted it to be like
that for me." Her mother remarried, and when Hely was fifteen,
the family moved to Orlando, Florida, where her stepfather had a
job at a waste-management plant. With two incomes, the family
became economically stable again.

Hely graduated from a two-year community college and decided against a four-year degree. "I was finding more life lessons
in the world as opposed to in school, for me personally." She loved
restaurant life — the regulars, the new customers, and the fast pace.
Over the years, she worked as a server and a bartender at a number
of different restaurants, ranging from a big chain in Atlanta to the
Crooked Bayou, a woman-owned barbecue joint in Orlando.

In 2005, Hely moved to New York to follow a boyfriend. It was
hard to break into the New York restaurant business, but she eventually succeeded, getting a job as a server at Salt, a small trendy bistro
in SoHo. Two months into the job, the general manager left, and
the owner asked Hely to take over. She did, becoming a jack-of-all-
trades: server, maître d', and hostess when required; she also handled

the inventory, payroll, and finances. Hely's relationship did not last, but several years later she met Tim, the man who would become her husband, at Salt's sister restaurant. In 2012, Hely was hired by the Bowery Group. She spent three and a half years as the general manager of a restaurant before taking on the same role at Cookshop, the company's flagship restaurant. Hely, who earns a salary in the low six figures, is now on track to become the director of operations and hopes to be considered for partnership someday. She outearns her husband, who works as Cookshop's beverage director. They split childcare and chores fifty-fifty.

Needless to say, Diana, Breegan, Hely, and the many other women whose stories I tell in this book do not stand for all women. There are plenty — millions — who prefer to stay home.[8] One of them, Lillian, who was also a guest on Tamron Hall's modern-motherhood show, was interviewed right after me. I watched along with the audience as clips played of Lillian holding her baby, helping her older daughter study, doing laundry, and vacuuming the carpeted stairs of her elegant home, smiling all the while, not a strand of her long dark hair out of place. She proudly called herself #TradMom (as in "traditional mom") and made widely watched videos about her life as a homemaker and homeschooler of her three young children. "We typically do three hours of formal instruction at home," she told Tamron. "In the afternoon, we add on Chinese, Spanish, piano, and violin." My heart sank thinking about my two kids, neither of whom had ever picked up an instrument and who were unlikely ever to be trilingual.

When Lillian met her husband, Felipe, they were both in school pursuing doctoral degrees, Lillian in choral music and music education. Her plan was to get a DMA — doctoral of musical arts — and become a college professor. After Felipe's job took them to Baltimore, Lillian temporarily put those plans on hold and taught in public schools. After becoming pregnant with their daughter, she left her job to stay at home. At first, she said, she questioned her decision, having mini–existential crises and asking herself, "What am I doing with my life?" What she ultimately came to appreciate, she said, was that this question was "not the right mindset." By downsizing, she and Felipe could live off his income. "There is a sacrifice we feel," she said. But it was all for a higher purpose: "This is your sacred duty, mothers out there, that you raise your children."[9]

Her children, she told Tamron, "get to see that Mommy stays home, that I submit to my husband, and that I look to him to make the major decisions in our family and, yeah, that I am inward-facing. I keep the home, I cook, I clean, I educate them and then my husband is the one who is outward-facing, so he does all the yard work but he is also the one who goes out and works and brings home the bacon." One of the rules of the marriage is that Lillian must seek Felipe's permission for any expense over a hundred dollars. Tamron asked, "Is he the CEO of the marriage and over raising the children?" "Absolutely," she replied, smiling. "So we call him the principal of our home school and I am the teacher. So he is the one who has the final say in what the children learn and kind of checks up on me and makes sure that I am doing a good job with them."

As I listened to Lillian, I found myself judging her and then judging myself. Everything she said sounded like an indictment of my own life. I was never going to "submit" to Matt — the use of that word in the context of marriage makes me queasy — but could I have at least considered being a touch more accommodating? Maybe if I had, my kids wouldn't be trundling back and forth between our two houses with no hope of switching effortlessly between languages or playing a Beethoven violin concerto. My attempts to "homeschool" Carter and Ella during COVID-19 amounted to checking up on them twice a day, at most, as they stared at teachers and classmates on Zoom. Half the time they were also on their own devices, texting with friends and playing video games. Had I done anything about that? No. I was just happy that they were occupied so I could do my job — no easy task, since I, too, was spending my days online — teaching, writing, in back-to-back meetings, all while seated on a stool in the kitchen of the twelve-hundred-square-foot condo we shared.

After the show, I watched some of the videos Lillian made of her life, hoping to gather evidence to discredit her, evidence that would reveal, somehow, that her choices were clearly wrong (or at least problematic enough that mine would seem less cringe-worthy). In one video, Lillian and Felipe sat side by side on the couch in their living room talking candidly. Felipe asserted that one reason women are driven to have careers is "as a safety net for when divorce happens." Lillian added, "And that's why people always advise you to have separate bank accounts. We don't, we decided to pool our money into the same place." Felipe explained, "We avoided all that advice that everybody gives that builds a sort of independence, a state of separation in the marriage for 'just in case.'"

It felt like they were talking directly to me. When Matt and I got married, we kept our money separate. This was by mutual agreement, but at the time I had far more money than Matt did. We are the same age, but when we met, I had been a practicing lawyer for five years and he was a debt-saddled law student who had spent his twenties working as a carpenter. Months before the wedding, I put my retirement money from my seven years at the federal public defender into an IRA under my name. It was a significant amount of money and I had earned it. Why should Matt have it? During the marriage, I inherited money after my grandmother's death, and I deposited it in a trust account that Matt could not access.

Felipe was saying the quiet part out loud. Yes, these decisions did create "a state of separation in the marriage," and yes, I made those decisions "just in case." Was that careful planning or a self-fulfilling prophecy? Was the demise of my marriage inevitable because I was too selfish and scared to throw my chips into the community pile? Was my refusal to go all in financially a prudent decision or a reflection of a fundamental lack of faith?

But then I recalled my mother's advice. *Never be at the financial mercy of anyone else. Find work you love. Help other people. Excel.* No, she didn't homeschool me, and no, she wasn't there when I got home from school. But I was so proud of her, of her busy career, her medical degree, and the *Dr.* in front of her name. When our elderly neighbor Roy Popper collapsed one morning and his panicked wife called us, my mother ran to his house and performed CPR until the ambulance came. He survived. When I was studying abroad at Cambridge during my junior year in college, I met a young woman in the computer lab. She was wearing a Bryn Mawr sweatshirt. I mentioned that Bryn Mawr was my mother's alma mater and that she now worked there as the head psychiatrist at the medical center. The young woman stared at me, eyes wide. "Your mother is Dr. Bazelon?" she asked. I nodded. She told me the story of a close friend at school who had been suicidal. "Your mother saved her life."

The financial independence my mother stressed felt important. What if Felipe left Lillian? What if he died suddenly and tragically, like my grandfather had? While the chances were low, the ravages of COVID-19 have brought mortality into sudden terrifying focus for all of us. You never know in this life. Isn't it better to be prepared for the worst-case scenario? To me, Lillian's trusting plunge into her marriage was the equivalent of buying a beach house at the Jersey Shore with no hurricane insurance. She might be fine. She'd probably be fine. But then there was Hurricane Sandy.

Still, Lillian had done the same math as me. Factoring these risks into her personal equation, she had chosen to pursue the path that was going to make her the happiest. She didn't fit my "ambitious mother" mold; in fact, her life was an open challenge to my thesis.

That didn't make her wrong. It was a pointed reminder that in writing this book, I should never presume to speak for all mothers.[10]

I interviewed other millennial and Gen X women whose choices were not as stark as Lillian's but who had opted to step back from their careers by working part-time or not at all for a combination of reasons. These included burnout, the crippling cost of childcare, the desire for more independence and flexibility in their schedules while their children were very young, and the need for the time to reflect before taking the next step in their careers. Many of them saw their time at home as temporary, and in their stories, I uncovered a different kind of ambition: nonlinear, intuitive. They were confident that new and different professional opportunities lay on the other side of that time at home. Ambition is like water — it has different temperatures, pressure levels, and pathways as it navigates around the solid objects that are spouses, family, friends, children.

Elea, a thirty-something stay-at-home-mom, spoke to me from the open sunny front room of the house where she now lives with her husband, Josh, and two-year-old daughter, Leona, in the foothills of the Blue Ridge Mountains in Clayton, Georgia, a city of just over two thousand people. Elea and her family moved to Clayton in the winter of 2020 after the pandemic made life in their tiny Brooklyn apartment unlivable. Josh's company, which has an Atlanta office, agreed to allow him to work remotely. Elea, who had been working full-time as a middle-school teacher, finished out the spring semester teaching online and then resigned. Since then she has worked as a freelance tutor and an online yoga teacher, and she's also collected unemployment under the CARES Act.

The move from a seven-hundred-square-foot apartment in a densely populated city to a roomy three-bedroom house in a small rural town within minutes of the Appalachian Trail brought Elea geographically closer to her family and her in-laws. It also made financial sense, and it appealed to her sense of adventure; Elea's mother had been a helicopter pilot in the U.S. Army whose postings took the family all over the world. For the first ten years of her life, Elea lived on military bases in Alabama, Germany, and South Korea. "I am used to moving and change," she said. "That kind of thing excites me."

But Elea also craved stability, both emotional and financial, and the opportunity to spend more time with her daughter. Elea describes herself as "very close" to her mother — "I looked up to her immensely" — but her mom's repeated deployments to war zones took a toll. Shortly after 9/11, when Elea was thirteen, her mother was sent to Afghanistan and Kuwait, where she spent the next two years, coming home for occasional visits after months and even a full year away. At the time, Elea's outward-facing life looked picture-perfect: she got top grades, took honors classes, and was a member of the varsity cheerleading squad. But she drank, smoked pot, and engaged "in other reckless behaviors." In part, she was rebelling against her father, whom she described as intemperate and authoritarian, traits she attributed to the fact that "he was jealous of my mom." Elea told me, "It is very hard to be without a parent who gives love, guidance, and support in the home."

Elea met her husband, Josh, when they were both attending college at the University of Georgia. After graduation, Elea was accepted into the competitive Teach for America program and placed in a charter school in the Bedford-Stuyvesant neighborhood in Brooklyn. She moved in 2010; after several years of a long-distance relationship, Josh moved there too.

Elea loved her work. After two years of teaching first grade and going to school at night to get a master's degree in education, she created a performing arts program for children in kindergarten through fourth grade, designing the curriculum and teaching classes in dance, yoga, and theater. She and Josh got married in 2016, when they were twenty-eight. Three years later, in August 2019, Elea gave birth to Leona. After twelve weeks of maternity leave, Elea started a new job at an all-girls middle school. It was miserable. "Middle school is intense," she said. Her students could often be cruel to each other and to Elea, mocking her for, among other things, not losing the baby weight. The comments about her body cut deep; Elea had always been in excellent physical shape but she was still recovering from a cesarean section and too exhausted and broke to make time for exercise. "What time or resources did I have to go to a Pilates class that costs forty dollars an hour?" she asked, throwing up her hands.

The financial strain and cramped quarters felt suffocating. Josh was working full-time at a sports marketing agency, so they created a nanny-share with their upstairs neighbors. Elea's job barely covered the cost, which was $550 a week. Their apartment seemed to shrink in size by the day. When COVID hit, in some ways Elea was relieved. With both Elea and Josh now working remotely, they moved south, first to live with her mother, who had remarried and moved to Kentucky, and then to live with Josh's parents in Atlanta. For a few months, Elea freelanced, working as a tutor for a pod of five second-graders in Atlanta and making more money than she ever had as a full-time teacher.

After the move, ensconced with her family and then her in-laws, Elea realized how lonely and disconnected she had felt. "Mothers aren't supported well at work," she told me, "and no one talks about it." Her life in New York "felt a little bit impossible." A tree that is part of a larger forest has roots that connect with other trees, she said. But a solitary sapling has no way to get that kind of communal nutrition. "Humans are like that. When we are alone, we can't get what we need."

The decision to buy a home in rural Georgia came from a desire to live a quieter life closer to nature with a far lower cost of living while still being relatively near family (Atlanta is a two-hour drive away). Elea describes her decision to stop working in the fall of 2020 as a way to recenter, reflect, and learn new skills. The mortgage was less than their monthly rent. Leona's part-time day care cost less per month than Elea and Josh had paid per week for the nanny-share. With that financial breathing room, Elea has used the past year to teach herself to compost, landscape, and, through trial and error, create a garden where she grows cucumbers, basil, thyme, tomatoes, peppers, broccoli, butter lettuce, strawberries, and watermelon. Elea is working outside in the sun, her hands in the soil, often next to her daughter — who loves worms — but she isn't doing it for money, and she goes at her own pace. "As a teacher at a high-performing charter school, you are conditioned to be a type A person whether you want to be or not. I used to work so hard my arms would go numb. I don't have to be at a hundred and ten percent. I don't have to draw my worth from constant output."

Elea describes her months staying at home as "a great challenge" that also gave her renewed faith in herself. She plans to reenter the workforce within the next six months to a year, confident that the opportunities are there for her or she will create them herself. "One of my husband's clients is LinkedIn, and I see the companies that are making changes and those that are not, and I am going to target those places that are going to give me family leave and flexibility with my work location. I think about these things when I think about going back. The confidence you are seeing is that I won't settle."

It occurred to me after interviewing Elea and comparing her to Lillian that there are as many variations of stay-at-home mothers as there are of working mothers. There is also a significant amount of overlap as women transition from one phase of their lives to another. We tend to simplify these two categories of women even as we pit them against each other — as Lillian and I were on Tamron Hall's show. We tend to tell women that stepping back even briefly will doom them professionally when in fact, for women like Elea, it may make sense financially, emotionally, and professionally because they have the space to figure out their next professional move. We are constantly asking what the right model is for motherhood and child-rearing, as if there were only one correct answer and every woman who failed to come up with the magic formula was worthy of censure.

For many years, Elea was in love with her job as a teacher, steadily assuming more responsibility, often through her own initiative and creativity. Then she wasn't. Her decision to step away, though, wasn't about giving up; it was about putting herself in the best position to fall in love with a different job — one she needed time to envision and prepare for. When I asked Elea if she would describe herself as ambitious, she didn't hesitate. "I would," she said. "My ambition is there, it is just expressed in different ways in various points in my life."

CHAPTER SIX

GETTING FREE

This is a chapter about getting free — free to re-imagine relationships or get out of them altogether; free to rethink what it means to be a "good mother" so that definition can include working with dedication and ambition outside the home; free to acknowledge the simple truth that happier mothers are better mothers and that constant self-sacrifice and self-abnegation are a road to nowhere.

Marriages can undergo strain and can even fracture when women continue to pursue their professional ambitions after becoming mothers. This choice challenges centuries-old gender norms, revealing unconscious but entrenched biases. Some partnerships don't survive. But others do — when there is a recognition that tired marital prototypes can be replaced by something different. The rebuilding process begins when men accept that their ambitious wives are good parents because of, not in spite of, devotion to their jobs. That recognition frees women from constantly feeling selfish and inadequate.

It also allows couples to reframe the dynamics of the relationship so that it can accommodate women's professional needs and desires.

I see this reframing as a way of playing the same game with a different strategy that produces better results. Take Boggle, a game in which lettered cubes are shaken up and land randomly in a four-by-four grid, and the players must spell as many words as possible before the sand runs out of the hourglass timer. The letters must be connected horizontally, vertically, or diagonally. The goal is to get more words than anyone else, which necessarily means finding words the other players did not. Growing up, my sisters and I played this game often with our parents; my best friend and I play to this day — and he always wins.

There's a point about halfway through a round of Boggle when the only words you can see are the ones you have already written down. Your mind traces the same routes, ending at the same result. It's maddening. But if you turn the Boggle board ninety degrees, you see the same letters from a different perspective, and an amazing thing happens. You find new words. So it goes in reconfigured relationships, with each other and with the institutions that dictate what is financially possible and socially acceptable.

The lack of institutional support for working parents is a perennial problem and a persistent roadblock to meaningful change interpersonally and systemically. The United States stands alone among industrialized countries in its failure to enact cost-effective, commonsense policies at the federal, state, and local level that provide crucial economic support for working parents, especially free preschool and subsidies for childcare. Because women tend to earn less than men and are expected to be the primary caregivers, that lack of resources prevents many mothers from working outside the home. Women's workforce participation peaked in 1999; it remained stagnant for the next ten years and then began dropping off, according to a report by the U.S. Bureau of Labor Statistics. Notably, "women

in the 25- to 54-year-old age group have experienced decreases in
their participation rates since 2000."[1] This cohort of women, who
are most likely to be the mothers of young children, made up almost
73 percent of working women in 2000. In 2015, they made up 63.8
percent.[2]

What explains this drop-off? There are many factors, including
the 2008 recession and the lower birth rates between 1965 and
1975, which left fewer of these women to begin with.[3] But a major
factor, according to experts, is the crippling cost of childcare.[4] "In
28 states and the District of Columbia, infant care costs exceed
the average cost of in-state college tuition at public four-year institutions," wrote the journalist Kerri Anne Renzulli in 2019, citing
data collected by the nonprofit organization Child Care Aware of
America. Since 2010, the cost of day care has ballooned to an average of nearly $10,000 annually; a nanny is closer to $30,000 per
year. Meanwhile, wages have remained stagnant.[5]

The costs are so prohibitive, they prevent poor women from entering the labor force. For women with slightly more money, childcare costs bite off a significant chunk of their pretax earnings, leaving
them barely able to scrape by, much less save money and move into a
higher economic bracket. Even for families that can afford it, quality
care can be devilishly difficult to find.[6] Because women are histor-
ically tasked with childcare — presumed to be biologically suited
for it, they are responsible for handling it themselves or outsourcing
it — solving this daunting equation falls primarily to them.[7]

The federal government and most state governments offer little help — embarrassingly little in comparison to other industrialized nations.[8] In 2017 and again in 2019, Senator Patty Murray
introduced the Child Care for Working Families Act, which was
intended to confront this problem head-on.[9] The bill aimed to help
lower- and middle-class families afford childcare by capping its total
cost at 7 percent of their income. The bill also raised the pay for

the childcare providers themselves, who often labor for poverty-level wages. The authors of the legislation estimated that between one and two million mothers with children under the age of thirteen would be able to join the labor force as a result, many then pulling their families out of poverty. Investments in childcare and early education were estimated to add seven hundred thousand jobs.[10] The Republican-led U.S. Senate never brought the legislation to the floor for a vote.

Then came COVID-19. One of the virus's devastating effects was driving mothers from the workplace. Women are overrepresented in pink-collar occupations such as retail and hospitality services, and many of those jobs vanished. For other women, including frontline workers, showing up for work became impossible because of overwhelming childcare obligations that could no longer be outsourced — childcare centers and schools were closed; grandparents and older relatives could not risk the exposure. Under COVID, the second shift metastasized, taking up so much space and exerting so much pressure that there was no room for anything else. According to a 2020 Brookings Institution report, "Between February and August, mothers of children 12 years old and younger lost 2.2 million jobs compared to 870,000 jobs lost among fathers."[11] One-quarter of these women cited lack of childcare as the reason.[12] Women of color suffered disproportionately, particularly those without a college degree.[13]

In part because of the gender-skewed fallout from the pandemic and the deleterious effects on the economy, there is now, finally, the real possibility of institutional changes — although federal legislation, modeled on bills like those introduced by Senator Murray remains maddeningly elusive. But as long as American society remains woefully backward when it comes to supporting working mothers, many women will remain shackled to unhealthy relationships and other misery-inducing "choices." Without help from the government, many couples — especially those without family support — are left to figure out the vexing division of marriage-children-work on their own. In the main, that division has not favored working mothers, hence the need to reframe these relationships. Professional working mothers who find themselves with partners who are unwilling to make that shift in perspective and allocation of time and resources have a tough choice: radically compromise who they are and what they want in order to stay in the marriage, or leave.

In the year leading up to Kash's release from prison, my marriage collapsed like a house falling in on itself. There were many reasons our brief union failed. But at the heart of it lay our fundamentally different ideas of what my role in our family should be. Taking the job in LA and leaving our family for the time it took to try Kash's case were simply the starkest examples in a line of decisions that put my career first. Matt was not unreasonable in wanting me to change after we had our children — not to give up working, but to stop chasing after bigger, harder projects so that I could be more present. *You are not present* was a phrase I heard a lot. Sometimes it was literal — away for long stretches, I was physically not in the picture. Sometimes it was metaphorical — my mind consumed by a case or piece of writing, I would retreat to an inner world that made it hard to focus on the people right in front of me. Not always, but enough to create plenty of resentment.

Kash's case cost me. It cost my children. But I believed they would be able to absorb those costs and even come to understand why I did what I did. And I also knew in my gut that my husband never would. I don't regret my choices. For me, advocacy is a kind of zealotry. I don't know how to be a good lawyer without the single-minded focus it sometimes requires, and I don't know how to live a purposeful life without doing my small but significant part to correct the staggering injustices I see around me. In the years since then, I have done the same for other clients who needed me at pivotal moments in their lives, needed me more than my children did. Sometimes, those clients got more of me — a lot more.

I made these decisions knowing that I would always come home to my children. Just as important as my fury and resentment about my father's monthly out-of-town trips was my delight when he came home. Just as important as his absences were the times we spent together. I never doubted that he loved and adored me. In making the same decisions with my own children, I hoped that they would feel the same way. I hoped they would understand, as I understood about my own parents, that it was important that I had a strong professional identity. Embedded in that understanding was an acceptance that sometimes — not all the time, but, yes, sometimes — my job was going to come first. Growing up, I had learned that lesson from both of my parents. Far from inflicting permanent damage on my psyche, it made me determined, resilient, and ambitious in my own right.

Matt had a different vision about the kind of mother I was going to be. But trying to force myself to be that kind of mother — the one who subordinated her ambitions — would be a Procrustean task. It would lop off a vital part of me. My spirit would be crushed. My visceral understanding of this truth was at war with my fervent desire to save my marriage and give my children an intact family. Despite all of our problems, I was still in love with Matt. Sometimes during those final months, after yet another argument or a week of frosty silence, I wavered.

If I quit and found a job in San Francisco, even if it meant work I did not particularly care for, maybe Matt and I could hold on. I could even work part-time, maybe join the PTA at Carter's school and start cooking dinner again. Then I would picture myself a few decades in the future sitting next to Matt at our daughter's wedding.

One of the guests, well-meaning, would raise a glass to toast our happy marriage — what footsteps the bride would be following in! And there I would be, skinny and shrunken in my seafoam mother-of-the-bride dress, the smile on my face freezing the resentment beneath it, a third vodka tonic sweating in my hand. Our daughter would know the truth — that it had not been a happy marriage at all. She would know, and my son would know. They would know in the same way that kids always know, on an intuitive level, what their parents are thinking and feeling.[14]

The collapse of a marriage isn't only heartbreaking, it is the end of a life plan. I had never dreamed of a white picket fence, but I had imagined an intact family of four. I had imagined for better or for worse, years of good sex and intimacy, growing old together — maybe somewhere in the Sierra mountains or a place with a view of the Pacific Ocean — after successfully launching our offspring. The avalanche of ruin threatened to overwhelm me. I made the deliberate choice to turn my face away so I could continue to function.

Throughout that extended period — our final weeks together, followed by eighteen months of "nesting," which meant Matt and I rotated in and out of the house while our children stayed put, followed by Matt's moving out and the finalization of our divorce — my work saved me. Every Monday when I got up to begin my downstate commute, I put on my beautifully tailored professional clothes — bought for me by my mother, of course — carefully applied my makeup, and strode forward, wedding ring still on my finger. I told almost no one outside of my family. At work, I was my old self: focused, competent, eminently capable. Having my job gave my life purpose, structure, and a welcome distraction from my personal pain. It also provided crucial independence.

Throughout this difficult period in my life, I was comforted by the fact that I had taken my mother's advice. I had spent my life working *not* to be at the financial mercy of anyone else, and I wasn't.

My money was separate; I had savings, and I could use some of what I had inherited to buy Matt out of our condo. As wrenching as the decision to divorce was, it was not complicated by economic considerations. Alimony and child support were not in the cards. But I didn't need Matt's financial help. I could do it on my own.

I am not advocating for divorce, never mind writing a how-to manual on it. Nor am I saying that every ambitious mother must sacrifice her marriage. But it is important to acknowledge that at the root of some unhappy heterosexual partnerships is a mismatch in expectations of how women will "balance" mothering — which is to say, there is still plenty of pressure in our culture to equate being a "good mother" with stepping back professionally. The gendered nature of this mismatch and its faulty premise must be addressed honestly by both partners, preferably before the babies arrive. These conversations are particularly important given the lack of government infrastructure to support working parents. Sometimes — especially for couples who do not live near their families — the only people they can rely on are each other.

To radically reinvent marriage so that it is truly equality-based when it comes to work and family, both partners need to accept these truths: (1) working mothers can be crucial to a family's economic well-being; (2) working mothers' happiness derives from feeling supported in that choice; (3) when working mothers are supported and happier, they are better mothers; (4) children benefit from seeing their mothers succeed outside of the home; and (5) the entire family benefits when household chores do not fall disproportionately on women's shoulders because children learn important lessons about shared responsibility and their mothers are not overburdened and resentful.

The point of this book is not to pass judgment on mothers who opt out because of a deep desire to be the primary caretaker of their children. The point of this book to encourage and support mothers who want to opt in. There is a way to be a working mother that isn't full of guilt, shame, and self-recrimination. There is a way to be a working mother that is full of pride, satisfaction, and self-love. To get there, we have to give up on the impossible — the work-life balance mirage — and embrace the simple truth that when we are happy and fulfilled, our children benefit, even though that necessarily entails imbalance. Part of that journey may involve the collapse of a marriage or a radical reframing of it. What is important is the recognition that when working mothers are strong and self-sufficient, our families benefit. When we succeed, our children are inspired.

In heterosexual relationships, a nongendered view of parenting allows mothers the freedom to reimagine their role without fear of judgment or recrimination from their male partners. Mashal, whose son is turning two, said, "I am outlandish; I am not the typical safe, secure mom." Recall Hely, whose son is nine, telling me, "I do have a tinge of guilt that I work so much but I see the little man he is becoming and I know I am doing a good job." Both women seemed relatively content on all fronts: with their steady rise through the ranks at work, with the amount of time they spend with their sons, and with the division of labor at home. Mashal's and Hely's husbands are not simply tolerant of how they choose to be mothers, they are proud and appreciative.

For some women, there is a learning curve, with divorces ultimately leading them to choose new partners with a more clear-eyed sense of what they need to feel supported as mothers and hard-working professionals. Leah Nelson, thirty-nine, married her first husband, a filmmaker, when they were both in their mid-twenties. In 2009, when she was twenty-eight, they moved from Brooklyn to Los Angeles for his career. Leah, who had graduated from the Columbia School of Journalism, struggled to find work in an industry that was radically contracting. After six months, during which she felt increasingly miserable and isolated, she and her husband separated. Leah moved back to New York and "sent out nine billion job applications." When she received an offer to move to Montgomery, Alabama, to work as a research fellow tracking hate groups at the Southern Poverty Law Center, she took it.

For a while, Leah saw the move as temporary, hoping to reconcile with her husband and persuade him to move back to the East Coast. But he didn't want to. "He was coming into his own, he was succeeding, and his career was in LA." It took Leah time to admit to herself that the marriage was over. But once she did, she said, "I started opening my mind. I've always been interested in the Deep South," where her parents had gone to graduate school. She loved her work at the Southern Poverty Law Center, which, she said, "was interesting and sexy in all the ways I thought it would be."

About a year after Leah moved to Montgomery, a friend and his wife persuaded her to go to a Wilco concert with them. A guy sitting next to Leah asked her if she liked Wilco. "I was like, I'm at an actual Wilco concert! But also, not really." The guy's name was James, and when he asked for Leah's number, she gave him her e-mail — with some suspicion. "I got chatted up by a lot of people who saw me as a curiosity. Jewish! New Yorker! Southern Poverty Law Center! I was on a lot of bucket lists." James, a Southerner who came from a religious Catholic family and who had gotten his undergraduate and law degrees from the University of Alabama, seemed an unlikely romantic prospect.

"I thought about his expectations early on," Leah said. She decided to be blunt, telling him she was an atheist who didn't know whether she wanted children. Her ambivalence stemmed from her lack of interest in the day-to-day grind of child-rearing that in her experience inevitably fell on mothers. As a kid, Leah said, "I hated field trips and I hated watching team sports, never mind playing them. I couldn't image doing any of that stuff, being a soccer mom, or the class parent. James was going to have to be in charge of those things. More generally, I hoped he would understand that it was the dads who got the privilege of not doing the logistical work." She continued, "I didn't want that. I wanted to work, and I also knew that if I was marrying a lawyer, I was never going to make as much, but it can't be about 'he makes more money, so his career wins.'" To her surprise, James was willing to sign on to her vision. "I was won over by his lack of horror over every signal I was putting out that I was an unsuitable match for him."

A little less than a year and a half after they met, Leah and James got married. They had two children, and Leah, who was working as a paralegal, took three months' paid maternity leave each time. When she returned to work, their children went to day care from 8:30 a.m. to 5:30 p.m. Over the years, Leah and James have generally divided the pickup and drop-off equally. In 2017, shortly after their younger child turned one, Leah was offered a position as the research director for Alabama Appleseed Center for Law and Justice, a small nonprofit that works to reduce poverty and incarceration rates within the state. "I mostly do these big reports that integrate historical research and qualitative research in the general area of economic justice as it relates to criminal justice," she said. Leah anticipated that the job would be demanding, and it is; she works fifty or more hours most weeks. She loves the work and the confidence that her boss — a working mother — places in her judgment.

In the main, James has stuck by his promise to be an equal partner who is supportive of Leah's career. Still, Leah said, "Sometimes I get mad about how much of the planning I do," particularly as their children have gotten older. Recently, she and James got into a heated conversation after she complained about it. James said lightly, "I guess my Y chromosome–addled body doesn't get it." Leah was annoyed. "Even though he was joking, it reflected dated thinking that this is 'women's work,' and I am like, 'No, this isn't genetic. You have chosen not to pay attention.'"

What has allowed the marriage to work, Leah said, is ongoing frank and difficult conversations where she feels she has James's attention and his willingness to be both more intentional and more appreciative. He is also unconditionally supportive of her career aspirations. For Leah, the importance of these qualities in a life partner was a hard-won lesson. "With my first husband, I made so much space for his ambitions that I never thought about what I was giving up along the way," she said. "This time I was explicit. I told James: I want to be able to do fulfilling work. I want to achieve a level of expertise that means I would be asked to travel and give my opinion and he would be excited for me. I wasn't sure I would accomplish enough to get these invitations, but I wanted to try. I needed him to be good with it, and he is."

Valerie, thirty-seven,[15] told me that a lifetime of hard work and love of her job allowed her the freedom to emerge from a profoundly unhealthy relationship financially intact and with the strength to heal emotionally. Born and raised on the East Coast by a stay-at-home mother and a father who taught high-school chemistry, Valerie had worked steadily since she was a teenager. The money she earned as a manager at a fast-food franchise helped pay her tuition at a parochial school. She continued to work while attending community college and then a state university. After she graduated, Valerie accepted an entry-level position with a midsize computer software company.

Advancing within the company, Valerie said, required that she "work very hard with old-school WASP-y men, and getting a place at the table meant that I had to keep pushing." Her father, she said, always advised her to work at 80 percent and keep 20 percent in reserve, "but I am not capable of anything less than a hundred percent and that is probably why I have gotten so far." Eight years later, Valerie was a member of the executive team.

During this steady upward trajectory within her company, Valerie met Dale, her future husband. She had just turned thirty. Dale, a police officer, had served in the Marines, joining straight out of high school. They moved in together after two months of dating. Looking back, Valerie said, "There were red flags I overlooked. I was telling myself, *You are running out of time, you need to have children, you are not going to have time to restart the clock.*" Their first son was born with special needs; he was followed by a second son two years later. Meanwhile, Valerie continued to rise through the ranks of her company, overseeing a division that grew from five people to fifty. She was in the office every day at 9:00 a.m. and made sure to be home by 5:30 p.m. to give her children dinner, have speech therapy with her older child, and put them to bed before getting back online with her staff.

Valerie's marriage, meanwhile, was on the opposite trajectory. Her husband was struggling with the stress of his job and going out drinking at night. He was also verbally abusive, constantly denigrating Valerie and playing on her insecurities. I asked her if her ex-husband was threatened by her professional success. "Yes," she answered, "but that was the story of every relationship I had ever been in." She described the divorce as "pretty awful" but said that the money she earned from her job allowed her to formulate "an exit plan." She explained, "He was someone who had nothing to lose and I was someone who had everything to lose, so I had to make sure that my kids were going to be okay." She paid off her student debt, their joint debt, and their car payments. "When I paid off the last bill, I sat down and in twenty minutes I wrote down our separation agreement."

When the divorce became final, the boys were four and two. Valerie assumed full physical custody. For a time, she moved in with her parents to save money. Later, she moved with her children to a small apartment in what she called "a second-tier neighborhood." She was, she said, the only divorced parent in her older son's kindergarten class. "It was tough," she told me, "and I lost a lot of friends. It is like a death — they are there when you first deliver the news, and then they just drop off." But Valerie, who describes herself as resilient, kept working and saving. Three years later, in 2019, they moved again, to a larger home in a nicer neighborhood in a better school district.

The same year, Valerie's company was bought by a large corporation. She was asked to start a new division overseeing over a thousand employees and working with clients that included Fortune 500 companies. She gladly accepted, excited for a new opportunity with a higher salary and more responsibility. "My kids know I am busy, but they also know that my job is part of my identity and what makes me satisfied. I love my job. I one hundred percent love it."

Her words resonated with me and, according to the research, speak to many other working moms. A 2009 paper by Professors Jayita and Murali Poduval that summarized numerous studies on this topic acknowledged the intense pressure working mothers experience as they juggle competing priorities while enduring the judgment of others but concluded, "The rewards are many, including personal benefits, financial rewards, and improved family life."[16]

When partnerships collapse, mothers who step back from their careers to stay home often fare poorly. As one divorce lawyer explained to *The Guardian*, "The money these women could have earned — and consequently their potential to save for their own future long-terms needs, including retirement — has been significantly compromised."[17] Then there is the problem of trying to get back into a competitive job market after years away. Skills atrophy, and younger people with gapless résumés and no "baggage" (read: childcare needs)[18] are angling for the same positions. There is also the "caretaker bias," a negative inference that many employers make about the choice to stay home: "Opting out of work to care for children is a direct violation of these pervasive expectations for employees to prioritize work above all."[19]

One woman told me, "I regret staying home for all these years — I am now in a divorce, and making my way back professionally is not only brutal, it's impossible. I can't support my children and, worse, I can't support myself. This means that my financial future is at the mercy of others and that at midlife I am starting from scratch."[20] This experience is all too common following the end of a marriage. While women with less education and lower economic means are more vulnerable, middle-class women without the ability to earn a living can also find themselves facing economic peril. My grandmother's experience in 1948 — having to move back in with her parents after losing her husband — is still a common coping mechanism for suddenly single mothers like Valerie more than seventy years later.[21]

Dimitri Mortelmans, a sociology professor at the University of Antwerp, assessed decades of studies on the subject in the United States and Eastern and Western Europe, including Norway, Sweden, and the Netherlands. "It has been consistently shown that these lone parents have a substantially higher poverty risk than the general population," he wrote, and he concluded that "women fare worse economically after a break-up than men. Throughout the literature, this simple yet far-reaching conclusion is replicated again and again, regardless of the time period, geographic focus, or methodology used."[22]

Stacy Francis, a certified financial planner and certified divorce financial analyst, launched Francis Financial two decades ago which is a wealth-management firm that specializes in helping women regain financial stability after divorce or the death of a spouse. "Many of us will take several financial risks in our lifetimes, but for women, getting married may be the biggest financial risk of all," she wrote in a piece published by CNBC in 2019.[23] A common pattern she sees among her female clients is a focus on caretaking and a decision to leave the money side of things — the earning, investing, and spending — to their husbands. This ceding of financial agency leaves women vulnerable. "As a result," she wrote, "a significantly large number of women stay in marriages that are unhealthy and even border on dysfunctional." Stacy's grandmother was among them, compelled by economic necessity, she wrote, to remain in an "unhealthy, toxic and abusive marriage."[24]

For most mothers, working isn't a choice or a part-time occupation, it is central to their lives and livelihoods. The money they earn helps fuel the nation's economy and sustain their families. "All across the nation — regardless of region and across a diversity of family types, racial and ethnic groups, and ages of children — mothers are driving forces of the American economy," according to the Center for American Progress.[25] In 1975, the year after I was born, only 39 percent of women with preschoolers worked outside the home. In 2018, that percentage had grown to over 65 percent and was as high as 71.5 percent for mothers with older children — a total of 23.5 million women.[26] Nearly 85 percent of Black mothers and more than 60 percent of Latina mothers work full-time; when all races and ethnicities are tabulated, "64 percent of mothers are the primary breadwinners or co-breadwinners in their households."[27]

For many, relying on a single income means slipping out of the middle class. In some heterosexual partnerships, women are the top earners. Karyn Ward, sixty-four, said that her job as an executive assistant to the co-CEO of a family-owned real estate firm, the Ashforth Company, has been a source of happiness and financial support for the past twenty-seven years. After graduating from Georgetown University in 1979, Karyn moved to New York City to be an office manager for a municipal-bond company. In 1984, the company got a new comptroller, Joe, who was ten years her senior and her boss. Karyn and Joe started dating two years later and got married in 1991, when she was thirty-four. Several years after that, they moved to Stamford, a Connecticut suburb. "Joe wanted a place to garden, and he liked the calmness that came with having a glass of wine on the back porch." Joe commuted to Manhattan, and for a year Karyn did too, before landing her job at Ashforth in Stamford, which she describes as "like having a second family."

It took years for Joe and Karyn to conceive their son, Anthony. Eventually, they turned to IVF. He was born in 1997, when Karyn was forty. Karyn said that Joe, who had always been supportive of her career and the income it provided, "expected me to turn into a 1950s mom. I told him, 'That ain't happening.' A lot of women, once they got married and had kids, they stopped working, but I knew I couldn't do that." Their marriage underwent a series of adjustments. Karyn learned to appreciate Joe's domestic contributions ("He was the cleaner. He loved to cook. He loved to garden") and accept that when it came to their son, she had all the responsibility ("I was the one who went to the pediatrician and the PTA").

Throughout, Karyn worked. When Anthony was in preschool, she was able to scale back to thirty-hour workweeks, but she was full-time when he was in kindergarten. By the time Anthony was in middle school, Karyn's responsibilities had increased to the point where a few nights a week, she would come home and have dinner with her family and then go back to the office, and she often went in on weekends.

In 2008, when Anthony was eleven, the family's economic circumstances changed. Joe, then sixty-two, had left his job and was having trouble finding another one. There were years when he wasn't working at all, and Karyn was the sole supporter of the family with a steadily increasing salary and benefits, including health care. "The job was a refuge financially, absolutely." And it was a place where she felt loved and appreciated; some of her best friends were her coworkers.

Joe found other employment eventually, but the jobs were short-lived and he didn't enjoy the work. Throughout, Karyn's job at Ashforth kept the family afloat. I asked Karyn about Joe's reaction to the shift in the economic-power dynamic. She said that once he gave up on the idea that she would be a stay-at-home mom and then suffered his own professional setbacks, Joe did a 180-degree turn. "He didn't feel threatened at all. Which was interesting, given his age and his generation." At one point, Joe told Karyn, "I never understood why men are scared of strong women."

In 2014, Anthony's senior year in high school, the family received the devastating news that Joe had colon cancer. A few months later, Anthony was diagnosed with both Addison's disease and Hashimoto's disease and was in the hospital for two weeks. Then Joe had surgery and underwent chemotherapy for his cancer. "The first year was a blur," she told me. "I barreled through it." In 2015 Joe got sicker; Karyn had a hysterectomy and had her gallbladder removed. "My boss was on the board at Stamford Hospital and so when I needed help with a test or getting in to see a doctor, that was huge." The connection proved especially important when the insurance company balked at covering certain tests and treatments, forcing Karyn to spend hours a day on the phone, arguing with customer service representatives and sitting on hold listening to elevator music. As maddening as it was, Karyn was still grateful. Without her job and the health insurance it provided, her family would have faced financial ruin.

Joe died on June 1, 2018. "He was at home because that's where he wanted to be," she said, "and Anthony and I were there." Afterward, Anthony, then a college student at Boston University, went back to school, and Karyn went back to work. Before COVID, she would arrive at the office at 9:00 a.m., work until 8:00 p.m., and put in at least four hours over the weekend. In December 2019, Anthony, who had graduated in June, was laid off from work. Then the pandemic hit, and he couldn't find another job until February of 2021. He moved back in with Karyn temporarily, which she said worked out well for both of them. Once again, her income and yearly bonus got her family through a difficult time. "Thank God I worked for who I work for," she told me. "My job allowed us to survive."

While we are making progress, we have a long way to go. Statistics deliver the undisputed message that working mothers like Karyn may not only contribute to their family's economic well-being, they may be 100 percent responsible for it. And yet. "The idealized vision of 1950s womanhood still permeates our politics," wrote the author Jill Filipovic in her book *The H-Spot: The Feminist Pursuit of Happiness.* Filipovic argued that the failure to offer "robust feminist ideals" to counter the *Leave It to Beaver* prototype helps perpetuate outdated stereotypes while heaping shame on the growing number of mothers who do not fit that mold.

Women like Leah and Karyn who demand marital partnerships that acknowledge the importance of their work not only benefit themselves and their families, they improve the prospects for other working moms. By normalizing the concept of full-time working mothers within their own homes, these women help ensure that their husbands are supportive of the working mothers who populate their own workplaces.[28] Citing a 2012 study of 718 married men,[29] Filipovic noted the converse: "Men who have stay-at-home wives are more likely than men with working wives to penalize their female co-workers, denying them promotions and viewing them unfavorably."[30]

Women who separate from partners who don't support their professional choices also separate themselves from constant judgments about their mothering within their own homes and may find it easier to push back against the judgments visited upon them from the outside. Working mothers who get divorced report that they are happier.[31] They are relieved of the pressure to subordinate their work and the crushing disapproval that comes when they don't. They are free to reject the trope that a good mother is always self-sacrificing and "present" physically and emotionally.[32] An associate dean at the University of Chicago who is a divorced mother with sole custody of her learning-disabled child finds strength in her work: "I tell my son that education opens doors to better choices for people who might not have the advantages that we have; that my work helps to make life more fair. I spend the day at work trying to figure out impossible solutions and then the evenings at home with my boy, learning fractions and solving equations with two variables. I lose my patience; I am not calm. [But] every day is a chance to do better for everything that I care about."[33]

For women, like me, whose marriages do not survive but who are fortunate to have a loving and involved co-parent, the reformation of the family brings unexpected benefits, particularly if the former spouses can maintain a cordial relationship. Matt and I have managed, with the occasional step backward, to rebuild our relationship. We agreed to fifty-fifty physical and legal custody. Once I stopped judging myself and letting other people's judgments affect me, I realized that the arrangement worked out surprisingly well.

Because our children were so young when we separated — only five and three — they have no fixed memories of all four of us living under the same roof. For that, I'm grateful. Our home life was tense and unhappy; had Matt and I stayed together, I have no doubt it would have poisoned their childhoods and soured them on the idea of marriage more generally. Despite what unhappily married parents tell themselves, kids know. They know everything. We had to remove the cracking shell of our nuclear family before the shards embedded themselves in the two little people nestled inside.

Rarely, if ever, do Matt and I allow our anger and disappointment with each other to get in the way of our co-parenting. We even take vacations as a "broken" family, and unlike the vacations we took when we were intact, they are happy ones. My most cherished memories of my time with Matt and our kids are post-divorce: swimming with them in an outdoor pool on the Northern California coast, completing a thousand-piece jigsaw puzzle, taking them to the Monterey Bay Aquarium. As I wrote in a *New York Times* Modern Love column after describing one such vacation: "Happy families are not all alike. Some are fractured and misshapen. To appreciate them, you have to adjust your line of sight, your level of expectation. They have seams and scars. But they are beautiful, still, in their odd imperfect way."[34]

I appreciate our family time together, the time I have alone with my children, and the time I have to myself. My children's absence creates protected time pockets where I can be productive. I can put my students, my clients, my writing first. I can put myself first. Never has this been more important than after COVID struck. "We're lucky," Matt pointed out more than once, noting that switching off every few days gave us each uninterrupted stretches to recover from the claustrophobia and stress of trying to work full-time and ride herd on our restless and increasingly screen-dependent children. During those endless eighteen months of quarantine, the divorce brought a precious gift: sanity.

One does not need to get divorced to have time alone. Spouses routinely trade off caretaking duties, and most rely on some kind of childcare. The mothers I interviewed, married and divorced, reflected mothers in the United States more generally in their approaches to childcare: they used a patchwork of options over time to stitch together a crazy quilt. Those who could afford it often employed nannies. Others found day-care options that ranged from very good to good enough. Many were lucky to have family nearby — often parents or in-laws — who were willing to help. Some women, like Diana, the esthetician who owns her own business, have husbands who stay home. Nicole DeVon, who went back to college to get her four-year degree when her daughter was a toddler, relied in part on a community of other single mothers who were willing to trade off care-taking duties. Some used some combination of all of these options over the years.

COVID destroyed many of these fragile ecosystems. Some of the mothers of younger children whom I had been following described their COVID workday as enervating and endless, much of it laboring without pay as a homeschool teacher, babysitter, house-cleaner, and short-order cook in addition to their actual jobs. (The older women I interviewed tended to fare better for the simple reason that their children were grown. Even if those children returned home — and many did — they were adults and could take care of themselves.)

The pandemic was, one hopes, a once-in-a-lifetime catastrophe. But as the authors of the Brookings Institution paper on COVID's effect on working women noted, the lack of support for working mothers "was a preexisting condition" that the virus took to the next level: "Our economy was doing a disservice to millions of working women before COVID-19 hit."[35] Before and after the coronavirus, the cost of childcare can make some lower-paying jobs seem financially questionable even if those jobs are emotionally rewarding and are part of a path to better-paying work.

My two-year teaching fellowship at Hastings paid so poorly that it barely covered the cost of sending our infant daughter and toddler son to day care. I stuck with it, though, in part because I believed it would eventually lead to a tenured job and the payoff on my Five-Million-Dollar Bet. Needless to say, my plan was ambitious, perhaps wildly so, and by no means guaranteed to succeed.

I can readily appreciate why other young mothers in my position, married to high-earning partners and guilt-ridden over leaving their children for a full workday, would make a different decision.[36] It is my hope that Congress will finally enact legislation that will allow the United States to join the rest of the industrialized world in providing crucial childcare infrastructure for working mothers: universal free pre-K and subsidized, high-quality childcare.[37] In the fall of 2021, the House passed a bill that included this critical legislation. But the Senate seems unlikely to enact a similar version.

That is infuriating because the $1.9 trillion stimulus bill passed by Congress in March of 2021 was a step in the right direction, providing monthly checks of around $300 to families of small children who qualify for aid. The *New York Times,* reporting on this benefit, interviewed a single mother of two boys who felt compelled to stop working during COVID because her childcare responsibilities had become overwhelming. Had the subsidy been available, she said, "I definitely would have kept my job" because it would have paid for childcare.[38] But this crucial benefit has expired. Without this kind of permanent government subsidy, some mothers will continue to opt out.

Two years ago, Valerie, the computer software executive, fell in love again, this time with a man who had been a longtime friend and coworker. "We became really close after I got a divorce, and he had separated from his wife around the same time. He is the opposite of me in many ways, but he's my best friend." Like Valerie, he has two children. Both have busy lives and competing demands, but her boyfriend makes her feel like a priority. "Every time we go out on a date, it is still so much fun." Crucially, and unlike any other relationship she's ever been in, she said, "This guy sees me as his equal."

After years of feeling isolated, Valerie has found women she calls "my circle of peers — they are all career-minded moms." The group has regular get-togethers that start with some kind of physical exercise — hiking, biking, swimming — and end with going out for drinks. The conversation ranges: politics, pop culture, work issues, romantic partners or dating prospects.

There is only one rule, Valerie told me: "No talking about the kids."

The friendship group Valerie describes is important. It provides camaraderie and, for younger women, role models. These "career-minded moms" don't just normalize ambition, they celebrate it — and each other. That kind of inclusive, mutually reinforcing sisterhood seems key to nurturing the drive that many working mothers feel they have to camouflage or downplay.

I've lived in San Francisco for more than a decade now and I have made a few close friends who are working mothers. But I don't have Valerie's "circle of peers." I haven't stopped looking, though. I'm still hopeful I will find them.

CHAPTER SEVEN

EMBRACING IMBALANCE

What Goes Down Will Go Up

THIS BOOK IS ABOUT REFRAMING A DEBATE THAT HAS BE-come stale and suffocating. It is about a feminism that dispenses with the false premise that women can live their lives in perfect equipoise if they only try hard enough. In real life, the pendulum swings wildly. Mothers who always make their children the primary focus are one extreme; mothers who never allow their children to be a primary focus are the other. Most of us live lives that are far more complicated: imbalanced but not unstable. It isn't about always or never, or a straight upward trajectory. It is about sometimes and this time, not all the time. It is about zigs and zags on a switchback path.

The idea that ambitiously pursuing a profession is the key, for many of us, to being a good mother is controversial. I have heard from children of ambitious mothers who felt abandoned. I have heard from children who felt burdened by their mothers' achieve-ments. I am not arguing that all ambitious working mothers do a fantastic job. I am writing this book knowing that the jury is out with my own children. But I am arguing — with the data behind me — that the sad outcomes are the exception.

Today, in my late forties, I am the happiest I have ever been. Because I worked hard and refused to give up on my ambition, I got what is most important to me: two beautiful children and a career as a tenured law professor. My path was not easy or certain, and I lost plenty along the way. I think it is important to tell that part of the story and to normalize the nonlinear journey of so many women. I did not get balance. I never will. But now I know that no one does.

Late in 2014, I realized that I had to leave my job at Loyola Law School. The commute and the stress of the divorce were making me sick. Literally. A mild sinus infection never fully resolved and took over the rest of my body. For months, I ran a low-grade fever. Often midmeal, I became nauseated and could not finish. Worst of all was a persistent cough that racked me until I doubled over. I coughed until I was breathless; I coughed until I gagged. No amount of Dayquil or Nyquil quieted it. I went to the doctor repeatedly and got various prescriptions. But the medicine didn't work.

Days turned into weeks. I lost weight. I no longer had the energy or ability to do what I loved — go running, read to my children. I even stopped drinking wine, which had been a nightly pleasure. By the time I finished the last leg of my journey every week, crossing the Bay Bridge to make the traffic-choked drive back home from the Oakland airport, I was on the verge of physical and emotional collapse. At night as I boiled hot dogs and microwaved chicken fingers for the kids' dinner, I counted down the minutes until bedtime. The three of us went to sleep at 7:30 sharp. I was too tired to go through the nightly ritual of settling them in their own beds. We all piled into mine instead. Lying between them, cocooned in the crescents of their warm bodies, I fell asleep inhaling the scent of incompletely rinsed shampoo.

Adding to my exhaustion was the fakery: I continued to pretend to everyone other than my family and a few close friends that everything was fine — or would be, once I kicked this pesky virus-or-whatever-it-was. That was especially true at work; I feared that if my boss knew the emotional strain I was under, she would think I was no longer competent to do my job and might hesitate to recommend me for another one.

The person who saw through this charade most clearly was Kash's mother, Wilma. Every time I saw her, she would cross her arms and look at me disapprovingly. "You're too skinny," she told me. And when I doubled over coughing: "You're working too much. You need to take better care of yourself." Then she would give me a searching look, the kind I would have gotten from my own mother had she not lived three thousand miles away: "Is everything really okay?" I assured her that it was.

But everything was not okay. "This is not going to break me," I told my mother when she called to check up on me. But it nearly did. Once, during our nesting days when Matt arrived to take up residence in the house, I broke down in tears in what had been our joint office, lying facedown on the couch in my suit and heels. "I can't get on the plane," I sobbed to my estranged husband. "I can't do it." My cough started up, which made me cry harder, which in turn made me cough more.

"Then don't," he said. "Tell them no."

But I wasn't raised to tell anyone no, especially myself. I was raised to keep going, to never, ever quit. And anyway, I had nowhere else to go — it was Matt's turn to live in the house. So I shook my head and kept coughing and wailing, the sounds bringing my children to the closed door. Matt got up and opened it. "Mom is sick," he told them. That was my cue to assure them that everything was fine, but I couldn't summon the words. If they saw my face — bright red, tearstained, mascara smeared and running — they would be frightened. I kept it buried in the couch cushion.

In the end, I got on the plane, just as I had every week for three years. But I knew I was done.

In the fall of 2015, I left my position as the director of the Loyola Law School's Project for the Innocent without anywhere to land. My thirties were over. My marriage was over. My job was over. My life plan was in ruins. But I had my children, I had my ambition, and I had not given up on my Five-Million-Dollar Bet. In my darkest moments, it was my love for them, my love for my career, and my determination to make it — to be the sole breadwinner doing work that I loved — that gave me the resilience and determination to keep going. But I needed to take a circuitous route.

I decided to write a book, hoping it would distinguish me from other candidates in a future academic job search. I also hoped it would be therapeutic. After diving into any topic that frightens, confuses, fascinates, and enrages me, I emerge feeling calmer; enervated, but also in a meditative frame of mind. The research forces me to question my assumptions. When I interview people with nuanced views of an issue I have always seen in black-and-white, it planes down the sharper edges of my anger and self-righteousness. Writing gives the Boggle board a quarter turn, allowing an escape from an ideological and emotional cul-de-sac. This book, I decided, would be my new professional purpose, an important credential, and a means of working through a thicket of conflicting emotions about crime, justice, love, work, and family — the issues that had dominated my consciousness for as long as I could remember.

I wrote about restorative justice, which reframes crime and punishment as harm and healing through the lens of family and community. The aftermath of Kash's case made me hungry for that reframing. Most people assume, based on the media coverage — the ecstatic embraces and the tears of joy — that exonerees ride off into the sunset to a life of "happily ever after." Kash was luckier than most — he had Wilma — but even for him, every day was a series of painstaking and painful adjustments.

Kash's exoneration felt more like an earthquake than a happy ending. Amid the rubble were the lives of the crime victim's family members, including the victim's daughter. She had been told for more than three decades, "We got the man who killed your father," only to watch as the lie was exposed day after agonizing day in court. What was her path toward healing?

Restorative justice, a centuries-old practice that originated with American Indians and other indigenous peoples, focuses on healing and repair, not blame and punishment.[1] It brings together the people who have been harmed by an offense and the person who committed it to get to the root causes of what happened. Together, they sift through the wreckage for the pieces to rebuild their lives and, in so doing, form a kind of family. As someone born and raised in the adversarial system, I found the concept of a universe that isn't neatly divided into good and evil, right and wrong, foreign. That was certainly true in my professional life and had become increasingly true in my personal life. Years of binary thinking had warped me.

In January of 2016, I sold my book proposal to a small independent press. The advance was a pittance, though, so I cast about for other ways to support myself and my children. I wrote freelance articles and began litigating cases for a fee, relying on referrals. But every month, my bank account balance dropped. I signed up for Covered California, the public health insurance option offered by my state, so that my children and I would have health care. I braced myself to apply to law firms, knowing that I would not enjoy the work or taking orders from senior partners after so many years of autonomy. But there were no academic jobs on the horizon, and I did not have another obvious way to make money.

In March, I got a call from Kash. The settlement from his lawsuit against the City and County of Los Angeles had come in: $16.7 million.[2] "I want to give you some money," he said. Clutching my cell phone to my ear, I shook my head vigorously even though he couldn't see me.

"You don't owe me anything," I said. He insisted. I pushed back: "I can't take your money."

"Yes, you can," he told me. "You need it."

Kash gave me $50,000. That, along with my other freelance work and my savings and investments, was enough to live on for the next twenty months. It was enough for me to concentrate my professional energy on researching and writing my book. And it was enough to push my own work-life imbalance in a badly needed counter-direction. For the first time in years, I didn't get on a plane to go to work; I walked down the hall to my home office. On my days with the children, I did pickup and drop-off. I read to them at night — all of the Laura Ingalls Wilder books, the entire Harry Potter series. We went to the zoo, to the Exploratorium, to the Koret playground in Golden Gate Park, where we barreled down the giant concrete slide on flattened cardboard boxes.

During that twenty-month period, my life changed radically. For years, I had been running from one task to the next — at times, literally running at full speed through the airport, dragging my roller bag behind me — and employing a rapid-response approach to every work demand. Just like that, it all stopped. I woke up in the early-morning darkness to the prospect of shapeless, silent hours stretching out in front of me. On the days without my children, the quiet was so thick it felt like I had been buried under a snowbank — I thought often of Pa Ingalls deep underground after he got caught in a blizzard just yards away from his home on Plum Creek.

Book writing happens alone and in silence. The distractions were minimal, as there were vanishingly few e-mails, calls, or texts to return. I had no classes to teach, no students to supervise, no clients with immediate and overwhelming needs. There were no planes to catch, no rental cars to return. On most days, I spent hours alone in front of a laptop, often in agony, waiting for the words to come out. On some days, they didn't.

Fear — of not finishing on time, of wasting Kash's money, of not delivering what I had promised to my publisher — kept me more or less on task. Occasionally, I got anxious, wondering about what would happen after it was over. I had stepped into a professional void with the hope that a combination of grit, determination, and luck would arrest my free fall. But what if I never landed? What if my Five-Million-Dollar Bet went bust?

The anxiety never abated, but it was tempered by two things: my confidence in my ability to rebound and the realization that I needed the silence and the stillness to begin to heal myself and my family. Divorce is a trauma. Yes, my children were very young, but that did not mean they were unaffected. My days of crying facedown on the couch were over; they needed me to step up. They needed me to prioritize them. To do that, I had to get my mind right.

Writing the book helped do that. The research meant spending hours with men and women who were engaged in the soul-baring work required to come to a more complete and complicated understanding of a life-shattering event. Observing them inspired me to apply the same practices in addressing the comparatively minor trauma in my own life. Adopting a restorative mindset brought a slew of realizations. For years, I had been telling myself a story in which I was the victim in the marriage, laying all the blame on Matt, and clinging to a narrative that was riddled with half-truths that conveniently absolved me of responsibility. I was equally accountable for the failed marriage, and I was certainly accountable to my children, not only for our fractured family but for their ability to cope and thrive moving forward.

During those twenty months, I slowly let go of my anger, bitterness, and disappointment. I weaned myself off my addiction to victimhood and vindictiveness. Slowly, over time, Matt and I became something we never had been during our courtship and marriage: friends. I worked as much as ever, but I worked differently, molding my time around my children's schedules. Once I stopped being sick, I appreciated my health rather than assuming it was a given. I started taking better care of myself, knowing that if I was well rested and in good physical shape, it would give me the physical and emotional stamina I needed to be a single parent.

I felt like someone learning how to make a French meringue after a lifetime of relying on store-bought doughnuts. Was I doing the right amount of recipe-following and improvising? Would the egg whites stand up? A benign event involving one of my children was fraught with assessment. I distinctly remember the day Matt and I went to Carter's first-grade parent-teacher conference. It felt like Judgment Day. Ms. Diane, Carter's teacher, was a woman I greatly respected, even feared. She did not make nice with parents. Mild-mannered but strict, Ms. Diane had high standards. As I took my seat beside Matt in one of the pint-size chairs, I felt my stomach tighten. For the next half hour, Matt and I listened as Ms. Diane described our son — diligent, kind, curious, intelligent. Carter was thriving and, in some areas, even exceeding expectations. I kept waiting for the "but" — *But he needs to work on . . . But he could improve in . . .* There were no buts. Walking out, Matt and I were mostly silent and lost in our own thoughts.

But before he got into his truck, Matt turned to look at me and held out his arms. "Great job, Mom," he said.

His praise meant the world to me because it was hard-won and well earned. I burst into tears.

In the fall of 2016, a friend sent me a job posting. There had been a retirement at the University of San Francisco, and the law school was hiring. It was a tenure-track position to run two clinics, one focused on criminal defense, the other on racial justice. They were looking for a candidate with a solid record of scholarship, teaching, and commitment to training students to be public-interest lawyers. Check, check, check. Amazingly, the law school, situated across the street from the beautiful main campus, was less than a mile from my house. *This is my job,* I thought. *Now I have to go get it.*

There are many successful women, celebrities in particular, who like to say, "The opportunity fell into my lap." They are "grateful," "lucky," and, always, "humbled." Hillary Clinton even felt compelled to say that it was a "humbling experience" to vote for herself when she ran for president.[3] As the journalist Cara Chocano wrote at the time, "This is a politician's answer, though you can also hear it as a woman's." Then there is the ever-trending #luckygirl, which the journalist Kaitlin Menza aptly described as "weirdly distancing — annoying in its refusal to take any credit."[4] According to a 2015 study, when someone uses the word *lucky* as a self-description on Twitter, there is a 67 percent chance that person is female.[5] There is a deep-seated, gender-based reason for women's adoption of this language: a well-grounded fear that owning their ambition and success will make others judge them as arrogant and obnoxious. According to the Center for Creative Leadership, "Research shows that there are multiple, measurable double standards impeding women's success, while similarly advancing men. It's a double-bind of being seen as competent or likable — but not both."[6]

I get it. But the only way to change the paradigm is to push back forcefully against it. So, please, well-meaning, self-abnegating women: Stop. These phrases — verbal tics, really — are a way of sublimating the ambition that got you to the place where the opportunity was not only available, but obtainable. There is an element of serendipity to any career story, no doubt, but for ambitious women, the vital ingredient is drive.

Compare Julius Caesar's famous words "I came, I saw, I conquered" to what you sometimes hear from high-achieving women: "I was there, I wasn't looking, I lucked out." All too often, women disassociate themselves from their achievements to avoid seeming arrogant. Men, meanwhile, proudly own their ambition and success. So let me own mine here: I had been scanning the horizon for a tenure-track position as a law professor and spent years building my résumé to qualify for it. When the position opened up, I came for it like a sprinter off the blocks, determined to be the first person to break through the tape at the finish line. In the end, it felt more like being the last person standing at the end of a marathon; the hiring process was long, competitive, and stressful. I wasn't the first choice, or even the second. It took months, rounds of interviews, and staying in the game. In the end, I got the job. Why? For a number of reasons, including the fact that I was exceptionally qualified. The opportunity did not drop down from the heavens while I was lying in a daisy field staring off into the distance. I drove toward it like a heat-seeking missile.

Women need to own their drive, ambition, and success. Owning the importance of work, an ability to do it well, and the fulfillment it brings can help empower women to dispense with the nonsense that their ambition is an indulgence that their children cannot afford. Success at work and success at motherhood are not mutually exclusive or even complementary. They are dual, mutually reinforcing strengths. Unfortunately, as the writer Jill Filipovic has pointed out, the feminist movement has fallen short in telling this all-important truth. That silence, and the insistence that working is a "choice" rather than an economic and psychological imperative, help explain why, she argues, that so little progress has been made in enacting legislation that supports working women and their children. "That feminists have been often unable or unwilling to say that working outside the home isn't just a necessity, but that it's good for women — that it's good for mothers — is perhaps one reason why we have not seen the political groundswell necessary to passing the workplace policies we so desperately need," she told me.

The acknowledgment by the feminist movement that having a career makes women equally good mothers, not worse ones, is long overdue. This acknowledgment is necessary for women to be able to celebrate the choices that got them to where they are rather than living in a shame spiral. Making the decision, at times, to put work before children is not wrong when coupled with the knowledge that the pendulum will inevitably swing back in the other direction. The words *at times* are doing a lot of work in that sentence, as they should. This isn't about always or never. It is about sometimes. It is an acknowledgment that work and life operate in tandem, not equipoise. Like an infinity symbol, one side comes up as the other side comes down to form two permanently interconnected loops. Work-life balance is a myth. Work-life *im*balance is a reality — messy and complicated at times, but also beautiful and true.

I started my job at the University of San Francisco School of Law on June 1, 2017. One month later, I handed in the manuscript for my book. Twenty months of working from home and around my children's schedules came to an end. Getting tenure meant economic security for my children and me. It meant I could spend the rest of my career doing a job I loved, free to take the cases I thought were important and to speak my mind on virtually any topic. Tenure was what I had been working toward since taking that lowly, poorly paid fellowship at Hastings all those years ago.

This was the Five-Million-Dollar Bet. To get tenure, I knew, I needed to say yes to everything: unwanted and tiresome committee assignments, teaching extra courses, any speaking engagement — in St. Louis, Chapel Hill, Newark, Duluth — where I could promote my book and the law school. I had to excel by producing scholarship, getting nearly perfect scores on my teaching evaluations (from

students and from the status committee of professors who were evaluating my tenure application), and maintaining a cheerful, competent demeanor and can-do spirit. But I knew this all-out effort
would be time-limited. The law school had given me credit for my
teaching and scholarship at Loyola, which meant I could submit my
tenure application in two years rather than five.

I had a steady income again, and so did Matt, who was working
at a small criminal defense firm. We hired a babysitter to pick the
kids up from school. On my days with my children, I usually arrived
home at 6:30; on my days without them, I stayed in my office well
into the night and went in on the weekends. For the next two years,
I worked my ass off. Sometimes, my children complained. Matt,
who went out of his way to accommodate my requests when my
schedule became overloaded — picking up our children when it
wasn't his turn and keeping them for an extra night — was not always thrilled, understandably. But the distance the divorce afforded
us, the downtime he knew would eventually come his way, and,
most of all, his commitment to being a good father made the un-
evenness in our parenting responsibilities during that time something he could accept.

The tenure vote came in the spring of 2019. That semester had
been particularly grueling: I was teaching an extra course — in academic parlance, an overload — and hustling to submit all of my materials to the committee that was evaluating my application. When
I walked into the closed-door session after the vote, my colleagues
applauded me. It had been unanimous. During those two years, I lost
time with my children. But what I gained — in skills, confidence,
and my ability to support us — was worth that sacrifice.

I interviewed other working mothers who had made similar decisions, some involving much greater sacrifices than any my children and I ever had to make. In early 2020, the air force offered
Daphne LaSalle Jackson an opportunity that frightened and exhil-

arated her: a six-month deployment to the Bagram Air Force Base in Afghanistan — a war zone — where she would be the top lawyer overseeing a legal team and handling issues ranging from environmental impacts to criminal prosecutions to approving contracts to advising enlisted men and women in a range of civil matters, including how to handle an overseas divorce. The position, staff judge advocate, translated, she said, into "district attorney for the base."

It was an honor for Daphne to be asked and a recognition of her achievements over the years. Succeeding in the role would bring gravitas and enhanced status. The new responsibilities excited her. But her children were six, four, and one. "Being deployed to the Middle East in support of a combat operation is something I have never done. It is a different level of service and I wanted to have that experience. But it is at the sacrifice of our family." After a series of conversations with her husband, Jared, she said yes.

Originally, Daphne was told the deployment would start in November 2020 and last six months. But with COVID came a change of plans. Because of the need to quarantine, Daphne had to spend weeks in isolation at Fort Dix, in New Jersey, starting in August. Six months away became eight. Complicating matters further was the fact that she had already agreed to a new stateside assignment at Eglin Air Force Base in Florida. Rather than uproot the family so close to her departure, she was commuting instead, staying with a friend in Florida and driving home to Alabama on weekends. One week before her departure date, Daphne took a leave to spend "intentional time" with her family. "We did a little impromptu birthday party for my baby girl because I am going to miss her second birthday."

In the weeks leading up to the deployment, she said, "I was Daphne the planner. Daphne the feeler was on hiatus. I was focused on making the house a home for a single dad." She got Jared comfortable doing the tasks she normally handled: doctor's appointments, meal planning, playdates. She felt a sense of relief when Jared's mother, with whom she was close, offered to move in, knowing that she would be a vital source of support. "My focus was on protecting my family from uncertainty, fear, and loneliness."

During her last week at home, Daphne said, "It started to hit me, and I was a hot mess. It would come in waves and I would just be so sad. Then I started asking myself, *Why?* Maybe it was all the things I put so much time and effort into, these huge themed birthday parties and individualized goody bags — maybe they don't need all of that. All the things we wrap ourselves around the axle about as mothers, maybe it's for us, not them. Is my daughter going to remember her mermaid-themed birthday party? No, she is not.

"Maybe," she added, "it is about my fear. If you can so easily remove me from the picture for eight months, then what am I actually doing? What has my motherhood been about?" Stationed in Qatar — she was sent there instead after President Trump ordered a drawdown of troops in Afghanistan — Daphne talked to her children daily, getting up at 4:00 a.m. in her time zone to say good night, reading to them over Zoom so that they could watch her turn the pages.

Daphne's days were packed with meetings on subjects ranging from contract extensions to sexual-harassment investigations. She issued ethics opinions and public policy declarations relating to the pandemic. But when the day was over, she had an unexpected gift — time to herself. "We have a tendency to lose ourselves and define ourselves in relation to our children," she told me one day more than halfway through her deployment. "Not having that and having this extra time has allowed me to refocus on Daphne and what Daphne enjoys doing. I've gotten amazing at yoga; I've started painting; there are things I can do here that I can't do stateside without feeling guilty. When people are vying for my time and attention at home, I was constantly trying to be everything for everybody.

Now I am like, I don't want to do that. I focus my time on things where either it has to be me to answer the problem or it is something that brings me joy."

In six years, Daphne will have completed two decades of service in the air force. At that point, she plans to retire, knowing that her family has the security of her vested pension and benefits. Her children will be fourteen, twelve, and nine. "Their whole lives, they have seen me get up every day and put on a uniform. They know the power of a woman. They know the power of their mom. They see my sacrifice and my dedication to my country. Then they will see the other side. They will see me take off my uniform and turn my attention back to my family." Daphne intends to pursue a new career at the age of forty-six. After the stress and fear of having all three of her children born premature and requiring extended hospital stays, she wants to go to school and train to be a nurse so that she can care for babies in a neonatal intensive care unit.

Daphne's devotion to birthday-party planning made me think of my own glaring deficits in this regard. Cherished rituals like these can showcase the controversial decision by some mothers to miss these milestone events because of pressing work. In February 2018, my clinic students and I took on a case in Humboldt County, six hours away from San Francisco. Almost immediately, it involved crazy-making sacrifices; more than once I had to call Matt and plead with him to take our children for an extra night because I wasn't going to make it home until long after bedtime. By early May, it became clear we were headed for trial — a brief but consequential one. On a conference call on May 14, the judge suggested a date later that week: Thursday, May 17. Opposing counsel, who were new to the case, asked for more time. I refused. After three months, my students and I knew the facts cold. The case was far too complex to digest in a matter of days, and therefore there was no way for our adversaries to prepare properly. I was not willing to give up that crucial advantage.

Afterward, I called Matt to rearrange the custody schedule. I needed to leave on May 16, I explained, to make the drive up and be ready for court the following day.

There was silence on the other end of the phone.

"What?" I said finally.

"What is May sixteenth?" he said.

I paused, trying to think. "A Wednesday," I said.

"May sixteenth is our daughter's seventh birthday."

My heart sank. Not only because of the conflict, but because I hadn't even realized one existed.

"Just go back and tell the judge you'll agree to a later date," he said.

"No," I told him. Silence fell, noisy with unsaid words. I knew what I was doing looked terrible — selfish, coldhearted, even cruel. Here I was, picking my job yet again. That choice and Matt's disapproval of it were why — more than any other reason — we were not together anymore.

At the same time, I never second-guessed myself, not even when Ella broke down in tears and I had to bite hard on the inside of my cheek to keep from crying myself. My daughter would have other birthdays. My client had one chance to beat this case. It was my job as his lawyer to make sure it was his best chance. So, after making Ella a chocolate chip pancake in the morning, I dropped her off at school, picked up my client, and headed north. When my daughter blew out the candles on her birthday cake, I was three hundred miles away in a hotel with my law students, huddled over a pile of documents, mapping out our final game plan.

After the *New York Times* published my essay in which I told this story, dozens of women wrote to say I was telling their story too. A veteran financial adviser, whose children are now thirty-four and twenty-nine, wrote that she had prioritized her career at times to climb the corporate ladder and "became a managing director at a top wealth management firm despite the odds against me." She worried about shortchanging her two sons. But, she wrote, "After reflecting back, I wouldn't do anything different." Victoria Mulhern told me, "I have been in leadership roles for many years. I felt so much better after reading your piece." As the executive director of faculty affairs and professional development at the Perelman School of Medicine at the University of Pennsylvania, Victoria said, "I have always loved my work, if not necessarily the 80-hour weeks. I object strongly to the term work-life balance, which somehow demeans work and celebrates life. I have always felt guilty that, at times, I was far more invested in my work than my children but never, not for one moment, would I have doubted my fierce devotion to and love for them. They are wonderful young men now, accomplished and invested in their work and their lives."

Stacy Francis, the financial planner whose expertise I cite in chapter 6, told me that in the early years of her son's and daughter's lives, she was absent much of the time as she built her company, Francis Financial, from the ground up. Watching her grandmother suffer in a marriage she could not afford to leave had lit a fire in Stacy. She decided to devote her life to helping women manage their finances, invest, and plan for retirement. Seventy percent of Stacy's clients are women who suddenly find themselves on their own after a divorce or the death of a spouse. All too often, they had delegated the important financial decisions to their husbands. "When you are both empowered," she said, "it leads to healthier marriage and more equitable partnerships."

Like many girls, Stacy told herself she was not good at math — languages were her gift, not numbers. But in college, she began taking classes in economics. "Seeing how finances can trap someone in a toxic relationship was enough for me to get over my fear of not being good enough. I realized financial independence was the difference between life and death, and if I didn't understand money and force myself to learn, I could end up the same way." As for math, she grinned and told me, "Turns out I am pretty darn good at it."

After Stacy's grandmother died in 2005 due to domestic abuse, she launched a charity called Savvy Ladies. "We have worked with twenty thousand women in need on a pro bono basis, some in abusive relationships, some who look like us: married moms, single moms, amazing women who struggle with a lack of financial security." Stacy uses her income from Francis Financial to keep the charity well funded and well run. "I could volunteer, I could work in soup kitchens or at a host of other nonprofits, but what moves the needle is not volunteering my time; it is giving dollars so that good work can be funded. Savvy Ladies gave me the passion: I want to make money so I can donate more money. I want to make a lot of money and there is nothing wrong with that."

Running two businesses — one that, by design, made no money — meant managing two payrolls, two budgets, two staffs, and two newsletters. The early years were "the hardest time in my life, no question," Stacy told me. Her husband, Michael, who also worked in finance, provided crucial financial and emotional support as Stacy took on these challenges as a new mother. "My maternity leave with my son was three days. With my daughter, I took three weeks. It was a heartbreakingly brutal time for me." Early on, after pouring her profits back into Savvy Ladies, her take-home pay was negligible. "There were years when my nanny made more money than I did." But Stacy was determined to succeed and never doubted she would. "I am one of the most ambitious people on the planet," she told me, "and I always knew that I was going to be successful. I was hell-bent on growing the firm early so that I could take time off later to be with my kids."

Stacy grew up in Howell, a small town in Michigan. The family lived on a farm where they grew most of their own food and chopped their own wood. Her parents raised her to believe in the importance of hard work and also in her own abilities: "I never thought there would be a limit for me." About seven years after she founded Francis Financial, Stacy started making as much money as she had in her previous job as an investment banker. Today, her business has thirteen employees and is worth $10 million. She outearns her husband, and her success gives him more flexibility in his career.

Years of putting her work first is what has allowed Stacy the freedom to put her family first today. She is still at her desk at 5:30 a.m., but she will take hours off in the middle of the day to attend PTA meetings, go on field trips, or take her daughter skiing when the family decamps to their house in Vermont. "I have found a balance that is not always in balance. When it is in balance, my work is exciting — it is invigorating, I can't get enough of it, and I love it, love it, love it. When I go too long without a break and I don't have enough time with my family, that is when I lose the energy and my passion for my work. That is what I have learned through the years."

I don't make nearly the money that Stacy does, nor do I have the bandwidth to run two businesses at the same time. But as they did for her, the early investment in my career, the grueling pace, and the prioritization of my work paid off. Tenure brought more than job security. Crucially, it gave me the freedom to make my own schedule. With tenure comes the ability to say no. Similar to Stacy, I can now mold my work around my children. I work just as hard as I ever did, but differently.

The payoff is more than financial, although financial stability is a key component. A tenured academic position lets me do what I love: write, teach, litigate, travel, and engage with the issues I care most deeply about. It gives me purpose and flexibility. I am proud of what I have achieved. Yes, it sometimes took me away from my children. That time away was necessary and important. I am not afraid or embarrassed to say so. Of course, I have my bad days and bad moods, but overall, I am a happy and fulfilled person, and that makes me a better mother.

Not every working mother is in a profession that offers her the kind of flexibility I enjoy. But in the hyperconnected twenty-first century and in the wake of the pandemic, working remotely and on a flexible schedule isn't just a pipe dream or an option available to only the privileged few; it is becoming increasingly acceptable, and some working mothers demand it. One of those mothers is Kenzie, whom I interviewed earlier on in the book with her wife, Abbie, and their newborn, Dashiell.

When Kenzie's employer announced on June 1, 2021, that everyone would be going back in person, she decided it was a dealbreaker. She was simply unwilling to spend eight to ten hours a day away from her baby. She did not think she needed to either. Months of working remotely had not changed her ability to be effective in her job. Going into the discussion with her boss, Kenzie drew from a well of internal confidence based on that experience. "I thought my skills [as a community organizer and policy maker] were in person, being out in the community, and now I know that I can deliver good work in this context. I can tell a better story about what I am able to do under more flexible conditions that could even empower me in future roles." To her surprise, her boss did not need any convincing. "We trust you," he told Kenzie. This was not blind faith; Kenzie had a proven track record that he could rely on.

Post-pandemic, it will be interesting to see if a significant number of young working mothers take an approach similar to Kenzie's, drawing on a personal record of excellence and changing norms about what it takes to excel at work to demand greater flexibility. An unexpected upside of the misery wrought by the coronavirus is the way it has upended traditional conceptions of work — namely, that it can be done only away from home. Of course, many working mothers do not have the option of working at home — their service-industry jobs require face-to-face contact. Others try to negotiate better pay and more reasonable hours only to be told no. For some women, the answer is to go out on their own. The number of women-owned small businesses has crept up slowly over the years and now stands at nearly 20 percent of all small businesses, bringing in over $1 trillion in revenue in 2018 alone.[7]

Diana left her job at the nail salon on May 26, 2018, to start her own esthetician business. In the weeks leading up to her departure, she let each client know of her plans. Though Diana never offered it, many clients asked for her contact information. "I wanted people to come willingly, not that I am forcing them, and I didn't want to make them uncomfortable or like I am trying to steal them." But when asked, Diana gave out her cell phone number, hoping that a few of them would follow her.

She threw herself into decorating her new work space, rented within the larger hair salon owned by one of her clients. She went for a tropical, relaxing vibe, putting up a picture of a waterfall and stenciling the words *Refresh, Relax, Renew* as a border on the white walls. "At night I couldn't sleep because I am thinking about how to organize the space and wanting it to be perfect." She also shopped for products; for the first time, she was responsible for buying and maintaining her own esthetician equipment.

Then the phone started ringing. "My kids would get so excited every time a client called for an appointment at the new place. It made me feel so good. My first successful steps and I realized it was because my clients loved me." Diana got to know the clients at the hair salon and picked up their business too. June was slow, but by July, she had gotten busier. Then the holidays came and she was booked solid. The business is seasonal, with clients coming in for waxing and other services when they are going on trips and attending holiday parties. January through April tends to be slower. When that time rolled around in 2019, Diana's husband started to worry. But even during the slower months, Diana said, she was making more than she had ever made at the nail salon, even after subtracting the cost of rent and supplies. Her regular clients provided a baseline source of income.

Diana realized the toll that the previous years had taken on her health. "My body was like an old lady's," she said. "I didn't take care of myself." A few months after starting her business, she signed up for yoga classes at a studio that was walking distance from work. Then she enrolled in a rhythm and dance class. It was, she said, "the very first time in my life that I got to do something for myself." Owning her own business made it possible because she could make her own schedule. On some days, Diana came in very early and worked until 9:00 p.m. On other days, she took afternoons off or came in later in the morning. "I am the one in control. Whatever I want to do, however I want to do it, is up to me."

At first, Diana kept her exercise routines a secret from her husband. She was worried he would say that she was wasting their money or that she should be spending that time at home with him and their children. "But I knew I needed it for my mental health and it has made a huge difference in my life." Because she has always managed their finances, she said, he did not question her decisions as long as she was able to earn enough money to support them. "I am buying my health and my happiness," she explained. Her new self-determined schedule also meant she got more sleep and had more time to spend with her family.

Then the pandemic hit. In March 2020, Diana was forced to close her business. She collected $175 a week in unemployment until the CARES Act took effect and increased the amount by $600. Relying on her savings, the family made it to September, aided by the fact that the salon owner was not asking her to pay rent. After she was allowed to reopen in September, Diana found her business reduced by half, with many clients too fearful to come in. She was able to negotiate better state unemployment insurance benefits when California's second shutdown took effect, with the state paying her $450 per week, but because Congress delayed enacting another relief bill, she went without supplemental federal benefits for weeks. By late January 2021, she had that additional money, and she and her family were living on $775 per week and a onetime family payment of $2,400. That money was helpful, Diana said, as was the extra income her husband earned by selling parrots he raised in their backyard, but she had to dip deeply into her savings.

Still, Diana is one of the lucky ones. California provides state unemployment benefits to 41 percent of its unemployed workers, the sixth-highest percentage in the country. Most states are far stingier. Florida, for example, covers only 11 percent of its workers, and North Carolina is dead last at 9 percent.[8] The lack of coverage applies regardless of gender, but the pandemic's disproportionate effect on women has left working mothers particularly vulnerable.[9]

Throughout these months of economic uncertainty, Diana struggled with stress and depression. She tried to occupy her days with cooking, cleaning, and doing art projects with her children after they finished yet another screen-filled day of remote school, but as the weeks passed in a colorless blur, her frustration and anxiety mounted. "At home, I am a wife. I'm Mom. There is no me time," she said. She stopped exercising; the dance studio was temporarily closed and the yoga studio had shut down permanently. Even if the expense of paying for online classes were affordable, she said, "I am not an at-home exerciser. I like to go out and be with people. I'm an extrovert."

Diana's COVID experience is all too common, particularly for nonwhite women with families to support.[10] Women of color absorbed 100 percent of the job losses in December 2020 while the employment numbers for men actually ticked up across the board, as did the numbers for white women.[11] Black, Latina, and Asian American women bore the brunt of the virus's impact on the economy, because they disproportionately hold jobs in some of the most severely affected industries: retail and hospitality. This is not work that can be done over Zoom.

Even without mandated business closings, millions of people opted out of travel, hotel stays, and in-person shopping for anything but basic necessities. In October 2019, the unemployment rate for Asian Americans was 2.8 percent; a year later, it stood at nearly 11 percent.[12] In December 2020, the unemployment rate for Latinas was over 9 percent; for Black women it was 8.4 percent, while for white women, it was 5.7 percent.[13] In February of 2020, one month before the worst of the pandemic hit the United States, women made up just over 50 percent of the workforce. Ten months later, the parity had eroded, with women losing nearly one million more jobs than men. Most of these women were mothers.[14]

The arrival of the vaccine has allowed the country to reopen, albeit in fits and starts and with significant restrictions in many states. Millions of jobs have come back and the unemployment rate has fallen from a pandemic high of nearly 15 percent to just over 5 percent.[15] But many businesses continue to struggle as they operate under a cloud of uncertainty with spiking cases of COVID-19 casting a complete reopening into doubt. It is not clear what the long-term impacts of the coronavirus will be for small-business owners like Diana who are struggling to keep their place in the middle class. President Biden's signing of the $1.9 trillion stimulus bill has been hailed by economic experts as a game-changer; the legislation not only addresses the impact of COVID but goes beyond with benefits designed to reduce child poverty and support working-class parents.[16] In 2021, there is also proposed federal legislation designed to repair the nation's tattered safety net with tax credits that would allow parents to offset the cost of childcare, enroll their children in free preschool, and get better medical coverage.[17] But the chances of passing such a comprehensive bill are dim, and even if pieces can be enacted, there is the question of how the money would be distributed and how far-reaching the policy changes will be.

Shortly before California allowed indoor hair and nail salons to reopen, in early March 2021, I asked Diana how she planned to move forward. Her eyes lit up. "I will be so much happier when I am not a housewife," she said. "I need to work for my mental health, not only for my financial health." But she also acknowledged that building her business back will not be easy. "It will be a long way to be back to normal even with the vaccine." How long? I asked. She thought for a moment, then shrugged. "At this point it is hard to say, but I keep hanging on tight. I keep hanging on."

Ambitious mothers without four-year-college degrees employed in the service economy have been disproportionately affected. As Diana noted: "Restaurants, hotels, beauty-business people, we got hit hard." Hely and her husband were both laid off from Cookshop in March 2020 after New York City became the epicenter of the pandemic and restaurants across the city shut down completely. At first, they were told the furlough would last four weeks; in fact, it went on for ten. "I told my husband, we are going to go crazy in this apartment." They moved in with Hely's sister, a stay-at-home mom who lives on a multi-acre property in Georgia with her husband and four children. During that time, they survived on unemployment insurance, which allowed them to continue to pay the rent for their Queens apartment. Hely spent more time with her son than she ever had, and she enjoyed it, even though she was anxious. But by the end, she was itching to get back. "It was the first time in my life since I was sixteen that I hadn't worked," she told me. When I talked to Hely in late January of 2021, Cookshop was open again, though only for takeout and outdoor dining. Her salary had been cut and she was not sure when the business would fully come back. She said that 2019 was Cookshop's best year ever; 2020 was its worst. "Looking at projections, to recoup what we lost will take at least two to three years. And that is best-case scenario." But Hely is optimistic. Cookshop's owners are willing to take a temporary hit. The restaurant's reputation, history of profitability, and loyal — even rabid — customer base bode well for a comeback. Even in these dark times, Hely still believes she is on track for her promotion. The idea that she would leave the industry — much less the workforce — has never crossed her mind.

For me, as for many white-collar professionals, the financial impact of the coronavirus has been negligible. But it has transformed my work and family life. For months, my children and I worked and learned in the same space: our one-floor condo. A few weeks into the pandemic, I converted my office into a bedroom for my son, who had previously shared a room with my daughter. For more than a year, I conducted all of my teaching and meetings virtually while sitting at the kitchen table as my kids wandered in and out during their separate lunch breaks and snack times. Unless I had a deadline, I wrote only on the days when they were with Matt.

The coronavirus obliterated the already porous wall between my work life and my family life. At first, I found the interruptions maddening. When I taught class, my son would occasionally pass by and toss out an editorial comment; once, when I was on a video call with a judge and a passel of lawyers, my daughter opened the refrigerator door behind me, exposing its contents to everyone, then scolded me for forgetting to buy maple syrup. It felt — it was — profoundly unprofessional. I missed the quiet and privacy of my own space, of just being able to shut the door and be alone.

And yet, there have been some unexpected upsides to having my kids routinely peering over my shoulder and popping up in the background. My work has come to life, providing them with a more complete understanding of why I do what I do. Carter and Ella have always known the basic outlines of my clients' stories; now they have seen their faces and heard their voices. They remain frustrated by my distractedness, but they also see with their own eyes the human beings whose lives are at stake.

One particular case captured their attention. In 2019, my clinic students and I took on the case of Yutico Briley Jr., who was convicted of an armed robbery in New Orleans that lasted less than two minutes and netted $102. Although Yutico was only nineteen at the time, he received a sixty-year sentence with no possibility of parole. The case against Yutico consisted of the white victim's cross-racial identification nearly a full day after the crime. Yutico, who is Black, was the only suspect the police showed him. Evidence in the form of surveillance footage, cell phone records, and eyewitness testimony would have established that Yutico was eight miles away when the crime was committed. But Yutico's lawyers did not present his alibi defense — or any defense at all. The trial lasted less than a full afternoon.

When the Louisiana prison that housed Yutico started allowing Zoom visits in 2020, my children met him online. They fell into playful conversation, with Yutico giving Carter a hard time about the San Francisco 49ers and telling Ella to stop sassing me. Was this appropriate? A year ago, I would have said, *Hell no.* But these relationships gave both my client and my children a healthy dose of human connection. When I went to New Orleans in December 2020 to investigate the case, my children did not complain about my absence. At the ages of nine and eleven, they understand the role of bad policing, bad lawyering, and indifference to Black lives that stole Yutico's freedom. They knew I had to go get the evidence to prove his innocence. At that point, Yutico wasn't just a name; he was a face, a voice, a person they had gotten to know. Their connection to Yutico, my students, and my work has brought us closer together.

In March 2021, I went back to New Orleans for a court hearing in Yutico's case. A new district attorney had taken over. Unlike his predecessor, he understood the gravity of the injustice and said that he would not oppose Yutico's release. The judge who had sentenced Yutico had been voted out of office several months earlier. The new judge was a well-respected former civil rights lawyer and public defender. Yutico's prospects, dim throughout the eight long years following his conviction, were suddenly bright.

Still, last-minute skirmishes had set me on edge, like the DA's eleventh-hour request to meet privately with the judge to reach an agreement on a secret matter before we went forward. For three nights, I barely slept. On the morning of the hearing, I woke up to the sound of my heart pounding and a text from my daughter. **Mommy!** she wrote. **Are you nervous? Are you going to puke?** She asked if I needed her. I told her I was scared. She replied by reassuring me, adding that she and Carter planned to watch the legal proceedings on Zoom.

When the time came to stand up and explain to the judge why Yutico should be freed, I used as many of his own words as I could, quoting his frantic recorded jailhouse calls to his attorney and a letter he wrote to a friend — the letter that convinced me that my law students and I needed to take his case. Describing the racist practices that led up to the wrongful conviction, I told the judge, "Yutico Briley was convicted in 2013, but it might as well have been 1813." It was a fiery speech, even by my standards. I even dropped the F-bomb — twice. But I think the tone was right. Yutico wanted his story — the true story — to be told, and there was no way to do that without expressing outrage.

When it was the prosecution's turn, the deputy district attorney conceded that Yutico was innocent and offered an apology on behalf of the state. Ruling from the bench, the judge called the case "appalling," and a "textbook example" of how the system too often fails catastrophically. She ordered that Yutico be freed. Walking out,

I saw a text from my son. **LEESSSS GOOOOOOO!** he had written, his ultimate expression of exhilaration and euphoria.

I missed Ella's fourth-grade parent-teacher conference, which was scheduled for the same time as the hearing. Ella was forgiving, if a bit angry and hurt. But from the expression on her face when she got to FaceTime with Yutico on the day of his exoneration, I think she understands. I am betting on it.

The most affirming words I heard about work-life imbalance came from Pamela Metzger. Like me, she is a trial attorney turned law professor with a son and a daughter. For nearly a year — from September 2005 to August 2006 — Pam commuted from Atlanta to New Orleans to do legal work after Hurricane Katrina. Today, she is director of the Southern Methodist Law School's Criminal Justice Reform Center in Texas. "Your kids will get it, I promise," she wrote to me. "My 21-year-old son is the first person on the street to stop and film a 'police-citizen encounter.' My daughter, who is 18, led Dallas's Students' March and organized the Students' March protest when the NRA met in Dallas. Yes, they bitch to me about how I was 'always gone,' but they also brag [to] their friends about 'that time mom sued all the judges in New Orleans.'"

She continued, "Our kids are always watching, even when we're not there. And we're not picking our jobs over our kids. The world we want for our kids has to be built, brick-by-brick. So we are showing them that justice and peace aren't free. We are showing them that those things carry a price tag, and we are willing to pay it. We are showing them that there is joy in the work of making others whole. You've made Tikkun Olam[18] real for your kids. In my book, that means that you're always choosing *them*."

CHAPTER EIGHT

THE KIDS ARE ALL RIGHT

CONVENTIONAL WISDOM TEACHES THAT MOTHERS WHO prioritize their careers do so at the expense of their children. This trope has been trotted out as truth for decades, leaving millions of working mothers feeling guilt-ridden and less-than, perennially anxious that their physical absence from the home equates to emotional neglect of their offspring. But the data does not bear this out.

Empirical studies showed that the children of working mothers were doing fine — in fact, many were thriving. The daughters of working mothers were more likely to be employed, earn higher wages, and have jobs with supervisory responsibilities, while their sons were more likely to devote time to caregiving and other domestic responsibilities than the children of stay-at-home mothers, according to a 2018 study. The study, led by Harvard Business School professor Kathleen McGinn, assessed a hundred thousand adult children across twenty-four developed countries and found that the children of working mothers were just as happy as the children of stay-at-home mothers.[1]

There are some qualifiers. The study relied on self-reports[2] and did not measure the intensity or hours of the working mothers' jobs.[3] Instead, the key question was whether working mothers served as role models for their children.[4] The answer to that question, resoundingly, was yes: "Employed daughters of employed mothers, when faced with the opportunities and challenges of having children themselves, appear both willing and able to emulate their mothers as they manage employment and caregiving roles simultaneously."[5] This was due in part to working mothers' "conveyance of egalitarian gender attitudes and life skills for managing employment and domestic responsibilities simultaneously." These results were not an indictment of stay-at-home mothers, the authors noted, but rather a refutation of the ingrained belief that the choice to stay at home — for those mothers who have a choice — is the better one.

Professor McGinn's findings replicated those of early studies of the same issue involving smaller sample sizes. Pamela F. Lenehan, the author of *My Mother, My Mentor: What Grown Children of Working Mothers Want You to Know,* surveyed one thousand adult children, some parented by stay-at-home mothers and others by mothers who worked. She found that there was no gap in happiness, education level, or employment between the two groups. Lenehan did find, however, that a higher percentage of the daughters of working women credited their mothers for teaching them independence. The persistent stereotype of the neglectful working mother, Lenehan theorized, was due in part to the hesitancy among the working women of her generation "to advertise" their success as parents — that is, to be loud and proud about their ability to raise healthy, well-adjusted kids.[6] She urged them to step forward, not only as examples but also to offer advice and support to the women coming after them.

In 2014, sociologist Amy Hsin and economist Christina Felfe published the results of a study they undertook to test the assumption that "maternal employment is detrimental mainly because it robs children of valuable time with parents."[7] What they found was a difference of quantity but not quality. Not surprisingly, the children of stay-at-home mothers spent more time with their mothers. But much of that time was spent on "unstructured activities," meaning activities that "require the least amount of verbal exchange" and "direct engagement." Working mothers and stay-at-home mothers spent roughly the same amount of "quality" time with their children, defined as being present and involved during "structured and educational activities" meant to promote a child's cognitive and behavioral development. The assumption that working mothers were harming their children, they wrote, was "unfounded."

A 2010 meta-analysis of sixty-nine studies performed over fifty years exploring the impact of mothers' careers on their children's academic and emotional development found more positive benefits than negative effects. In single-parent households across socioeconomic class, the children of working mothers performed better in school and had fewer behavioral problems. While some studies found that in two-parent households there was a net negative effect when mothers worked during their children's first year of life, the authors cautioned that the small sample sizes did not allow for the drawing of definitive conclusions. Their takeaway after this exhaustive review of the literature was that "the associations between achievement and behavior problems and maternal employments are predominantly insignificant."[8]

I began to read about the outcomes for the children of working mothers with trepidation and came away feeling relieved. The data tracked my own experience as a child. The quality versus quantity of time analysis, in particular, resonated with me. When I talked to my mother about this study, she pointed out that my sisters and I complained constantly that she worked too much, even though in her mind she bent over backward to carve out that "quality time" with us that the researchers emphasized was so important.

"Do you think I worked too much?" she asked me. I paused to think it over. "At the time, yes, but now, no," I said. My mother worked a lot when I was growing up. She still does, well into her seventies. From early on, even when I resented the time she was away, I understood the importance of her job, which involves healing people and teaching medical students to heal others. I have always been intensely proud that my mother is Dr. Bazelon. That title signified academic achievement and grit, an escape from poverty, and a forceful rejoinder to the sexist belief that women could not or should not be physicians.

My mother made time for me. Not in the same way that the stay-at-home mothers (or, for that matter, the mothers who had fewer children) did for their kids. But when I needed my mother, she was there. I associate my father with my greatest triumphs, and to this day, he is the first person I call with good news. I associate my mother with my greatest vulnerabilities, and she is the person I call when I am frightened and desperate and don't know what to do. Among the children of ambitious mothers whom I interviewed, reliance on one's mother — on her sound judgment, her resourcefulness, and her support — during life's worst moments was a recurring theme.

In some ways, I am a lot like my mother. I have worked steadily, even relentlessly, throughout my children's lives. But there are also significant differences. Because of my divorce, I spend less time with my children than she spent with my sisters and me. Because of my work choices, I travel far more than she did — more, even, than my father ever did (although that is less true these days and neither of my children has clear memories of the years I spent commuting from San Francisco to Los Angeles). What is similar, to some degree, is the way that I parent. I treasure the time I spend with my children and try to make it count. Just as I did with my parents growing up, we talk about sports, politics, celebrities, true crime, school, and work. We share fears and laughter and inside jokes and creative ideas. We laugh until we cry. Yes, we fight; they talk back; I yell. No, I am not solely responsible for the fact that they are doing well. They have an amazing father, a loving larger family, and a warm community.

I do not take my children's current well-being for granted; the world can be a dangerous place, convulsing with violence and strife. Even if they are fortunate enough to escape the direct impact of an earthquake-scale life event, tremors and fissures will inevitably appear in their own lives in the form of struggle, disappointment, conflict, and loss. That's life, as they say. But as their mother — their busy, ambitious working mother — I know that I play a key role in their present happiness. I give myself credit for that. I give myself credit for listening to my inner voice and making my own way. My life is an embrace of imbalance. Not teetering, but like the infinity symbol, one part coming up as the other comes down, rising and falling and rising again.

Twenty-first-century feminism is rightly focused on equal pay at work, equal division of labor at home, and the eradication of so many of the abuses and chauvinist metrics that have driven women out of the workforce or caused them to switch to lower-paying, part-time work. But feminism in the twenty-first century must also be about more than that. We have to redefine what it means to be a good mother.

Being ambitious and seeking fulfillment at work are not antithetical to good parenting — we know that because society rewards these qualities when fathers exhibit them. Mothers aren't selfish to want these things too. In fact, they should be *encouraged* to go after them. Empowered, economically secure women are happier, and children understand that and benefit from it even if it means less quantity time as a family.[9] If the dual desires to be mothers and successful professionals are viewed as compatible rather than at odds, women will experience more joy at home and at work. Holding themselves to a standard that is attainable rather than seeking a mythical work-life equipoise frees women from the impossible and exhausting project of being physically and emotionally present at all times in all spheres.

The proof, though, is in the pudding. How are the kids doing? And what do they have to say when asked about their ambitious mothers? I did not interview my children or any children too young to make an informed decision about whether they wanted to participate. But I did want to hear from the adult children of ambitious mothers directly, including the children of the mothers I interviewed for this book. How did they experience their mothers' decisions to prioritize their careers? As an absence and a source of hurt and frustration? With pride and as a source of inspiration? Did they aspire to be like their mothers or to rebel against the example they set? Were they close with their mothers as young children? Are they close with them now? If so, in what ways? If not, why not?

The answers, as it turned out, were all of the above. The children I spoke with were thoughtful, reflective, and honest about what their mothers had and had not given them. In the main, the adult children I interviewed spoke of their mothers with great admiration and affection. Most had felt deeply bonded with their mothers growing up, even though they were often absent, and most felt close to their mothers as adults. Many told me that their mothers were role models. These adult children were also ambitious and successful in their own right, some with hard-driving careers and families of their own.

These interviews are not meant to be representative of a larger trend; I was not conducting an empirical study. The stories of the children pick up where their mothers' left off. Their voices give a fuller picture and, in some respects, render a verdict. In the same way that I have tried to do with my own mother, I wanted to draw connections and gain insight by following that line of succession. As adult children, we are the legacies of our ambitious mothers. What is that legacy and what does it mean for our own children? Gathering the answers was often an emotional experience, for them and for me. I was not prepared for how much their words and experiences would resonate with my child and adult selves. I alternated between celebrating their mothers' choices while feeling good about my own and cringing at an unflattering reflection in the mirror they held up. At times, I revisited my proud, bold thesis and wondered if I would live to see it punch me in the face.

I was particularly interested in talking to the daughters of Gretchen Rossman, the Mother on the Card who was not — who was, in fact, willing to take risks and make breaks with tradition that my own mother never would. In the way that one is always curious about people from the distant past, I wanted to know what had happened to Dara and Tamara. But I also wanted their perspective on the kind of mother Gretchen had been. I was so certain of the correctness of my memories and perceptions, and I had been wrong.

Dara and Tamara both described themselves as very close to Gretchen growing up; Tamara used the word *enmeshed*. However, their mother's decision to move to Massachusetts to pursue the academic position she had sought for so long and her ensuing divorce from their father, Milt, were extremely difficult. "It was traumatic, there is no other word for it," Dara said. "She moved in January, when I was in the middle of tenth grade. Tamara went with her after she finished the school year." Gretchen and Milt sat the girls down and told them that the decision to stay or go was theirs to make. Dara chose to remain behind in Philadelphia. She was settled, with a boyfriend and a solid academic track record. She did not want to start over. But, most important, Dara felt that she could not leave her father alone.

Looking back on the dissolution of her parents' marriage, Dara told me that "it seems to me now as though the rules changed on them, like they did for a lot of people who got married in the late sixties: she was supposed to stay at home but then she realized that wasn't what she wanted. That is a huge change and they just couldn't absorb it." When the tenure-track offer to teach at the University of Massachusetts appeared on the horizon, she said, "Our mom at that point, I think she had a sense of destiny and urgency and she bound us up in that narrative. At the time, I didn't question it." Now, she said, as the mother of seventeen- and fourteen-year-old daughters, "I do. It was incredibly hard and I was incredibly sad."

Still, as an adult, Dara is well acquainted with the vagaries of the academic job market and the once-in-a-lifetime opportunity that presented itself to her mother. Since 2013, Dara has been a tenured professor of English at NYU, but the road to getting there took a decade and a half and involved two cross-country moves. After getting her PhD in Victorian literature from Brandeis University, Dara taught at Princeton on several one-year renewable contracts while her husband, Greg, worked at a white-shoe law firm in Manhattan. But when they had their first child, he left to work remotely for a nonprofit based in London.

"Those were related decisions," she said. "I had not signed up in our marriage to have children with someone who was working seventy hours a week." Even with Greg working from home, maternity leave was difficult. Dara didn't qualify for parental leave, and three weeks after a C-section, she found herself back in the classroom and nursing on her breaks. Laboring in this low-status position, Dara spent five years on the job market and did not land a tenured position teaching Victorian studies. "I felt like a failure," she told me.

In 2005, Pomona, a liberal arts college in Claremont, California, made Dara an offer to direct its writing program. It was not a tenured position, but it was prestigious and the work appealed to her. Greg, still working remotely, was supportive and willing to move. So they did, hoping it would eventually lead to a tenured position back on the East Coast where they could be close to their families again. Nine years later, Dara got the job at NYU.

"You can't step out of academia and then step back in as though nothing happened. I had no illusions about that. But the other part of it is that I just don't think I would have been happy." With her second daughter, who was born in 2006, Dara was able to go part-time for a few months, "but part of what made it awesome was that I got to use my professional brain for half the day. I love the ease when I am on sabbatical or in January when it's winter break, but I would get restless and bored and depressed if I did not also have my own creative and intellectual projects."

Dara pointed to the examples of her mother, grandfather, and great-grandfather, all of whom were prominent academics, and told me, "I think that was always my plan." Her mother, Dara said, inspired her and also taught her crucial life lessons. "Growing up, I felt like my mother always knew what to say and knew how to help me think things through. There were moments after she moved when it felt wobblier, but it came back again once I was older and in college. She has a kind of emotional intelligence where I feel like she has taught me to pay attention to who I am, to who I try to be as a teacher and who I try to be as a parent."

Tamara, who lived with Gretchen in Amherst from eighth grade until high-school graduation, described herself as "the good kid who did whatever I wanted. I was friends with everyone, I played sports, I was artsy, I was in orchestra. I got good grades. My mom and I were very close the whole time. She was a very approachable mom for other kids — not buddy-buddy, but supportive." At the same time, Tamara described Gretchen as "distracted." She had several serious long-term partners, and she was focused on those relationships and on her career. Tamara, meanwhile, went a little wild. "If I was spending the night at my friend Kathy's house, my mom would be like, 'Great, I can spend the night at [my boyfriend's] house,' and Kathy lived a quarter of a mile away, so we would sneak out and meet boys and drink at my house."

I asked Tamara whether Gretchen had some inkling of what she was up to. Tamara said, "I think she chose not to see." I winced, thinking about my own children and how they describe me: "distracted," "blurry," "obsessed" with my job. It was all too easy to imagine my own children, my daughter in particular, behaving just like Tamara in their teenage years. Of course, it was normal to act out — God knows I did — but what gnawed at me was the sense Tamara had of parental permissiveness through inattention. And what she said next felt like a body blow. "There is a part of me that understands why my mom would want to claim her life in the ways that she did, but there is a lot of me now that I am a parent that is a harsher judge of that."

Tamara met her husband, Matt, in tenth grade. From the start, the relationship was "very mature," she said. "We always knew we loved each other." He was two years older, and they stayed together until Tamara went to college. "We broke up because I had no idea who I was outside of Matt-and-Tam — we were one entity." Eight years later, when Tamara was living in Colorado and working as a public-school teacher and Matt was in the navy training in Florida, he wrote Tamara an e-mail thanking her for what she had given him during the years they were together. It had set the standard, he told her, for what love was. Tamara, who was struggling to extricate herself from an abusive relationship, was deeply moved.

A year later, Tamara met up with Matt for an afternoon in Maryland, where they were both visiting family. "Both of us knew," she said. They got married less than a year later, in 2002. Tamara, twenty-eight, relocated to Texas, where Matt was in flight school, then followed him to the Central Valley in California. After Matt returned from his first deployment, flying combat missions over Iraq and Afghanistan, Tamara got pregnant. They learned it was a girl, and they decided to name her Mackenzie. But Mackenzie was stillborn. "Matt was scheduled to deploy in two months, and I was in such a dark place, the darkest place I had ever been, and he was leaving for six to eight months. I knew I needed to get pregnant again to have any shred of sanity."

It was March 2006. The doctors told Tamara to wait six months to let her body heal, but one month later, Tamara was pregnant again. This pregnancy, too, was traumatic: "Because my body hadn't healed, weird things started happening." Her baby, Buzz, was born prematurely in October at twenty-six weeks, weighing only two pounds, and stayed in the NICU until the following January. Shortly after Buzz came home from the hospital, Matt deployed again.

Tamara describes Mackenzie's death as the turning point in her life. "Mackenzie dying made me wake up to the fact that everything is not going to go the way that I unconsciously assumed it was going to go. At that moment, I knew I had to stay home." That feeling intensified with Buzz's first few weeks of life, which were touch and go, and the months that followed, with Matt gone and Buzz on a heart monitor and an oxygen tank. "At that point, my purpose in life was to keep Buzz alive and to keep Matt mentally okay because it tore him apart to leave us. I had no family [nearby] and a really sick baby. My 'big P' Purpose was lightning clear, there was just no question."

When Buzz was thirteen months old, Tamara got pregnant again. This time, she carried the pregnancy to term and gave birth to their daughter, Mikayla, in 2008. For the next five years, Tamara was mostly on her own with two children born less than two years apart as Matt deployed again and again. "For the first three years of Mikayla's life, I think he was home for less than six months." Despite the stress of Matt's continuing absences, Tamara said they maintained a family unit, in part because she was very intentional about including him. "I was in the weeds doing the everyday stuff and [would] be stuck with a toddler-behavior thing and I would ask Matt's advice, kind of like throwing him a bone to make him feel included. But Matt could see the forest because he wasn't in the trees. He would offer this fantastic advice and we were co-parenting with him half a world away."

Over the years, the family has moved again and again: to Montgomery, Alabama; Virginia Beach, Virginia; Meridian, Mississippi; and, most recently, Louisville, Kentucky. "It is impossible to have a career with all these moves," Tamara told me. She has worked periodically as a substitute teacher and yoga instructor. When they were living in Virginia Beach, her yoga-therapy practice started to flourish. "The opportunity for growth was huge, but I couldn't transplant it when we moved to Mississippi." That was the one time, Tamara said, when the marriage was in real trouble. She had felt settled in Virginia Beach; the kids were doing well, and she was commuting to Washington, DC, to get a master's degree. Initially, Tamara told Matt that she and the kids would stay behind. But when she saw how heartbroken he was, she reconsidered. "Things were deteriorating in the relationship because we were focused on what we were doing and not how we were doing it." In the end, they all went to Mississippi, then moved to Kentucky after Matt retired from the military and took a job with Amazon. Tamara has started up her yoga practice again and now works full-time as a third-grade teacher at a school in downtown Louisville that is majority minority. Many of the children suffer from homelessness, abuse, neglect, and poverty. "It is all the things," she said, "hard, stressful, rewarding." Tamara cares deeply about her students, but "if it becomes too much, it is a no-brainer to choose my own health and sanity and my family's health and sanity over work," she told me.

"We have a history in our family of women who are strong-willed and have a strong work ethic," she said. Gretchen had taken her husband's last name, Rossman, but with a twist, as Tamara described it: "Growing up, my mom, Dara, and me called ourselves Ross-women. For them, these aren't jobs; they are careers, they are passions, it is *the* thing about them. And I tend to describe myself and make decisions in my life in opposition to that family legacy."

Military life, which Tamara had regarded with suspicion and misgiving at first, showed her that there was a different way of living than the coastal urban model she'd grown up with among liberal, career-oriented parents like her own. (And like mine.) "Moving around and living in all different geographic areas as a military spouse, I saw people from all walks of life: Christian, working class. I saw other patterns. And I thought, *Oh, growing up, we mocked those patterns.* Staying close to home, staying in the same town, maybe even living at home in college to save money — it can be healthy and nurturing and lovely in a lot of ways."

"You're bad for my thesis," I told her. I was sort of kidding, but not really.

She laughed. "I feel good about that."

In truth, my conversations with Tamara moved and unsettled me, much as my conversations with Gretchen had, but for wholly different reasons. Looking at Tamara's life, I could see the path not taken. A few days later, Matt — my own Matt — came over to pick up the kids one evening, and, as has become a routine since COVID, he stayed for dinner. What if I had been less driven and binary in my thinking? I asked him. What if I had said no to the job in Los Angeles? What if I had defined myself in opposition to the Bazelon women — my mother and my sisters — rather than believing my purpose in life was to compete for a place among them? What if I had tried harder to make the sacrifices necessary for our marriage to work?

Tamara had a deep, abiding, romantic love with her husband and a life centered on their children's well-being. I did not. My marriage, to quote Hobbes on a different subject, was nasty, brutish, and short. Which is not to say that Matt and I were not in love. We were. In fact, I was still in love with Matt when we got divorced. But I loved myself more. Yielding to his vision of what I should be like as a wife and mother meant a loss of independence and a ceding of ambition that would have left me resentful and unfulfilled. I simply wasn't willing to make those sacrifices or to have our children be the central organizing principle of my life.

I also did not experience the tragedy that crystallized Tamara's life purpose. Matt and I were fortunate — so fortunate — to have two healthy children. For a time, that outcome was in doubt. Deep into the second trimester of my pregnancy with Ella, I had abdominal surgery to remove a mass on my ovary the size of a tennis ball. My doctor — Laurie Green — could not rule out the possibility that I had ovarian cancer or that the mass would rupture my ovary and cause life-threatening internal bleeding.

The surgery, which sliced me open from navel to pubic bone, also carried a real risk of fetal death. The weeks leading up to it were terrifying. During the day, I coped by pretending it wasn't happening, which meant I worked harder than ever at my job. At night, I would lie in bed with my hand on my swollen belly, whispering, "We will make it, we will make it," while reminding myself that the odds were overwhelmingly in both of our favors.

In the end, the mass was benign, and Ella survived. But looking at the livid red scar served as a daily reminder that I had been cut open with my baby inside of me. I felt mutilated, and the recovery was a weeks-long, agonizing process. When I woke up from surgery, nauseated and in terrible pain, my mother was sitting in the chair next to my bed, having flown across the country that morning. She held the steel bowl under my chin while I vomited and smoothed back my hair while I cried like a child. She held my hand when I took my first steps, nearly doubled over, and slept in a chair in the hospital for days until I was allowed to go home. She was the person I wanted with me — more than I wanted Matt, who had to take care of our son — because I had complete faith in her ability to help me heal.

Maybe that should have been a sign to slow down, pay more attention, count my blessings. I did none of these things. Three weeks later, I had improved enough to go back to work. My mother went home. Four months later, after a mercifully uneventful delivery, I returned text messages for work from my hospital bed while Ella slept. The epidural had not even worn off.

Matt listened to me talk about this with a mixture of amusement and disbelief on his face. "That's not you," he said, referring to Tamara's life. "That was never going to be you." He was right, of course. And yet, Tamara seemed so happy and fulfilled; her children, now in seventh and eighth grades, were, she said, "still wonderfully innocent and that is important to me." I thought about what Carter and Ella had been through: my prolonged absences from their lives, their parents' divorce, and an up-close view of the criminal justice system through the lens of two criminal defense attorney parents. They were wonderful, yes, but "wonderfully innocent"? Not so much.

"Mom, I am getting sick of Jesse," Ella told me one day, referring to the client whose legal troubles had caused me to miss her birthday. "Can his case be over soon?" It was, but then there was another one. There was always another one. Recently, though, Ella had been pushing me to adopt Yutico, who had taken to calling me

Wonder Woman and her Baby Wonder Woman. The fact that he was twenty-seven, lived in Louisiana, and already had a mother did not deter her from continually bringing it up. Shortly before Yutico was released from prison, they both got in trouble: Yutico for a conflict with one of the prison wardens, Ella for a conflict with her teacher. Talking to Yutico afterward over Zoom, Ella said, "Don't worry, everybody loses control of their feelings sometimes." Yutico, meanwhile, told her to behave better and show me more respect. He told her that when he got out of prison, he planned to get tattoos of her name and mine on his back. (Reader, he did.) When Ella told me about this, my eyebrows shot up, but I was also moved by their emotional connection and shared belief that Yutico's release was not a question of *if* but *when*. They both operated under the absolute conviction that this Wonder Woman lawyer — me — would be able to prove his innocence. And they were right.

Of course, that is not the whole story. Both of my children complain about the hours I work and my distractedness. This, too, was a theme among a number of children of hardworking professional mothers who reached out to me after my *New York Times* essay ran. Some spoke poignantly of missing their mothers. Others wrote that they felt their mothers were distant and cold. One woman, Rachel, who was raised in a small town in Vermont and now lives and works in Tel Aviv, wrote, "I'm the daughter of a career-minded mom who chose her job over her kids. My mom was never there for me, and to this day has remained a distant, awkward parent." After her parents divorced, Rachel was raised primarily by her father, whom she described as "my best friend, a fantastic parent, a fervent supporter of everything I do."[10]

At the same time, Rachel, twenty-four, described herself as ambitious. She graduated from a competitive college and got a master's in government with a focus on counterterrorism. She is now in the process of applying to PhD programs in political science. Rachel, who is queer and engaged to marry a medical student, is ambivalent about having children. "The way I saw my mom being a parent, I do not want to replicate that. She is not maternal and did not have that instinct. I worry that I am that way too." Today, Rachel and her mother have a cordial relationship, and they talk regularly, even FaceTiming to bake together, which is a pastime they both enjoy. But, Rachel said, "I don't see her as a parent, I see her as a nice lady that I know."

Most of the adult children of hardworking professional women expressed great pride in their mothers. They missed them, they wanted more time with them, but they understood why their mothers needed to be away. The relationships were complicated, as many mother-child relationships are, but I was struck by how many of these children spoke of their mothers as role models, icons, even; the degree to which they were inspired to pursue their own careers with passion and intensity; and their preference for a partner who felt the same way.

Samuel Rickless, the son of a famous opera singer, is a professor of philosophy at the University of California San Diego. He wrote:

> I remember when my mother . . . would leave for months at a time, to sing in opera houses all over the world. I missed her terribly, I hid her clothes when I was very young, in the hope that she couldn't leave without them. But later I grew to understand that she had a passion and a calling, that this was something she loved and at which she excelled. And now, with my own passion (philosophy, and law!), I understand why she had to do what she did, and I am grateful for everything she was able to give me.

Allison Singleton, twenty-one, the daughter of Verna Williams, is a senior at Brown University. Growing up, she was one of the last kids to get picked up from school and spent many afternoons in her mother's office doing her homework, impatient to go home. When Verna became the dean of her law school, her work hours intensified. At times, Allison was frustrated and less than thrilled with how busy she was. But she also spoke lovingly of her mother and of their rituals, including going to the hair salon every other weekend, going to the art museum afterward, and regularly eating dinners together as a family. She is inspired by Verna's ambition and "super-proud" of her achievements.

When Allison was in eighth grade, Verna invited her to sit in on a presentation she was giving to her colleagues about a paper she was writing about reproductive rights. At the time, Verna was a faculty member. The dean started to aggressively challenge her mother's ideas with, in Allison's words, "not super-kind critique. I know in academia people tear each other apart, but I really didn't like seeing him talk that way." Listening as the dean went after her mother, Allison, who describes herself as "very introverted," felt a growing sense of outrage. In a roomful of law professors, she raised her hand. "I gave my feedback about why it was a good idea for an article, and I said that my mom did a phenomenal job."

Anthony Gentile, the son of Karyn Ward, was also one of the last kids to be picked up from school. Like Allison, he wished he could go straight home like his friends whose mothers did not work outside the home. But Anthony and Karyn also had rituals, including watching baseball and football religiously. "She's a massive New York Jets fan, unfortunately for her," he said dryly. During his senior year in high school, Anthony became deathly ill with Addison's disease and spent three and a half weeks in the hospital. Karyn — who, you'll recall, regularly worked seventy-hour weeks at her job as an executive assistant — was there.

"My mom is a very caring person and charismatic as hell. She got along with the nurses and she was very good at advocating for me, but not in a pushy way. If I needed something, she would make sure I got it immediately." When Anthony came home, he had lost fifty pounds. "I couldn't eat. I couldn't walk because I was so weak." A few days later, his father required emergency surgery for his cancer. Throughout, Anthony relied on his mother, even when she had to have surgery herself later that month. He described his father's death two years ago as "horrible, but I don't know what I would have done if it had been her. She is the person I go to when I have anything wrong in my life." During COVID, Anthony and his girlfriend moved in with Karyn, and every night, they cooked and ate together. It felt, he said, like having a family again.

Jonathan, twenty-four, is the son of Beth Fouhy, the NBC/MSNBC politics editor. Of his mother's travel for work, he said, "It doesn't cloud my memory like I had some absentee mother." Her guilt, he said, struck him as "rooted in this ridiculous and antiquated structure of the town where we lived, which can be somewhat conservative and reactionary at times. The idea that when my globe-trotting mom who is interviewing world leaders and asking Obama questions gets judgment from these suburban moms is infuriating to me. My mom's work became a fun part of my life. I used to take the train up to Thirty Rock and we would get lunch. It was always so fun to me." Jonathan, who graduated from NYU, is now getting a master's degree in urban planning at Columbia University. He sees his parents regularly for dinner and told me, "It is obnoxious how much I love them." He added, "There is no part of me that imagines marrying someone where I am the sole breadwinner and she is at home all day long."

Listening to Allison, Anthony, and Jonathan, I felt intermittent currents of recognition. I could imagine my daughter speaking up in my defense too. When she was a year old, she sat in my lap while I dressed down my bosses for what I thought was unequal and unfair treatment at my low-paying fellowship. I was leaving and had another job, so it felt safe to do so, but I was still shaking with nerves.

My daughter's tiny body, though, seemed to radiate power. It felt like she was the one giving me strength, not the other way around. I, too, like to watch sports with my son, who will still occasionally lean his head against my shoulder or even reach for my hand. When he and my daughter were sick — eye surgery for her, a misdiagnosis for him that required a battery of tests, including an MRI — I was just like Karyn: a relentlessly persistent advocate. I think my children were proud when they watched me in court arguing for Yutico's release, and I believe my example will inspire them to have their own big ambitions and find partners who feel the same way.

Peighton DeVon, who was a toddler when her mother, Nicole, went back to college, told me that they have always been very close, even through a childhood that was at times deeply traumatic. This included a custody battle initiated by Peighton's father when she was in first grade (he and Nicole had split up six months after she was born). Peighton did not see her mother for more than two months while the legal battle played out. "He told me my mom didn't want me anymore and convinced me that she was too busy and wanted a different life."

In the end, the court determined that the allegations were unfounded and the only trauma Peighton suffered was the forced separation from her mother. Nicole told me that the day they were reunited, "I held her, and she let out this guttural cry that should not have come from a child. Basically, since then we have been inseparable." Over the next few years, Peighton continued to see her father but the relationship deteriorated. Now twenty-four, she hasn't interacted with him since she was ten. But she did have the unconditional love and support of Nicole's biological mother, adoptive father, and Nicole's long-term partner, Derek, all of whom pitched in to babysit.

Peighton's central relationship, though, has always been with her mother. This remained true during the thirteen years that Nicole worked at her alma mater, Eastern Washington University in Spokane. When Peighton was in elementary school, Nicole began as a coordinator for American Indian studies and later created the position she moved on to hold as the director of Native American Affairs and trial liaison to the university's president. "She was constantly working," Peighton said, "but it wasn't to a point where as a single mom she was nonexistent." Peighton liked hearing her mother's stories about her work, and she could see how much Nicole meant to her students.

Like her mother, Peighton was a standout athlete, earning a full athletic scholarship to the University of Nevada Reno as a Division 1 volleyball player. She graduated in less than four years and went on to get a master's degree in athletic administration. Today, she lives in Los Angeles. After Peighton worked for several years as a hostess at a restaurant, Nicole helped her find a job in branding and communications for a nonprofit that acts as a liaison between Native tribes and the federal government in Alaska, Oregon, and Idaho. "This is my first big-girl job," Peighton told me proudly. "I make twenty-six fifty an hour," with benefits and a 401(k). Her ultimate goal is to work her way up through the sports industry; she views her ability to develop her marketing skills as an asset.

For about a year, mostly during the coronavirus pandemic, Peighton lived with her boyfriend. When she was laid off from her restaurant job, he supported her. When he was laid off from his job at a luxury gym, she supported him. Neither one of them was comfortable being dependent on the other, but it was especially problematic when Peighton was the breadwinner. "It made him feel emasculated, and we have a lot of issues in our relationship anyway, because I am so independent and I do my own thing." In February 2020, Peighton got her own place, which she described as necessary to save the relationship. "I need my own space and it is a huge step for me because I will literally be living on my own for the first time and paying for all my own stuff in a city as expensive as this." She beamed as she told me this.

Nicole, meanwhile, is getting what Peighton describes as "her second wind." In April 2021, she left Eastern Washington and moved across the country to take a job working as an executive officer in tribal affairs and diversity, equity, and inclusion in the Louisiana Department of Children and Family Services. Nicole says she is nervous but excited about the seismic change in her life; after fifteen years of living and working in Spokane, she is selling her house and most of her belongings to start a different life. When she gets fearful, she reminds herself that "I have that X factor, the thing that makes people pay attention. I have the ability to command attention and respect. It's just me being real and being authentic. So I have to believe that I will do amazing wherever I go. I have taken care of everyone else for so long and now that Peighton is on sure footing I figured I would take my career out for a spin."

Peighton has mixed feelings — "I don't want to be that far from her" — but mainly, she is proud that at fifty, her mother is embarking on a new adventure. "My mom loves the South," she told me, and then, smiling slyly, added "She loves Southern men."

Laurie Green's son, Ross, is now in his mid-thirties. "I am a mama's boy," he confessed. This is true, he said, even though his mother regularly worked seventy-hour weeks and never took time off. "I have friends who have stay-at-home moms and I've been to dinner at their houses and gone on vacations with them and it is different. We didn't have family dinner and we didn't have family vacations." Dinners for Ross and his sister, he said, often consisted of tortillas with string cheese and rice with carrots; dessert was ice cream sandwiches. At the time, he said, they loved it. "I didn't realize how bad the food situation was at our house until I got school lunches in first grade and they were actually better."

From a very young age, he was aware of his mother's identity as Dr. Green. His sister, Monica, would sometimes refer to Laurie that way to needle her, but it was a source of pride for Ross. Like many of the adult children I spoke to, Ross was aware that his mother carried a burden of the internal and external judgments that came with not being a traditional mom. "She knows there is some element of truth to the fact that it might have been better for her kids if she were not as hardworking. She took weekend call, spent nights at the hospital, missed sports games and a graduation. She didn't go camping, skiing, or take vacation." At the same time, it didn't occur to Ross that his driven, ambitious mother could ever trade being an ob-gyn for anything else. "Work-life balance suggests that work isn't life, but childhood intuition told us that just wasn't true. Our mom loved her work, and her patients loved her back. She was 'balanced' by practicing medicine; she had a calling."

As for what he is looking for in a partner, Ross told me, "Outside the coastal bubble there are a ton of people with traditional families." He said that there are compelling arguments for a relationship that involves a stay-at-home parent but added, "I don't know how to live like that and I have never dated anyone with that goal. I self-select for people who are ambitious and driven."

I spoke with David and Joe Granzotto, the sons of trial attorney turned appellate judge Elizabeth Gleicher. They are now in their thirties. David, who is the vice principal of a large public school in the Bay Area, said his mother "worked her ass off" when he was growing up. He described her as "at a nine [out of ten] all the time in terms of stress level, and, man, could she go off." Recently, David texted with a childhood friend who reminded him that "even the way your mom would say your name was terrifying." At the same time, David recalled the family eating together every night when his mother was not traveling and said, "It was very impressive that she was able to be who she was and create a family." It was his mother's earnings that allowed David and his brothers to attend an exclusive private school in Bloomfield, Michigan, a wealthy Detroit suburb. "Ninety percent of the moms were stay-at-home moms," he said. "And I remember being like, *My mom is way cooler than this.* The work she did was for principled causes. Her breakthrough case was a class-action lawsuit against Blue Cross Blue Shield because they didn't cover bone marrow transplants for breast cancer survivors. Her best friend had died of breast cancer, and after that lawsuit, Blue Cross had to cover those treatments."

David excelled in high school and attended his mother's alma mater, Carleton College, where he majored in religious studies; he learned to speak Arabic and read the Koran. He thought seriously about law school and even took the LSAT but had an epiphany when he went on a road trip and spent six weeks driving around Utah, camping out in various national parks. "I was thinking, *If I become a lawyer, I won't be able to do this.* My mother could never do this. I realized that time was more valuable to me than the money or the prestige." The best thing that ever happened to their family, he said, was his mother's appointment to the bench when he was in high school. As a judge, she had more manageable hours, and her stress level decreased markedly. "No one was happier than us," he said, referring to his father and brothers. "I was like, where is the governor so I can go shake her hand."

After college, David was accepted into the Teach for America program, where he was placed in a high school in Richmond, California, that was one of the worst-performing in the state. "We had riots. I taught special ed and some of my students were straight up Norteño gangsters." At times, he said, he felt "more like a bouncer than a teacher, but I felt like I was doing really good work. I loved my kids." He stayed six more years. Along the way, he fell in love, and he and his girlfriend had a son, Leo. He and Leo's mother are not together anymore. He describes her as driven in the same way his mother was and talks about her achievements with the same pride. Now he is dating someone he hopes to marry. The sticking point, though, is what David perceives as her more traditional values. "She wants to take my name and I am like, 'I don't want you to. What if we have a daughter? I don't want her thinking she has to take some dude's name.'" He firmly believes that both parents should work.

Joe, the middle child, is a Harvard Law School graduate who works at Paul, Weiss, and Rifkind, one of the country's largest and most prestigious firms. He, too, remembers his mother's constant travel and whirlwind schedule. Joe was something of a jock, lettering in soccer, basketball, and lacrosse. His mother didn't go to any of his sports events except Senior Night, a celebration for athletes and their families, when she watched him play his last soccer game. Afterward, Joe remembers her looking mildly surprised and telling him, "It turns out you're pretty good." But his mother's absence, he told me, "wasn't something I considered a hole in my life." His father was there, and in any event, "I was more interested in girls coming to my games than my mom."

Growing up, Joe had no intention of going to law school. But he, too, had an epiphany. After his mother was appointed to the court of appeals, there was a formal event where she was officially sworn in, her investiture ceremony. "It was a heartbreaking afternoon for me," Joe said, "because they made me skip a playoff soccer game to go. I was very, very upset and mad at my parents." But as he sat in the audience and listened to one speaker after another describing his mother's life-changing work, he was deeply moved. "I knew that she had done all this medical-malpractice litigation and worked for breast cancer survivors and women's organizations, but for the first time it was being told as a cohesive story of her career."

As Joe spoke, his voice began to break. "I'm sorry," he told me, "I am about to cry." He paused. "There was this story about how after she lost a trial, she was sitting in her car in the garage with her client and they were both crying. And I hadn't seen my mother like that ever. She had never been that way in front of us." Joe did cry before resuming. "I thought it was very admirable and I thought that becoming a lawyer would be a career well spent."

As I was conducting these interviews, I kept coming back to what Sarah Viren, an Arizona State University professor and creative-nonfiction writer, told me about how she and her wife, Marta, approach parenting their two children. Sarah has distinct memories of her own mother writing her dissertation at night as she pursued a PhD in psychology. When she had to study for an exam, she made parts of the drudgery into a game for Sarah and her siblings. "She showed us how she used mimetic devices to memorize diagnoses and we tried to help her think of crazy phrases to use. When she was learning how to give gifted tests, she tested them on the three of us, which I thought was super-fun. A lot of what she was doing spilled over into our life — we were involved. She was ambitious but we got to be there. I think that's nice. Marta and I try to talk about our work with our kids. What we are doing and what that means."

Sarah remembers her mother feeling guilty for taking short-cuts — pasta dinners with cream of mushroom soup for sauce, fish sticks. "But you know, we loved it," she said. "We had no idea there was this other world of organically grown vegetables." Sarah and Marta have different approaches to parenting their two children. "I think about this a lot — if I were married to a man, would I feel more guilty and would I be judged more? I don't want to do the Fun Run. Or the Turkey Trot. I don't think it is very important and I don't enjoy it. But Marta does. She likes to do the Turkey Trot."

She continued, "'Having it all' never resonated with me. I have ambitious friends who have to be good at everything — excellent at motherhood, excellent at their profession, excellent in their relationship. And so they feel like they are failing all the time. And for me,

I just want to be excellent in my profession. It is fine to be just okay as a mom. I don't want to be awful, and if I didn't do certain things like read to them, I would feel like I was failing, but I don't have to be the best. I don't care if I am not succeeding at mom-dom."

Sarah and Marta's children are now seven and four. Recently, Sarah watched them playing together and asked them what they were doing. "Work," they told her. I laughed, thinking about watching my daughter frantically typing on a "laptop" she had constructed out of two sides of a cardboard box. "I'm writing, Mommy," she'd told me proudly. "Just like you."

When my children are adults, what will they remember about my mothering? The Mother on the Card? No. Perfectly curated photographs of family joy of the kind used to sell fancy gilt picture frames? Probably not. Blurry images of absence and distraction, the times I was missing? Maybe, but not mostly, I don't think. My hope is that they remember a textured patchwork, the yelling and the fighting and the miserable parts, yes, but also, and more important, the many times we laughed so hard that tears rolled down our faces — at episodes of *The Office*, at inside jokes, or just at each other — the visit to the zoo when a seagull swooped down and ate our pizza, the time that Matt and I carried them on our backs across an icy stream in Yosemite National Park years after we had divorced, the day we brought our puppy home, the many nights we snuggled together in bed.

What they will also remember, I hope, is my work and how much it meant to my clients, to my students, to my readers, to me. And I hope that those memories will make them proud and also inspired to be equally ambitious in their own right.

The truth is that I love my children beyond all reason.

I feel the same way about my job.

And that's not only okay, it's awesome.

Acknowledgments

This book would not exist without my mother. Because of the example she set, because of her generous cooperation with the project, because of her unwavering support for the idea behind it. Throughout, my mother has encouraged me to tell the truth. Beyond measure, I am grateful to my mother.

I am also grateful to the "Ross-women": Gretchen, Dara, Tamara. You gave me hours of your time and taught me a great deal. It can be affirming to have one's fixed beliefs entirely upended.

To my writing partner, Valena Beety, who held me accountable even when the words were coming at a trickle and the world was crashing down all around us. Looking at your beautiful picture in the corner of my Zoom screen, I knew you were right there with me, even with the sound off. Our friendship was a lifeline, for my writing and for my soul. We found each other, held on tight, and crossed the finish line holding virtual hands.

To the dozens of incredible women across the United States who made the time to talk to me, with candor and vulnerability, about their work, their children, and their partners. About their hard, hard choices. You showed me how much more there is to ambition and to being a mother. The great pleasure of writing this book was the time I spent with each of you.

To my former editor at the *New York Times,* Jen Parker, who published my defense of working mothers. To my agent, Emma Patterson, who convinced me that there was a whole book inside of my op-ed and found the right home for it. You are always responsive to me, even when I am unreasonable. To my editor, Marisa Vigilante, I could not have asked for a sharper mind or a gentler scalpel-wielder. The book is so much better because of you. To Tracy Behar, Fanta Diallo, Lena Little, and the rest of the mighty Little, Brown Spark team. To Elizabeth Shreve and her team. To my intrepid researchers and fact-checkers: Elizabeth Bowman, Lila Garlinghouse, and Charlie Nelson Keever. Especially Charlie, who helped connect me to the next generation of mothers.

I am grateful to my sisters, Emily, Jill, and Dana. And to my father, who always told me I could do whatever I set my mind to do, including and especially taking the hardest cases and never, ever giving up. I forgive you for Florida, as I hope my children will forgive me for LA.

To my Boggle-playing bestie, Ben, who taught me that if I wanted to find new words, I had to change my point of view by turning the board.

Finally, to my beautiful children and two favorite people, Carter and Ella. You give me reason to live. And to Matt, who gave me my children. Without you, my life would be impossible.

Notes

PREFACE

1. Lisa Belkin, "Opting Out," *New York Times Magazine,* October 26, 2003, https://www.nytimes.com/2003/10/26/magazine/the-opt-out -revolution.html.

2. Judith Warner, "The Opt-Out Generation Wants Back In," *New York Times Magazine,* August 7, 2013, https://www.nytimes.com/2013/08/11 /magazine/the-opt-out-generation-wants-back-in.html.

3. Lara Bazelon, "I've Picked My Job Over My Kids," *New York Times,* June 29, 2019, https://www.nytimes.com/2019/06/29/opinion/sunday/ive -picked-my-job-over-my-kids.html.

4. Shelley J. Correll, Stephen Benard, and In Paik, "Getting a Job: Is There a Motherhood Penalty?," *American Journal of Sociology* 112, no. 5 (March 2007): 1297–339.

5. Lara Bazelon, "All the Single Mothers," *Slate,* May 11, 2019, https:// slate.com/human-interest/2019/05/single-moms-fewer-chores-free-time -married.html.

6. Sarah Jane Glynn, "The New Breadwinners: 2010 Update," *American Progress,* April 16, 2012, https://www.americanprogress.org/issues/economy /reports/2012/04/16/11377/the-new-breadwinners-2010-update/.

7. Rebecca J. Rosen, "Money-Rich and Time-Poor: Life in Two-Income Households," *The Atlantic,* November 4, 2015, https://www.theatlantic.com/business/archive/2015/11/work-life-balance-pew-report/414028/.

8. Kim Parker, Juliana Horowitz, and Rachel Minkin, "How the Coronavirus Outbreak Has—and Hasn't—Changed the Way Americans Work," Pew Research Center, December 9, 2020, https://www.pewresearch.org/social-trends/2020/12/09/how-the-coronavirus-outbreak-has-and-hasnt-changed-the-way-americans-work/.

9. James McDermott, e-mail to the author, June 30, 2019.

10. Yi-Jin Yu, "How Can We Help Working Women? Proposal Calls for a 'Marshall Plan for Moms,'" *Today,* March 8, 2021 (the article notes that women lost one million more jobs than men).

11. Austan Goolsbee, "The Battle to Come Over the Benefits of Working from Home," *New York Times,* July 20, 2021, https://www.nytimes.com/2021/07/20/business/remote-work-pay-bonus.html.

12. Adam McCann, "States Offering the Most Support During the COVID-19 Pandemic," WalletHub.com, April 28, 2020, https://wallethub.com/edu/states-offering-the-most-coronavirus-support/73333 (ranking the states that have provided the most support during the pandemic, including COVID-19-related medical services, food and housing assistance, and unemployment support); "State Paid Sick & Leave Provision Enactments Due to COVID-19," Partners Group, https://www.thepartnersgroup.com/state-paid-sick-leave-provision-enactments-due-to-covid-19/.

13. I corrected my daughter's creative spelling for clarity.

CHAPTER ONE: LOVE, MARRIAGE, BABY CARRIAGE

1. Gretchen Livingston, "They're Waiting Longer, but U.S. Women Today More Likely to Have Children Than a Decade Ago," Pew Research, January 18, 2018, https://www.pewresearch.org/social-trends/2018/01/18/theyre-waiting-longer-but-u-s-women-today-more-likely-to-have-children-than-a-decade-ago/.

2. Ilse Delbaere, Sarah Verbiest, and Tanja Tyden, "Knowledge About the Impact of Age on Fertility: A Brief Review," *Upsala Journal of Medical Sciences* 125 (2020): 167–74, https://www.tandfonline.com/doi/full/10.1080/03009734.2019.1707913.

3. ESHRE Capri Workshop Group, "Fertility and Ageing," *Human Reproduction Update* 11 (May/June 2005): 273.

4. Ibid.

5. "Infertility Causes," Cleveland Clinic, last reviewed December 2020, https://my.clevelandclinic.org/health/diseases/16083-infertility-causes; Chantel Cross, "Why Can't I Get Pregnant?," Johns Hopkins Medicine, 2021, https://www.hopkinsmedicine.org/health/wellness-and-prevention/why-cant-i-get-pregnant.

6. Hallie Levine Sklar, "Is It Too Late for a Baby?," *Health,* last updated December 19, 2019, https://www.health.com/condition/pregnancy/is-it-too-late-for-a-baby.

7. Rebecca Macatee, "Halle Berry Pregnant at 46: Here Are 5 More Stars Who Had a Baby After 40!," E! Entertainment News, April 5, 2013, https://www.eonline.com/news/405353/halle-berry-pregnant-at-46-here-are-5-more-stars-who-had-a-baby-after-40.

8. Marinus J. C. Eijkemans et al., "Too Old to Have Children? Lessons from Natural Fertility Populations," *Human Reproduction* 29, no. 6 (June 2014): 1304–12, https://doi.org/10.1093/humrep/deu056.

9. Sylvia Ann Hewlett, *Creating a Life: Professional Women and the Quest for Children* (New York: Hyperion, 2002), 33.

10. Ibid., 3.

11. Ibid., 7–8. Hewlett attributes this "extremely concrete piece of advice" to Cathryn Palmieri.

12. Caroline Bologna, "23 Times Tina Fey Hilariously Summed Up Parenting," *Huffington Post,* May 16, 2019; Zach Seemayer, "'Saturday Night Live': Maya Rudolph Gets Some Support from Her Kids in a Sweet Monologue," *Entertainment Tonight,* March 27, 2021; Lesley Messer, "Rachel Dratch Reveals Her Son's Father," *People,* December 2, 2020; Jacqueline Tourville, "Celeb Moms Who Had Babies After 35," Mom .com, October 27, 2014.

13. Jean M. Twenge, "How Long Can You Wait to Have a Baby," *The Atlantic,* July/August 2013, https://www.theatlantic.com/magazine/archive/2013/07/how-long-can-you-wait-to-have-a-baby/309374/.

14. Rachel Gurevich, "What Are the Chances of Getting Pregnant After 40?," Verywellfamily.com, updated November 30, 2020, https://www.verywellfamily.com/what-are-the-chances-of-getting-pregnant-after-40-1960287.

15. Reyhan Harmanci, "The Truth About Pregnancy Over 40," *New York Times,* November 12, 2019 (updated August 29, 2020), https://www.nytimes.com/2020/04/15/parenting/pregnancy/baby-after-40.html.

16. Twenge, "How Long Can You Wait."

17. Division of Reproductive Health, *2016 Assisted Reproductive Technology National Summary Report,* October 2018, https://www.cdc.gov /art/pdf/2016-report/ART-2016-National-Summary-Report.pdf.

18. Evita Almassi, "What Is a 'Geriatric Pregnancy'?," National Women's Health Network, May 14, 2019, https://nwhn.org/what-is-a-geriatric -pregnancy-at-35-can-i-have-a-normal-pregnancy/.

19. Virginia Sole-Smith and Nicole Harris, "Are You at Risk of Having a Baby with Down Syndrome?," Parents.com, last updated September 9, 2020, https://www.parents.com/health/down-syndrome/are-you-at-risk -of-having-a-baby-with-down-syndrome/.

20. "Percentage of Childless Women in the United States in 2018, by Age," Statista, October 28, 2021, https://www.statista.com/statistics/241535 /percentage-of-childless-women-in-the-us-by-age/.

21. Roni Caryn Rabin, "Put a Ring on It? Millennial Couples Are in No Hurry," *New York Times,* May 29, 2018.

22. Drew Desilver, "For Most U.S. Workers, Real Wages Have Barely Budged in Decades," Pew Research Center, August 7, 2018, https://www .pewresearch.org/fact-tank/2018/08/07/for-most-us-workers-real-wages -have-barely-budged-for-decades/.

23. Claire Cain Miller, "The 10-Year Baby Window That Is the Key to the Women's Pay Gap," *New York Times,* April 9, 2018, https://www .nytimes.com/2018/04/09/upshot/the-10-year-baby-window-that-is-the -key-to-the-womens-pay-gap.html.

24. Sara Eckel, "Sometimes, It's Not You, or the Math," *New York Times,* September 23, 2011, https://www.nytimes.com/2011/09/25/style /modern-love-sometimes-its-not-you-or-the-math.html.

25. Judith E. Owen Blakemore et al., "I Can't Wait to Get Married: Gender Differences in Drive to Marry," *Sex Roles* 53 (2005): 327–35. This study sampled 395 single people between the ages of eighteen and thirty-one who were "psychology students from a regional commuter campus of a state university in the midwestern United States." The racial breakdown was as follows: 88.6 percent were white, 6.1 percent were Black, 2 percent were Hispanic, and 1.5 percent were Asian.

26. S. M. Stanley, "What Is It with Men and Commitment, Anyway?," working paper based on a keynote address to the sixth annual Smart Marriages Conference, Washington, DC, last updated November 2019, 2002, http://www.box.net/shared/1zketqdii1ccnqb5vlf9.

27. While recent scientific research suggests that, like women's eggs, male sperm declines in quality as men age, the changes come later in life

for men than for women. See, e.g., Harry Fisch, *The Male Biological Clock* (New York: Free Press, 2015); Ana Swanson, "Why Men Should Also Worry About Waiting Too Long to Have Kids," *Washington Post,* October 27, 2015, https://www.washingtonpost.com/news/wonk/wp/2015/10/27/men-have-biological-clocks-too-so-why-does-no-one-talk-about-them/.

28. R. Sylvest et al., "Attitudes Toward Family Formation Men Attending Fertility Counseling," *Reproductive Biomedicine and Society Online* (July 2018), https://www.ncbi.nlm.nih.gov/pmc/articles/PMC6120434/.

29. Profile America Facts for Features, August 16, 2017, https://www.census.gov/content/dam/Census/newsroom/facts-for-features/2017/cb17-ff16.pdf.

30. William Safire, "On Language; A Woman of a Certain Age," *New York Times,* July 2, 1995.

31. Carol C. Nadelson et al., "To Marry or Not to Marry: A Choice," *American Journal of Psychiatry* 138, no. 10 (October 1981); see also Janet Cockrum and Priscilla White, "Influences on the Life Satisfaction of Never-Married Men and Women," *Family Relations* 34, no. 4 (1985): 551–56. The authors noted that single women were "seen as less feminine, less loving and nurturing, less sexually attractive, and more selfish."

32. Claudia Goldin and Lawrence F. Katz, "Putting the 'Co' in Education: Timing, Reasons, and Consequences from 1835 to the Present," *Journal of Human Capital* 5, no. 4 (2011): 412–23, https://scholar.harvard.edu/files/goldin/files/putting_the_co_in_education_timing_reasons_and_consequences_of_college_coeducation_from_1835-_present.pdf.

33. "Percentage of U.S. Population Who Have Completed Four Years of College or More from 1940 to 2020, by Gender," Statista, https://www.statista.com/statistics/184272/educational-attainment-of-college-diploma-or-higher-by-gender/.

34. Nadelson, "To Marry or Not to Marry."

35. Arline L. Bronzaft, "College Women Want a Career, Marriage, and Children," *Psychological Reports* 35, (December 1974): 1031–34. Dr. Bronzaft went on to win the American Psychological Association's Presidential Citation in 2018 for her lifelong professional achievements, which included serving as an adviser to five New York City mayors on children's health, city noise, and psychological development; see https://www.apa.org/about/governance/president/citation/arline-bronzaft.

36. "Percentage of the U.S. Population Who Have Completed Four Years of College or More."

37. Quoctrung Bui and Claire Cain Miller, "The Age That Women Have Babies: How a Gap Divides America," *New York Times,* August 4, 2018, https://www.nytimes.com/interactive/2018/08/04/upshot/up-birth-age -gap.html.

38. W. Bradford Wilcox and Wendy Wang, "The Marriage Divide: How and Why Working-Class Families Are More Fragile Today," Institute for Family Studies, September 25, 2017.

39. Naomi Cahn and June Carbone, *Red Families v. Blue Families* (New York: Oxford University Press, 2010).

CHAPTER TWO: THE CULT OF MOTHERHOOD

1. Sharon Hays, *The Cultural Contradictions of Motherhood* (New Haven, CT: Yale University Press, 1996).

2. Bethany L. Johnson and Margaret M. Quinlan, *You're Doing It Wrong! Mothering, Media, and Medical Expertise* (New Brunswick, NJ: Rutgers University Press, 2019).

3. Alexandra Sacks, "The Birth of a Mother," *New York Times,* May 8, 2017, https://www.nytimes.com/2017/05/08/well/family/the-birth-of-a -mother.html.

4. Julie Ma, "25 Famous Women on Becoming New Moms," *Cut,* May 28, 2018, https://www.thecut.com/article/celebrity-moms-quotes-about -motherhood.html.

5. Jaime Harkin, "The Thoroughly Modern Mogul," *People,* January 27, 2020.

6. Jen Juneau, "Cardi B Says 'I Met My Match' in Newborn Daughter Kulture: 'I Can't Believe I Have a Boss,'" *People,* July 27, 2018, https:// people.com/parents/cardi-b-met-her-match-baby-girl-new-motherhood/.

7. "Salma Hayek: I Would Give Up Acting for Valentina," *People,* updated December 2, 2020, https://people.com/parents/savages-usa-today -salma-hayek-quit-acting-for-valentina/.

8. Lisa Belkin, "What Does She Mean by 'Mom in Chief'?," *Huffington Post,* November 5, 2012.

9. Rasha Ali, "Larry King Has 'Less of a Fear of Dying Now' After Near-Fatal Stroke, Talks Recent Divorce," *USA Today,* February 5, 2020, https://www.usatoday.com/story/entertainment/celebrities/2020/02/05 /larry-king-talks-surviving-stroke-health/4665721002/.

10. Melissa Seelye, "The Cult of Motherhood: A Century of Mother's Days," *Feminist Wire,* May 11, 2014.

11. Allison Aubrey, "Xanax or Zoloft for Moms-to-Be: A New Study Assesses Safety," NPR, September 18, 2017, https://www.npr.org/sections/health-shots/2017/09/18/551020800/xanax-or-zoloft-for-moms-to-be-a-new-study-assesses-safety.

12. Bruce Drake, "Few Americans Say a Mother Working Full-Time Is Good for Her Children," Pew Research Center, April 3, 2013, https://www.pewresearch.org/fact-tank/2013/04/03/few-americans-say-a-mother-working-full-time-is-ideal-for-children/.

13. Jerry A. Jacobs and Kathleen Gerson, "Unpacking Americans' Views of the Employment of Mothers and Fathers Using National Vignette Data Survey," *Gender and Society* 30 (2016): 413–41. It is worth noting, however, that when the authors drilled down into the data, they found that support for young mothers working full-time outside of the home varied depending on the specifics of their jobs, their job satisfaction, their marital status, their financial contribution to the household, and their childcare arrangements.

14. Denise-Marie Ordway, "What Research Says About the Kids of Working Moms," *Journalist's Resource*, August 6, 2018, https://journalistsresource.org/economics/working-mother-employment-research/.

15. Kathleen L. McGinn et al., "Learning from Mum: Cross-National Evidence Linking Maternal Employment and Adult Children's Outcomes," *Work, Employment and Society* 33, no. 3 (2019): 374–400, https://journals.sagepub.com/eprint/DQzHJAJMUYWQevh577wr/full; Dina Gerdeman, "Kids of Working Moms Grow into Happy Adults," *Working Knowledge*, July 16, 2018, https://hbswk.hbs.edu/item/kids-of-working-moms-grow-into-happy-adults.

16. Susan Douglas and Meredith Michaels, *The Mommy Myth* (New York: Free Press, 2005).

17. Cressida Leyshon, "This Week in Fiction: Lauren Groff on the Cult of Motherhood," *The New Yorker*, May 16, 2016.

CHAPTER THREE: LEARNING FIRSTHAND
ABOUT THE SECOND SHIFT

1. In the 1970s, few were publicly advocating for gay civil partnerships, much less gay marriage, and the percentage of gay partners with children was tiny. It was not until the early 2000s that acceptance of gay rights, including the concept of gay families with children, began to take hold.

2. Jennifer Szalai, "The Complicated Origins of 'Having It All,'" *New York Times Magazine*, January 2, 2015.

3. Ruth Rosen, "Who Said We Could Have It All?," Open Democracy, August 2, 2012, https://www.opendemocracy.net/en/5050/who-said-we-could-have-it-all/.

4. Melissa Kirsch, "Why 'Free to Be . . . You and Me' Was the Most Important Album of Our Youth," *Scary Mommy,* August 5, 2005, https://www.scarymommy.com/why-free-to-beyou-and-me-was-the-most-important-album-of-our-youth/.

5. George Guilder, "Women in the Work Force," *The Atlantic,* September 1986, https://www.theatlantic.com/magazine/archive/1986/09/women-in-the-work-force/304924/.

6. Ibid.

7. Cynthia Hess, Tanima Ahmed, and Jeff Hayes, "Providing Unpaid Household and Care Work in the United States: Uncovering Inequality," briefing paper C487, Institute for Women's Policy Research (January 2020).

8. Kayla Van Gorp, "The Second Shift: Why It Is Diminishing but Still an Issue," *The Review: A Journal of Undergraduate Student Research* 14 (2013): 31–37.

9. Actual names and identifying details have been changed at the request of the interview subject.

10. Gretchen Livingston and Deja Thomas, "Among 41 Countries, Only U.S. Lacks Paid Parental Leave," Pew Research Center, December 16, 2019, https://www.pewresearch.org/fact-tank/2019/12/16/u-s-lacks-mandated-paid-parental-leave/.

11. Economic News Release, U.S. Bureau of Labor Statistics, last modified July 22, 2021, https://www.bls.gov/news.release/atus.t09.htm.

12. Findings from the 2017 Kaiser Women's Health Survey, March 13, 2018, https://www.kff.org/womens-health-policy/issue-brief/women-work-and-family-health-key-findings-from-the-2017-kaiser-womens-health-survey/.

13. Darcy Lockman, "Too Often Working Mothers Do Far More of the Childcare Than Their Husbands. Here's How to Fix That," *Time,* May 16, 2019.

14. Perhaps not surprisingly, some men push back when confronted by these studies and self-reports by women. Seventy percent of fathers say that they split domestic chores equally while only 44 percent of their female partners say they do; see "Women in the Workplace 2020," McKinsey and Company (2021), https://wiw-report.s3.amazonaws.com/Women_in_the_Workplace_2020.pdf.

15. Jessica Bennett, "'I Feel Like I Have Five Jobs': Moms Navigate the Pandemic," *New York Times,* March 20, 2020.

16. "Seven Charts That Show COVID-19's Impact on Women's Employment," McKinsey and Company (March 8, 2021), https://www.mckinsey.com/featured-insights/diversity-and-inclusion/seven-charts-that-show-covid-19s-impact-on-womens-employment#; Nicole Bateman and Martha Ross, "Why Has COVID-19 Been Especially Harmful for Working Women?," Brookings (October 2020).

17. It is also notable that the economic devastation wrought by the pandemic has had a disproportionate impact on women's employment. Because women are overrepresented in service industries, such as restaurants and retail, which have been hardest hit, women have lost a net of 5.4 million jobs during the pandemic, compared with 4.4 million lost by men. See Diana Boesch and Shilpa Phadke, "When Women Lose All the Jobs: Essential Actions for a Gender-Equitable Recovery," Center for American Progress, February 1, 2021, https://cdn.americanprogress.org/content/uploads/2021/01/29041540/WomenLoseJobs-brief.pdf?_ga=2.212257948.966411441.1616111546-2002805608.1615425830.

18. Melanie E. Brewster, "Lesbian Women and Household Labor Division: A Systematic Review of Scholarly Research from 2000 to 2015," *Journal of Lesbian Studies* 21 (2017): 47–69, https://www.tandfonline.com/doi/full/10.1080/10894160.2016.1142350; Charlotte J. Patterson, Erin L. Sutfin, and Megan Fulcher, "Division of Labor Among Lesbian and Heterosexual Parenting Couples: Correlates of Specialized Versus Shared Patterns," *Journal of Adult Development* 11 (2004): 179–89.

19. Abbie E. Goldberg, JuliAnna Z. Smith, and Maureen Perry-Jenkins, "The Division of Labor in Lesbian, Gay, and Heterosexual New Adoptive Parents," *Journal of Marriage and Family* 74 (August 2012): 812–28, https://onlinelibrary.wiley.com/doi/abs/10.1111/j.1741-3737.2012.00992.x.

20. Claire Cain Miller, "How Same-Sex Couples Divide Chores and What It Reveals About Modern Parenting," *New York Times,* May 16, 2018.

21. Tiffany Dufu, "I Was the Family Micromanager—Here's How I Learned to Let Go," *Good Housekeeping,* February 13, 2017, https://www.goodhousekeeping.com/life/parenting/a42864/tiffany-dufu-drop-the-ball/. See also Tiffany Dufu, *Drop the Ball: Expect Less from Yourself and Flourish in Work and Life* (New York: Flatiron Books, 2017).

22. Oliver Burkeman, "Dirty Secret: Why Is There Still a Housework Gender Gap?," *The Guardian,* February 17, 2018.

23. "Statistics on Stay-at-Home Dads," National At-Home Dad Network, last accessed March 18, 2021, https://www.athomedad.org/media-resources/statistics/.

CHAPTER FOUR: THE TOXICITY OF FEMALE AMBITION

1. Mimi Hu's education was paid for by the Freeman Foundation.

2. Robin Romm, ed., *Double Bind: Women on Ambition* (New York: W. W. Norton, 2017).

3. Robin J. Ely and Irene Padavic, "What's Really Holding Women Back?," *Harvard Business Review* 98, no. 2 (March–April 2020): 58–67.

4. Gwen Ifill, "The 1992 Campaign: Hillary Clinton Defends Her Conduct in Law Firm," *New York Times,* March 17, 1992. Clinton was also criticized for keeping her maiden name, Rodham, for ten years after her marriage to Clinton. Voters' disapproval with that choice, she said, was a factor in her husband's failed bid for reelection as governor of Arkansas in 1980. When Bill Clinton ran again in 1982, he announced that his wife would "heretofore" ask to be addressed as Hillary Rodham Clinton. According to the *Washington Post,* "It was a bow to tradition but it was also a political play. It was an attempt to disrupt the idea that she was an excessively ambitious woman or disinterested in the traditional role of the state's first lady"; see Janell Ross, "The Complicated History Behind Hillary Clinton's Evolving Name," *Washington Post,* July 25, 2015.

5. "For the Record: Obama Endorses Clinton as 'Likable Enough,'" *USA Today,* June 10, 2016, https://www.usatoday.com/story/news/politics/onpolitics/2016/06/10/record-obama-endorses-clinton-likable-enough/85675584/; Rebecca Sinderbrand, "Analysis: Why Clinton's Bid Failed," CNN Politics, June 6, 2008, https://www.cnn.com/2008/POLITICS/06/06/clinton.race/index.html; Patrick Healy, "After Delay, Clinton Embarks on a Likability Tour," *New York Times,* December 19, 2007, https://www.nytimes.com/2007/12/19/us/politics/19clintons.html; Sady Doyle, "America Loves Women Like Hillary Clinton, as Long as They Are Not Asking for a Promotion," *Quartz,* February 26, 2016, https://qz.com/624346/america-loves-women-like-hillary-clinton-as-long-as-theyre-not-asking-for-a-promotion/.

6. Amy Chozick, "Hillary Clinton and the Return of the (Unbaked) Cookies," *New York Times,* November 5, 2016.

7. Daniella Diaz, "Trump Calls Clinton a Nasty Woman," CNN, October 20, 2016.

8. See, e.g., Farida Jalalzai, "A Comparative Assessment of Hillary Clinton's Presidential Race," *Socius* 4 (January 2018). In it, she argues that gender, "evident in the persistent negativity that Clinton faced in the media coverage and among the general public, contributed in part to the electoral outcome." See also Clare Foran, "The Curse of Hillary Clinton's Ambition," *The Atlantic,* September 17, 2016, https://www.theatlantic .com/politics/archive/2016/09/clinton-trust-sexism/500489/, and Doyle, "America Loves Women Like Hillary Clinton."

9. Meghan Keneally, "Hillary Clinton's Progress Trying to Shatter That Highest, Hardest Glass Ceiling," ABC News, November 9, 2016.

10. Ruth Graham, "For Conservative Christian Women, Amy Coney Barrett's Success Is Personal," *New York Times,* September 28, 2020. "What does she have, six or seven children?" asked Pat Robertson on the Christian Broadcasting Network in 2018 when Barrett was first mentioned as a potential Supreme Court pick. "That's got to be tough, to be a judge and take care of all those kids, won't it?"

11. Brian Schwartz, "Some Biden Allies Wage Shadow Campaign to Stop Kamala Harris from Becoming Vice President," CNBC News, July 29, 2020.

12. Jessica Grose, "Ambition Has Always Been 'Ladylike,'" *New York Times,* August 11, 2020.

13. Keneshia Grant, a professor of political science at Howard University, noted that the white women under serious consideration for the vice presidential slot did not receive the same critique. "This [ambition] narrative that explicitly puts Sen. Kamala Harris in a special place to suggest that her ambition is wrong or not welcomed is problematic. And I think it signals a worry about a Black woman president and whether it's time for a Black woman president." See Eugene Scott, "In Accusations of Being Too Ambitious, Some Black Women See a Double Standard," *Washington Post,* August 3, 2020.

14. In a first-person essay she wrote for *Elle,* Harris described missing her stepdaughter's high-school graduation to grill FBI director James Comey on Capitol Hill. "I agonized over this scheduling conflict," she wrote, and then went on to state, "but [I] made it home in time for our time: Family dinner that night." See Kamala Harris, "Sen. Harris on Being 'Momala,'" *Elle,* May 10, 2019.

15. Lilee Williams, "VP Candidate Kamala Harris' Favorite Title Is Momala," Moms.com, August 13, 2020, https://www.moms.com/vp-candidate-kamala-harris-favorite-title-is-momala/.

16. Colby Itkowitz et al., "Vice Presidential Debate: Highlights and Fact Checks," *Washington Post,* October 7, 2020.

17. Claire Cain Miller and Alisha Haridasani Gupta, "Why Supermom Gets Star Billing on Résumés for Public Office," *New York Times,* October 14, 2020.

18. Ibid.

19. Steven Mintz, "The Other Gender Gap," *Inside Higher Ed,* August 4, 2019, https://www.insidehighered.com/blogs/higher-ed-gamma/other-gender-gap.

20. Mark J. Perry, "Chart of the Day: The Incredible 13M Gender College Degree Gap Since 1982 Favoring Women," *AEIdeas,* February 20, 2019, https://www.aei.org/carpe-diem/chart-of-the-day-the-incredible-13m-gender-college-degree-gap-since-1982-favoring-women/.

21. Facebook COO Sheryl Sandberg brought renewed attention to this study in her bestselling book *Lean In.* See also Danielle N. Sunday, "Challenges Women Face Leading in Work and Life," Penn State University, August 14, 2013, https://sites.psu.edu/daniellesunday/2013/08/24/challenges-women-face-leading-in-work-and-life/.

22. Lyn Turknett, "Who Are Heidi and Howard and Why Does It Matter?," Turknett Leadership Group, January 2020, https://www.turknett.com/wp-content/uploads/2020/01/Who-are-Heidi-and-Howard-and-Why-Does-It-Matter_.pdf.

23. Katherine Rosman, "Abby Phillip Is Next-Gen CNN," *New York Times,* November 13, 2020.

24. "Women in Politics, the Workplace, and Family Life," Associated Press and NORC Center for Public Affairs Research, March 2019, https://apnorc.org/wp-content/uploads/2020/02/APNORC_GSS_gender_equality_2019.pdf.

25. Leonardo Bursztyn, Thomas Fujiwara, and Amanda Pallais, "'Acting Wife': Marriage Market Incentives and Labor Market Investments," *American Economic Review* 107, no. 11 (November 2017): 3288–319.

26. Anna Fels, *Necessary Dreams: Ambition in Changing Women's Lives* (New York: Pantheon 2004).

27. Lara Bazelon, "What It Takes to Be a Trial Lawyer if You're Not a Man," *The Atlantic,* September 2018. Several paragraphs in this chapter are paraphrased or taken verbatim from this piece.

28. Catherine Saint Louis, "Up the Career Ladder, Lipstick in Hand," *New York Times,* October 12, 2011.

29. Debora L. Spar, "Aging and My Beauty Dilemma," *New York Times,* September 24, 2016.

30. See S.B. 188, Reg. Sess. § 2, § 3 (Cal. 2019-2020), amending § 212.1 of the California Education Code and § 12926 of the California Government Code, respectively. Similar legislation has been passed in New York and New Jersey and is pending in other states. See 2019 Assemb. Bill A07797A (N.Y. 2019); S.B. S3945, Reg. Sess. (N.J. 2019); S.B. No. 165, Reg. Sess. (N.C. 2021); Aimee Simeon, "Connecticut Is Officially Making Natural Hair Discrimination Illegal," Refinery29, March 2, 2021, https://www.refinery29.com/en-us/2021/03/10339549/connecticut-natural-hair-discrimination-crown-act.

31. S.B. 188 § 1(b) (Cal. 2019-2020).

32. Samantha Grossman, "The Insidious Sexism of Resting Bitch Face," *Week,* January 10, 2019. She notes that the phrase is "actually insidious and sexist" and that there is a double standard because "if a man's neutral expression seems unpleasant or annoyed, that's him getting to be a person."

33. Name and identifying details have been changed at the request of the interview subject.

34. Emma Gray, "Every Woman Should Read Reese Witherspoon's Stunning Speech About Ambition," *Huffington Post,* November 10, 2015.

CHAPTER FIVE: I'M IN LOVE . . . WITH MY JOB

1. "Family and Medical Leave Act," U.S. Department of Labor, last accessed September 29, 2021, https://www.dol.gov/agencies/whd/fmla.

2. Since 1993, only fifteen states and the District of Columbia have expanded unpaid leave benefits beyond FMLA standards by either increasing the amount of leave time offered or expanding the definition of an eligible family member; see "Paid Family and Sick Leave in the U.S.," Kaiser Family Foundation, December 14, 2020, https://www.kff.org/womens-health-policy/fact-sheet/paid-family-leave-and-sick-days-in-the-u-s/. A company offering even as little as sixteen weeks of paid leave will easily make it into the top twenty U.S. companies with the best family-leave policies in the United States; see Richard Feloni, "These Are the Top 14 US Companies Giving New Parents at Least 4 Months of Paid Time Off," *Business Insider,* June 24, 2019,

https://www.businessinsider.com/best-parental-leave-policies-from-large
-us-companies-2019-6.

3. Linda R. Hirshman, *Get to Work: A Manifesto for Women of the World* (New York: Viking, 2006), 3.

4. Ibid., 16.

5. Ibid., 3.

6. Sharon Hays, *The Cultural Contradictions of Motherhood* (New Haven, CT: Yale University Press, 1998).

7. Roos IJsendijk, e-mail to the author, July 1, 2019.

8. Gretchen Livingston, "Stay-at-Home Moms and Dads Account for About One-in-Five U.S. Parents," Pew Research Center, September 24, 2018, https://www.pewresearch.org/fact-tank/2018/09/24/stay-at-home-moms -and-dads-account-for-about-one-in-five-u-s-parents/.

9. "Why Lillian Gave Up Her Career, Part 1," Postmodern Family, July 2, 2017, http://thepostmodernfamily.com/2017/07/02/why-lillian -gave-up-her-career-part-1/; "Why Lillian Gave Up Her Career, Part 2," Postmodern Family, July 2, 2017, http://thepostmodernfamily.com/2017 /07/02/why-lillian-gave-up-her-career-part-2/.

10. According to a 2021 news report, "Attacks on feminists, queer people and people of different cultural backgrounds are not difficult to find under the #tradwife hashtag"; see Anna Kelsey-Sugg and Siobhan Marin, "For Some Being a Tradwife Is About More Time with Family. For Others, It's a Dangerous Far-Right Ideology," ABC Radio National, August 21, 2021, https://www.abc.net.au/news/2021-08-22/tradwife-movement -personal-pleasures-or-extreme-right-ideologies/100356514. One of Lillian's posts from 2019 links to an article that states: "You no longer have the right to pull your child out of relationship and sex education (now under the banner of 'health education'). Your 4 year old will now be taught in a classroom . . . affirming that some children don't feel the gender they were born into. They're being taught from the very first year of school that biological sex is different from mental gender—an IDEOLOGY, not fact." Another news report says that "the #tradwife movement is especially popular among white supremacists, who are extremely down with the message that white women should submit to their husband and focus on making as many white babies as possible"; see Hadley Freeman, "'Tradwives': The New Trend for Submissive Women Has a Dark Heart and History," *The Guardian*, January 20, 2020. Neither Lillian nor Felipe is Caucasian.

CHAPTER SIX: GETTING FREE

1. Mitra Toossi and Teresa L. Morisi, "Women in the Workforce Before, During, and After the Great Recession," U.S. Bureau of Labor Statistics (July 2017).

2. Ibid.

3. Ibid.

4. Elisabeth Jacobs and Kate Bahn, "Women's History Month: U.S. Women's Labor Force Participation," Washington Center for Equitable Growth, March 22, 2019.

5. Kerri Anne Renzulli, "This New Bill Before Congress Could Save Parents Thousands of Dollars a Year—Here's How," CNBC, February 27, 2019.

6. Brigid Schulte and Alieza Durana, "The New America Care Report," New America Foundation, September 28, 2016, https://www.newamerica .org/better-life-lab/policy-papers/new-america-care-report/.

7. Maggie Germano, "Women Are Working More Than Ever, but They Still Take on Most Household Responsibilities," *Forbes,* March 27, 2019, https://www.forbes.com/sites/maggiegermano/2019/03/27/women-are -working-more-than-ever-but-they-still-take-on-most-household -responsibilities/?sh=19bd77c952e9; Darcy Lockman, "Too Often, Working Mothers Do Far More of the Childcare Than Their Husbands. Here's How to Fix That," *Time,* May 16, 2019, https://time.com/5589770 /parenting-working-women-domestic-balance/.

8. Francine D. Blau and Lawrence M. Kahn, "Female Labor Supply: Why Is the U.S. Falling Behind?," discussion paper no. 7140, presented at the American Economic Association Meeting in San Diego, January 2013.

9. "Senator Murry Reintroduces Comprehensive Child Care and Early Learning Bill to Ensure #ChildCare4All, Builds on Momentum from Washington State Stories," news release, Murray.Senate.gov, February 26, 2019, https://www.murray.senate.gov/public/index.cfm/2019/2/video-senator -murray-reintroduces-comprehensive-child-care-and-early-learning-bill-to -ensure-childcare4all-builds-on-momentum-from-washington-state-stories.

10. Chaudry and Hamm, "The Child Care for Working Families Act."

11. Nicole Bateman and Martha Ross, "Why Has COVID-19 Been Especially Harmful for Working Women?," Brookings (October 2020); Tim Henderson, "Mothers Are 3 Times More Likely Than Fathers to Have Lost Jobs in the Pandemic," Pew Research Center, September 28, 2020.

12. Alicia Sasser Modestino, "Coronavirus Child-Care Crisis Will Set Women Back a Generation," *Washington Post,* July 29, 2020.

13. Tyler Atkinson and Alex Richter, "Pandemic Disproportionately Affects Women, Minority Labor Force Participation," Federal Reserve Bank of Dallas, November 10, 2020.

14. Much of this section appeared in slightly different form in Lara Bazelon, "Divorce Can Be an Act of Radical Self-Love," *New York Times,* September 30, 2021.

15. Names and identifying details have been changed at the request of the interviewee to preserve anonymity.

16. Jayita Poduval and Murali Poduval, "Working Mothers: How Much Working, How Much Mothers, and Where Is the Womanhood?," *Mens Sana Monographs* 7, no. 1 (January–December 2009): 63–79, https://www.ncbi.nlm.nih.gov/pmc/articles/PMC3151456/.

17. Tracy McVeigh, "The Biggest Financial Risk for Women Today? Embarking on a Relationship," *The Guardian,* March 18, 2017.

18. Poduval and Poduval, "Working Mothers."

19. Katherine Weisshaar, "From Opt Out to Blocked Out: The Challenges for Labor Market Re-Entry After Family Related Employment Lapses," *American Sociological Review* 83, no. 1 (2018).

20. Julia Zimbalist, e-mail to the author, June 30, 2019.

21. Dimitri Mortelmans, Gert Thielemans, and Layla Van den Berg, "Parents Returning to Parents: Does Migration Background Have an Influence on the 'Boomerang Effect' Among Parents After Divorce?," in M. Kreyenfeld and H. Trappe, eds., *Parental Life Courses After Separation and Divorce in Europe* (Cham, Switzerland: Springer, 2020), 83–102.

22. Dimitri Mortelmans, "Economic Consequences of Divorce: A Review," in ibid., 23–41; Ben Steverman, "Divorce Destroys Finances of Americans Over 50, Studies Show," *Bloomberg News,* July 19, 2019.

23. Stacy Francis, "The Biggest Financial Risk a Woman Can Take Is Getting Married," Francis Financial, last accessed November 18, 2021, https://francisfinancial.com/the-biggest-financial-risk-a-woman-can-take-is-getting-married/.

24. Stacy Francis, "Money Stress Traps Many Women into Staying in Unhappy Marriages," CNBC, August 13, 2019.

25. Sarah Jane Glynn and Katie Hamm, "The Economics of Caregiving for Working Mothers," Center for American Progress, December 10, 2019.

26. Ibid.; Cheridan Christnacht and Briana Sullivan, U.S. Census Bureau, May 8, 2020.

27. Sarah Jane Glynn, "Breadwinning Mothers Continue to Be the U.S. Norm," Center for American Progress, May 10, 2019. The higher number of breadwinning Black mothers is explained, in part, by the fact that the majority of Black mothers are raising families on their own; see "Breadwinner Mothers by Race/Ethnicity and State," Institute for Women's Policy Research, September 2016, https://iwpr.org/wp-content/uploads /2020/08/Q054.pdf. Similarly, households headed by Latina mothers constituted 24.4 percent of Latinx family households (in a 2018 study). In contrast, that same study found that white women headed only 12.7 percent of households and Asian American women headed 11.7 percent of Asian American family households; see Jocelyn Frye, "On the Frontlines at Work and at Home: The Disproportionate Economic Effects of the Coronavirus Pandemic on Women of Color," Center for American Progress, April 23, 2020, https://www.americanprogress.org/issues/women /reports/2020/04/23/483846/frontlines-work-home/.

28. Sreedhari D. Desai, Dolly Chugh, and Arthur Brief, "Marriage Structure and Resistance to the Gender Revolution in the Workplace," UNC Kenan-Flagler research paper no. 2013–19 (March 2012).

29. Jill Filipovic, "Are Women Allowed to Love Their Jobs?," *New York Times,* April 28, 2017.

30. Ibid.

31. Sonyan White, "The Brighter Side of Single Mom Life: Why Women Are Living Happily Ever After Divorce," *Connected Women,* June 7, 2017, https://www.connectedwomen.co/magazine/the-brighter-side-of -single-mom-life-why-more-women-are-living-happily-ever-after-divorce/.

32. Lara Bazelon, "Confessions of a Part-Time Mom," *Slate,* June 13, 2017, https://slate.com/human-interest/2017/06/divorce-and-shared -custody-suits-me-and-it-suits-my-kids-too.html.

33. Mary Daniels, e-mail to the author, July 4, 2019.

34. Lara Bazelon, "From Divorce, a Fractured Beauty," *New York Times,* September 24, 2015.

35. Bateman and Ross, "Why Has COVID-19 Been Especially Harmful."

36. The authors Hana Schank and Elizabeth Wallace tell many of these stories in their book *The Ambition Decisions: What Women Know About Work, Family, and the Path to Building a Life* (New York: Penguin, 2019).

37. "Senator Murray, Senator Cantwell Introduce Bill to Help Families Pay for Child Care," news release, February 10, 2021, https://www .murray.senate.gov/public/index.cfm/mobile/newsreleases?ID=67704AE2

-AE85-40E4-B837-7BCA7371AAAE#:~:text=In%202019%2C%20she%20
also%20introduced,wages%20for%20early%20childhood%20educators.

38. Jason DeParle, "In Stimulus Bill, a Policy Revolution in Aid for Children," *New York Times,* March 7, 2021.

CHAPTER SEVEN: EMBRACING IMBALANCE

1. J. F. Meyer, "History Repeats Itself: Restorative Justice in Native American Communities," *Journal of Contemporary Criminal Justice* 14, no. 1 (February 1998): 42–57.

2. Emily Alpert Reyes and Matt Lait, "LA to Pay $24 Million to Two Men Imprisoned for Decades After Wrongful Murder Convictions," *Los Angeles Times,* January 19, 2016.

3. Cara Chocano, "Calling Yourself 'Humbled' Doesn't Sound as Humble as It Used To," *New York Times Magazine,* January 24, 2017.

4. Kaitlin Menza, "#LuckyGirl Is the New #Humblebrag," *Cosmopolitan,* June 6, 2013.

5. Hannah Seligson, "The #LuckyGirl's Lie," *The Atlantic,* September 21, 2015.

6. Shannon Bendixen, "Women Leaders and Luck," Center for Creative Leadership, November 20, 2020, https://www.ccl.org/articles/leading-effectively-articles/women-luck-credit-success/.

7. Andrew W. Hait, "Number of Women-Owned Firms Increased 0.6% from 2017 to 2018," U.S. Census Bureau, March 29, 2021.

8. Eduardo Porter, "How the Unemployment System Failed," *New York Times,* January 21, 2021.

9. Andrew Stettner and Elizabeth Pancotti, "12 Million Workers Face Jobless Benefit Cliff on December 26," Century Foundation, November 18, 2020; Christopher Rugaber, "Trump's Hesitation on COVID-19 Relief Bill Will Delay Stimulus Payments for Unemployed," Associated Press, December 29, 2020; Diana Boesch and Shilpa Phadke, "When Women Lose All the Jobs: Essential Actions for a Gender-Equitable Recovery," Center for American Progress, February 1, 2021. See also Nicole Bateman and Martha Ross, "Why Has COVID-19 Been Especially Harmful for Working Women?," Brookings (October 2020), https://www.brookings.edu/essay/why-has-covid-19-been-especially-harmful-for-working-women/.

10. Boesch and Phadke, "When Women Lose All the Jobs."

11. Annalyn Kurtz, "The U.S. Economy Lost 140,000 Jobs in December. All of Them Were Held by Women," CNN, January 8, 2021.

12. Scott Horsley, "'Overlooked': Asian American Jobless Rate Surges but Few Take Notice," NPR, October 20, 2020; Erica Hellerstein, "'I'm So Scared': California Nail Salon Workers Face Ruin as Pandemic Wears On," *San Francisco Chronicle,* September 19, 2020.

13. Kurtz, "The U.S. Economy Lost 140,000 Jobs in December."

14. Tim Henderson, "Mothers Are 3 Times More Likely Than Fathers to Have Lost Jobs in Pandemic," Pew Research Center, September 28, 2020, https://www.pewtrusts.org/en/research-and-analysis/blogs/stateline /2020/09/28/mothers-are-3-times-more-likely-than-fathers-to-have-lost -jobs-in-pandemic; Boesch and Phadke, "When Women Lose All the Jobs."

15. Rakesh Kochhar, "Unemployment Rose Higher in Three Months of COVID-19 Than It Did in Two Years of the Great Recession," Pew Research Center, June 11, 2020, https://www.pewresearch.org/fact-tank/2020 /06/11/unemployment-rose-higher-in-three-months-of-covid-19-than -it-did-in-two-years-of-the-great-recession/; "The Employment Situation," U.S. Bureau of Labor Statistics, September 3, 2021, https://www.bls.gov /news.release/pdf/empsit.pdf.

16. Dylan Matthews, "Joe Biden Just Launched the Second War on Poverty," *Vox,* March 10, 2021, https://www.vox.com/policy-and-politics /22319572/joe-biden-american-rescue-plan-war-on-poverty; Heather Long, Alyssa Fowers, and Andrew Van Dam, "Biden Stimulus Showers Money on Americans, Sharply Cutting Poverty and Favoring Individuals Over Businesses," *Washington Post,* March 6, 2021, https://www.washingtonpost.com /business/2021/03/06/biden-stimulus-poverty-checks/.

17. Jonathan Weisman, "From Cradle to Grave, Democrats Move to Expand Social Safety Net," *New York Times,* September 6, 2021.

18. *Tikkun olam* is a Hebrew phrase meaning "repair the world," synonymous with the principle of social action and the pursuit of social justice in modern Judaism.

CHAPTER EIGHT: THE KIDS ARE ALL RIGHT

1. Kathleen L. McGinn et al., "Learning from Mum: Cross-National Evidence Linking Maternal Employment and Adult Children's Outcomes," *Work, Employment and Society* 33, no. 3 (2019), https://journals.sagepub .com/eprint/DQzHJAJMUYWQevh577wr/full.

2. Jacqueline Howard, "Having a Working Mother Has Benefits for Kids Later in Life, Study Says," CNN, July 18, 2018, https://www.cnn.com /2018/07/18/health/working-moms-kids-study.

3. McGinn et al., "Learning from Mum."

4. Carmen Nobel, "Kids Benefit from Having a Working Mom," *Working Knowledge,* May 15, 2015, https://hbswk.hbs.edu/item/kids -benefit-from-having-a-working-mom.

5. McGinn et al., "Learning from Mum."

6. Pamela Lenehan, "I Surveyed More Than 1,000 People to Find Out How Having a Working Mom Really Affects Kids," *Time,* March 1, 2016.

7. Amy Hsin and Christina Felfe, "When Does Time Matter? Maternal Employment and Child Development," *Demography* 51 (October 2014): 1867–94.

8. Rachel G. Lucas-Thompson, Wendy A. Goldberg, and JoAnn Prause, "Maternal Work Early in the Lives of Children and Its Distal Associations with Achievement and Behavior Problems: A Meta-Analysis," *American Psychological Association* 136, no. 6 (2010): 915–42.

9. Denise-Marie Ordway, "What Research Says About the Kids of Working Moms," *Journalist's Resource,* August 6, 2018, https://journalists resource.org/economics/working-mother-employment-research.

10. Names and identifying details have been changed at the request of the interviewee to protect her anonymity.

Index

About the Author

LARA BAZELON is a writer, teacher, and advocate for racial and social justice. A professor at the University of San Francisco School of Law, she directs the criminal and racial justice clinical programs and holds the Barnett Chair in Trial Advocacy.